The Use of English

The Use of English

RANDOLPH QUIRK
Professor of English Language · University of London

WITH SUPPLEMENTS BY
A. C. GIMSON
Professor of Phonetics · University of London
AND
JEREMY WARBURG
Sometime Professor of English · Earlham College, Indiana

LONGMANS

LONGMANS, GREEN AND CO LTD
48 Grosvenor Street, London W1
Associated companies, branches and representatives
throughout the world

Printed in Great Britain by
Richard Clay (The Chaucer Press), Ltd.,
Bungay, Suffolk

Preface to the Second Edition

Even in the six years since the first edition was published, there has been considerable achievement in the study of the English language. In a serious attempt to reflect the new and important work that has appeared in this period, a thorough revision has been carried out which has resulted in extensive alteration and expansion. For example, the greatly increased study (particularly in Europe) of the impact of English on other languages has meant a considerable extension of Chapter 2, and the fruitful resurgence of grammatical research—especially stimulated by M.I.T. and one or two other leading centres—has led to the expansion of the material suitable for more advanced students by the inclusion of a new chapter (Chapter 12) and by the enlargement of other parts; Supplement I has been extended to take account of the increased interest in writing systems. And of course English has continued to add speedily to its enormous word-stock, new dictionaries have appeared, there have been new departures in lexicology, stylistics, phonological theory, and general linguistics as a whole. Within the limits of a single volume, we have sought to reflect, not least by supplying a new bibliography, what seem to us the most significant of the new developments; and we have been determined that in its new guise (totally reset in a somewhat more economical format) this book should be worthy of the reputation it has won among students of English language and literature as well as of linguistics.

In preparing the new edition, my co-authors and I have drawn gratefully on the valuable comments of Barbara M. H. Strang, John Lyons, Y. Olsson, M. A. K. Halliday and other friends and colleagues, especially in Britain and the United States; we are very conscious also of our debt to those who, in all parts of the world, have contributed to the present edition through their reviews of the first. Particular thanks must be expressed to past and present associates of the Survey of English Usage at University College London (Valerie Adams, David Crystal, Derek Davy, Sidney Greenbaum, Geoffrey Leech, Joan Mulholland, Jan Svartvik), many of whose ideas, communicated in the course of daily contact, are otherwise silently incorporated in the pages that follow. Finally, three exemplary native informants, Jean, Eric, and Robin Quirk, have been shamelessly exploited (as only a family can be) for their invaluable help in criticism, checking, and proof-reading.

R.Q.

University College London,
March 1968.

Preface to the First Edition

The Use of English began as a series of talks commissioned by the BBC and broadcast in the summer of 1961. On that occasion, as in the subsequent revision and expansion of the material, I enjoyed the co-operation of my colleagues, A. C. Gimson and J. Warburg, so that a wide coverage could be given to the many important aspects of the language and so that differing viewpoints might be presented on the complex instrument that is English. The aim has been to stimulate a mature and informed approach to our language, so that we can understand the nature of English, be encouraged to use it more intelligently, respond to it more sensitively, and acknowledge more fully the implications of its international use today. In short, this book seeks to satisfy our natural curiosity about language and to supply just such knowledge of the mother-
vi

tongue as R. G. Latham claimed (a century and a quarter ago) should be the familiar equipment of every educated person.

Nothing beyond such 'natural curiosity' and an ordinary working knowledge of English will be required in order to begin profitable work on the book. On the other hand, the range of the subject is vast—as is the range of the language itself. We have tried to provide for those whose interest may be limited to the practical everyday use of English as it impinges on the lives of us all. But we have tried to provide also for those whose interests will extend rather further. There is material in every chapter, as well as in the exercises at the end of every chapter, which will readily carry such students into advanced work both on the subtler use of language (as in literature) and on the contributions that modern linguistic science is making to the study of English. Moreover, in the Supplements, we have been able to give to topics of great importance a fuller and more specialised treatment than might have seemed appropriate in the body of the book.

One need hardly say that this volume does not attempt to be definitive or to provide a description of the manifold uses of English. It would be futile to have such aims in writing a book of these modest dimensions. What is more, it is only recently that scholars have begun to realise just how immensely complex the uses of English are. The present book sets out some provisional observations and suggestions, many of them made in the course of work upon the Survey of English Usage which is being conducted at University College London and which will eventually yield more precise and detailed information on the nature, use, and range of English than is at present available.

It would be impossible to do justice in a concluding paragraph to the many who have directly or indirectly contributed to this book. There is special pleasure in acknowledging the stimulus provided by Professor A. H. Smith, whose firm but friendly insistence, indeed, caused the book to be written. But warm thanks are due also to my colleagues on the Survey of English Usage (Anne P. Duckworth, J. P. L. Rusiecki, J. Svartvik) for lengthy discussions which have clarified many points; to Jean Rowntree and Rosemary Jellis of the BBC for much of the original conception of the work; to Roy Yglesias for guidance at every stage of the writing; to George Perren for numerous suggestions; to Donald J. Taylor, who has given a wealth of advice, especially on the exercises; to the lively students both in London and in Durham whose response to earlier versions of several sections has led to improvements in many respects; to scholars in English studies and linguistics all over the world, whose help and influence can to some inadequate extent be seen in the notes and in the bibliography; Jean and Erik Quirk for their devoted and skilful help in checking quotations, correcting typescript, and many another task cheerfully undertaken for all its tediousness. But of course no helpers, named or unnamed, are responsible for the blemishes that nevertheless remain.

R.Q.

University College London,
February 1962.

Contents

1 : From 'Small Reach' to Large

L ET us begin by considering the following proposition:
   1   Most people who were born in Sweden are Swedish
       and speak Swedish.
We may fairly claim that this is a statement of fact and
that the exceptions allowed by the wording, 'most people',
will not be very numerous: some thousands of Lapps in
northern Sweden are Swedish citizens but have their own
language, and of course a child may be born in a foreign
embassy in Stockholm without becoming Swedish or learning Swedish. We note in passing that it is rather neat that
the names of country, citizenship, and language should all
be linked with a common root. Let us now re-arrange this
proposition to make a new one:

   2   Most people who speak Swedish are Swedish and were
       born in Sweden.

Here we realise at once that the qualification 'most' is
more obviously necessary: Minnesota and Finland spring
to mind. There are a million Swedish speakers in North
America, most of them born there and holding United
States or Canadian passports. There are half a million
Swedish speakers who were born in Finland and who are
Finnish citizens. For all these people, the links between the
names for country, nation, and language become obviously
less relevant, and in fact the 'nation' meaning of *Swedish*
splits into two, genetic and political: 'of Swedish background' and 'owing allegiance to Sweden'. Even so, the
second proposition is also a statement of fact, and we need

1

scarcely consider other exceptions such as university students in Germany or Britain who learn to speak Swedish as part of their studies.

Now, what has all this to do with the use of English? The answer is twofold. First, as with 'Swedish', the word 'English' is the name both of a language and of a nationality and is linked with the name of a country, England; but there is the important difference that, since England is not a political entity (as a part of Great Britain or the United Kingdom), 'English' corresponds only to the genetic half of the two national meanings of 'Swedish'. Secondly, if in propositions 1 and 2 we replace 'Sweden' and 'Swedish' by 'England' and 'English', we find that they are no longer both true. The first proposition remains true enough, of course, but the second is now wildly out: most people who speak English are *not* English and were *not* born in England. Not only has the 'national' sense of 'English' no official political meaning: the 'language' sense of 'English' (importantly, as we shall see) has no necessary link with the genetic sense either.

Proposition 1 can be framed and found valid for the names of many countries, peoples, and languages. 'If he is French, he speaks French'—and we may go on doing this in turn with 'German', 'Swedish', 'Spanish', and many others. But such a correspondence does not always hold, and an attempt to follow through with this experiment for a few minutes will help us on the road to getting rid of the identification of nation and language which causes a good deal of trouble in the world. One soon comes up against examples like 'If he is Swiss, he speaks—?', 'If he is Welsh, he speaks—?', 'If he is Belgian, he speaks—?', 'If he is Canadian, he speaks—?'.

So far as 'English' is concerned, therefore, the truth of proposition 1 simply points to one happy fact for the people of England which is by no means paralleled in all countries:

2

one way in which the national life of England is not complicated as it is in many places. But the truth of proposition 1 is unfortunate to the extent that we are inclined to identify the name of our language with the name of *one* of the races using it: to think of English as the private property of the English. In other words, we are in danger of taking the second proposition as a corollary of the first.

With the names of many languages and peoples, this order is sound enough. There are probably not a great many exceptions to the generalisation 'If he speaks Welsh, he is Welsh'—though, as we should have noted already, there would be many exceptions indeed if we were to say 'If he is Welsh, he speaks Welsh'. On the other hand, if we try proposition 2 with French, we see that this would be a very risky deduction, since parts of Switzerland, Belgium, Canada, and other countries are French-speaking without owing national allegiance to France. And of course, many of us in Britain and America speak French without being French. A few interesting and highly informative minutes with a good encyclopedia are all that is necessary to fit us for arguing the probability or improbability of proposition 2 in relation to such languages as German, Finnish, Irish, Portuguese. For example, we may find that 'If he speaks *Hausa*, he is a *Nigerian* or a *Sudanese*'—and this of course would be excluding numerically smaller possibilities such as 'anthropologist' or 'former colonial civil servant'.

The desire to use language as a sign of national identity is a very natural one, and in consequence language has played a prominent part in national movements. Men have often felt the need to cultivate a given language to show that they are distinct from another race whose hegemony they resent. At the time when the United States split off from Britain, for example, there were proposals that independence should be linguistically acknowledged by the use of a different language from that of Britain. There was even

3

one proposal that Americans should adopt Hebrew. Others, again, favoured the adoption of Greek, though, as one man put it, things would certainly be simpler for Americans if they stuck to English and made the British learn Greek. In the end, as everyone knows, the two countries adopted the eminently practical and satisfactory solution of carrying on with the same language as before. For nearly two hundred years now, they have shown the world that political independence and national identity can be complete without sacrificing the enormous mutual advantages of what has remained in all but some trivial details a common language.

More recently, we have seen in Ireland, a thorough-going attempt to make *linguistic* independence an emblem of political independence. In Czechoslovakia during the years before the Second World War, the fact of linguistic identity between residents of Sudetenland and Germany contributed powerfully to the events leading up to Hitler's annexation of the area. Since 1945, Israel, Norway and Yugoslavia are among the countries witnessing far-reaching developments in establishing a language which can identify the nation. At the same time, Afrikaans and English have continued to emphasise the division between races in South Africa, and in several parts of the Indian subcontinent there have been serious troubles arising from attempts to establish political entities where there are linguistic entities. Language riots in Louvain caused the fall of the Belgian Government in February 1968. Language again is an important factor in the problems which confront Italy in the German-speaking South Tyrol. Like religion, language is clearly a powerful unifying—and dividing—force.

As we have seen, however, there is nothing about language as such that makes linguistic identity conterminous with national identity. 'If he speaks French, he is by no means necessarily French.' French is not the private pro-

4

perty of Frenchmen, and still less is English the private property of Englishmen.

This should be obvious when one reflects that English is the mother-tongue in Canada, the United States, Australia, New Zealand, and many other areas of the world. Yet many of us still half-consciously feel that when anyone other than an Englishman uses English, we have a special right to criticise his usage because he has been privileged to handle something which is in the English-man's gift. We feel that he must necessarily look to us for a 'standard', because it is 'our' language. Quite frequently, in fact, such feelings are not merely half-conscious: they may be given full expression. Not long ago, an Englishman ended a letter to the press with the following uncompromising sentence:

> If other nations wish to borrow or adopt our language, it is up to them, but let it be understood that the language remains fundamentally ours. (*Daily Telegraph*, 4 July 1955.)

It is high time that such narrowly parochial and naïve notions about English were firmly scotched. They do not even remotely correspond to linguistic realities and they can do nothing but harm to the cause of human relationships and international harmony. There is no copyright in the use of English and we cannot demand of users in other countries that they pay royalties of obeisance as though the language carried a British patent.

It is unreasonable to regard any language as the property of a particular nation, and with no language is it more unreasonable than with English. This is not to say that English is used by a greater number of speakers than any other language: it is easily outstripped in this respect by Chinese. But it is the most *international* of languages. A Dane and a Dutchman meeting casually in Rome will almost

5

automatically find themselves conversing in English. The crew of a Russian airliner approaching Cairo will use English to ask for landing instructions. Malayan lecturers use it as the medium of instruction when addressing their Malayan students in Kuala Lumpur.

Such examples are striking and significant because they show that the use of English in the world has no immediate connexion with the economic or political supremacy—past or present—of an English-speaking country. To people in Africa or Pakistan or Chile, English is the obvious foreign language to master, not merely because it is the native language in Great Britain and the United States, but because it provides the readiest access to the cream of world scholarship and to the bulk of world trade. It is understood more widely than any other language.

These points are made crystal-clear in the British Council's Annual Report for 1960-61:

It has been customary to speak of teaching English as a foreign language, often merely to emphasise that the process is by no means the same as teaching it to those who already have it as their mother tongue. More recently, the term English as a second language has been employed to describe English taught or learnt for practical and necessary uses of communication—whether to serve as the language of instruction in education, for specialised studies, or as a *lingua franca* among those to whom English is an acquired tongue. The distinction is important: for example, English in France or Germany is still largely learnt for reasons comparable to those for learning French or German in Britain—as a foreign language, as a humane discipline and as an introduction to a foreign culture. In many countries, however, the place of English in education may be more important, and indeed more fundamentally necessary, because it is either the medium of education itself or a necessary link with resources beyond the borders of the country where it is learnt. When it is used thus as a second language English is not necessarily the vehicle of distinctively British or American cultural values; it may well be the means of expressing those of the country where it has been adopted. The educational use of English as a second language today varies from the level of the university to that of the primary school; its social or economic functions range from the needs of internal administration to those of external trade.

In June 1965, the United States Government issued a policy statement showing a striking similarity of view and commitment:

English has become one of the most important world languages. The rapidly growing interest in English cuts across political and ideological lines because of the convenience of a *lingua franca* increasingly used as a second language in important areas of the world. Demands for help in learning English are, therefore, widespread. The United States ought to respond to these demands. English is a key which opens doors to scientific and technical knowledge indispensable to the economic and political development of vast areas of the world. An increase in the knowledge of English can contribute directly to greater understanding among nations. It can also be the means of assuring access to a treasure house of man's knowledge about himself—about his political experiments, his philosophies, and his inner human needs.

(The statement is reprinted here from the Spring 1966 issue of the U.S. Government publication, *International Education and Cultural Exchange*.)

The importance and the international status of English today come home to us particularly clearly when we compare the use of English in Shakespeare's time. In 1600, 'He speaks English' and 'He is English' were very close to being interdependent statements: *if* the one, *then* the other. English was almost unknown outside the British Isles—and

7

by no means universally spoken within the British Isles, as Richard Mulcaster tells us in 1582 : 'our English tung is of small reatch, it stretcheth no further than this Iland of ours, naie not there over all'. The number of English speakers in the world when Shakespeare was writing has been estimated at five million. The increase during the intervening years to the present is quite phenomenal. There are now something like 250 million people for whom English is the mother-tongue or 'first language': and this of course means, for the most part, their *only* language. If we add to this the number of people who have a working knowledge of English as a second or foreign language (many Indians, Africans, Frenchmen, Russians, and so on), we raise the total to about 350 million.

Such numbers are naturally difficult to estimate, and they must in any case embrace a wide range of competence. At one end are those with a native-like command of English, and at the other those with only a slow and painful reading-knowledge or even only a smattering of the language adequate for coping with tourists' needs. To say that one 'speaks' a language may well relate more to the latter end of the range than the former, as any of us may testify who have been asked 'Do you speak French?' Certainly, if we answer 'yes', we know full well that 'yes' would have meant something very different if the questioner had asked whether we spoke English.

The increase from 5 million to 350 million speakers has not come about because of any special merits in the language itself, but because of increases in the influence exerted by the *speakers* of English. It is to an important series of historical events that we must look in order to understand the development of English, and, although this is not a book to deal with history, we may pause to glance at one or two significant points.

Mulcaster explained the 'small reatch' of English in

8

1582 (the year Shakespeare married Ann Hathaway) by saying that 'our state is no Empire'. But he was writing at the beginning of the settlement of America by English speakers—the greatest single event which has given English the enormous number of users it has today. Jamestown in Virginia was settled in 1607, and the Plymouth colony in Massachusetts was founded in 1620. In addition, Mulcaster pointed out that there was no valuable learning written in English that might stimulate foreigners to learn the language. We recall that as late as 1620 Francis Bacon felt it necessary to write in Latin when he was laying the foundations of modern science in such works as the *Novum Organum Scientiarum*, with its emphasis on the need for careful observation of natural phenomena: 'Naturae enim non imperatur, nisi parendo'—'For we cannot *command* nature unless we *obey* nature.'

But Bacon's successors in the sciences wrote in English and soon made Mulcaster's remarks obsolete in this field too. Within three or four decades of Bacon's death, the Royal Society came into being, and it was in English that such foundation Fellows as Robert Boyle formulated and published fundamental theories. We are all familiar with Boyle's formulation of the law about gases; here is his less well-known definition of chemical elements, modern for all its three hundred years:

I mean by elements certain primitive and simple, or perfectly unmingled bodies which not being made of any other bodies . . . are the ingredients of which all those called perfectly mixed bodies are immediately compounded, and into which they are ultimately resolved.

From Boyle to Newton (who died in 1727); from Newton to Joseph Priestley (who died in 1804). By this time there was a great deal of such valuable learning in English as Mulcaster had missed in his time, and in consequence—

9

true to the implication of Mulcaster's words—there were large numbers of foreigners eager to learn our language. In 1762, Thomas Sheridan (father of the dramatist who wrote *The Rivals* and *The School for Scandal*) published a book on the needs of such foreigners and the difficult problems involved in teaching English as a foreign language.

These needs have increased beyond all measure since Sheridan's time and innumerable books are being written on aspects of the problem of teaching the language. It is not generally realised that the English Departments of several universities in this country are deeply engaged in these problems, or that an important part of the British Council's and (in America) the U.S.I.A.'s work is concerned with remedying the desperate lack of English teaching all over the world. Nor is it generally realised how many and how attractive are the careers open to young men and women who have an interest in their language and in the cultural needs of their fellow-men abroad.

A measure of the importance of English today even in the highly developed countries of Europe can be seen in this: A Norwegian or Finnish scientist who a century ago might have published his work in French, and three centuries ago in Latin, will often today seek to achieve the maximum circulation of his ideas by publishing it in English. Swedish scientists in the distinguished and venerable University of Uppsala may be heard discussing atomic physics among themselves—in English, since English is the language they associate with such scholarship. Yet in Mulcaster's time there was scarcely *any* scholarship to be associated with English.

When Thomas Sheridan wrote his book on English for foreigners, another of the conditions noted by Mulcaster had changed likewise. Our state *was* by now an empire, and—again as Mulcaster had rightly implied—this had carried our language far and wide. One very important

10

part of the empire was in fact just ripe for secession and soon became the United States of America. Within a very few years, the English language in America had been provided with grammars, spelling-books and even a dictionary —all, or nearly all, the work of the zealous and energetic Noah Webster.

In the eighteenth century, too, English was already firmly established in Canada, and English had spread to India. Before the century ended, it had spread to Australia and South Africa as well.

In most of these areas to which English had been newly exported, the situation was a fairly straightforward one. There was a large-scale settlement from the British Isles of people who took their language with them and who preserved that language (with varying degrees of adaptation) in an expanding colony of European people whose numbers and power made the language supreme there. India was different. Here was a very numerous and highly cultivated native population, and no large-scale immigration of English speakers as colonists. English therefore remained the language only of trade and government, spoken by few Indians; there was no question of its becoming the first language of ordinary people throughout the sub-continent. It is for this reason that India became the first area to encounter the problem of using English as the commercial, educational and scientific medium in what came to be called 'developing' countries: a problem which was to be acute by the middle of the twentieth century in many parts of the world.

The first man to grapple seriously with the question was Thomas Babington Macaulay. A Minute which he wrote in 1835 is of considerable historical importance and is worth quoting from at some length.

The problem in India [he says] is that we have to educate

11

a people who cannot at present be educated by means of their mother tongue. We must teach them some foreign language. The claims of our own language it is hardly necessary to recapitulate. It stands pre-eminent even among the languages of the West. It abounds with works of imagination not inferior to the noblest which Greece has bequeathed to us; with models of every species of eloquence; with historical compositions . . . ; with just and lively representations of human life and human nature; with the most profound speculations on metaphysics, morals, government, jurisprudence, and trade; with full and correct information respecting every experimental science. . . . Whoever knows that language has ready access to all the vast intellectual wealth which all the wisest nations of the earth have created and hoarded in the course of ninety generations . . . [English] is likely to become the language of commerce throughout the seas of the East. It is the language of two great European communities which are rising, the one in the south of Africa, the other in Australasia. . . . Whether we look at the intrinsic value of our literature or at the particular situation of [India], we shall see the strongest reason to think that, of all foreign tongues, the English tongue is that which would be the most useful to our native subjects.

We no longer have ' native subjects ' in India or Pakistan, but English has retained a good deal of the importance that Macaulay outlines with such clarity and foresight. Some of its present importance, however, oddly results from the large number of other languages available in India—Hindi, Bengali, Tamil, Telegu, Gujerati, Kannade and several others, each spoken by millions of people. When India became independent in 1947 it was decided to make Hindi the national language, but for various reasons (such as the numbers of administrators and other professional men for whom English was more convenient) English was given equal status temporarily. It was then intended that English should cease to be one of the two official languages in 1965, but when 1965 came, the Indian Government—in the face of bloodshed in Madras and elsewhere—had to give assurances that English would continue as a working language for official purposes.

This is because it has been found that Hindi is not being universally adopted as swiftly as had been hoped. At present, English—formerly much identified with foreign rule—is paradoxically the only language which tends to encourage unity and discourage separatist movements. Reference has already been made to the language riots in Assam. In June 1961, *The Guardian* announced that quarrels over the relative status of Hindi, Assamese, and Bengali had been settled by the intervention of the Indian Home Minister: 'The Minister's formula ensures that, at state level, English will be used exclusively now, and even later will continue to be used along with Assamese.' Obviously, the feeling is that any particular Indian language puts at a disadvantage people who are not native speakers of it, whereas English puts everyone on a common footing.

Moreover, English is still closely bound up with education throughout the sub-continent, in Pakistan as well as India, and it is frequently—especially in higher education —the medium of instruction in all subjects. In India, for example, training in the armed forces is given in English, and so are examinations in the universities, for entry to the public service, for commissions in the forces; English is required in commerce, and business firms insist on a good command of it in filling all but the humblest posts. It is significant that, in a current handbook for Indian university students, a model essay should be included on 'The future of English in India' (strongly arguing its retention), with a note that this has been set several times as an essay subject in final degree examinations (D. C. Saxena, *New College Essays*, Jallundur, 1963). And of course English is still the language of the law, external affairs, and much day-to-day

13

administration. It is even used as the literary language by a number of Indian authors. The well-known novelist and short-story writer, R. K. Narayan, does his literary work in no other language than English, and here are some lines by that great philosopher-poet, the late Sri Aurobindo:

Time waits, vacant, the Lightning that kindles, the Word
    that transfigures:
Space is a stillness of God building his earthly abode.
All waits hushed for the fiat to come and the tread of the
    Eternal;
Passion of a bliss yet to be sweeps from Infinity's sea.

Nor, indeed, is this true only of Indian writers: in other Asian and in African countries where English is used as a second language, valuable work has been published by authors for whom English is the adopted medium. One may mention the Nigerian novelist Chinua Achebe, or his compatriot Wole Soyinka, the poet and dramatist, in whose verse one finds English effectively expressing tropical scene and Yoruba culture:

A dawn of bright processions, the sun peacocked
Loud, a new mint of coins. And those were all
The night hours, only the dissipated gourds,
Rain serried floor, fibre walls in parsimonious
Sifting of the sun, and she . . .

To our store of written English, as the British Council Report puts it, 'which comprises an international heritage of arts and sciences, notable contributions by those who have themselves learnt English as a new language are common and likely to increase'.

Although the English of cultivated writers like Sri Aurobindo looks on paper very similar to cultivated English anywhere, the spoken English of the sub-continent differs very much from English in any of the 'native English' countries such as Britain or the United States. Moreover, it must be remembered that English is in any case known to only a tiny minority of the population (however important a minority), and that it is in serious danger of declining from even its present degree of currency unless something can be done to relieve the desperately acute shortage of teachers. Nevertheless, even if a plentiful supply of excellent teachers becomes available (with help from Britain, the U.S.A., Australia and elsewhere), we must plainly recognise that an independent, *Indian* standard of English may well crystallise. 'Obviously,' says the British Council Report, 'fresh dialects of English will arise abroad—as they have always done in English-speaking countries. Standards of acceptable speech will vary—as they do in Britain itself.' The language's 'assets may indeed be increased rather than diminished by wider use; overseas varieties of English may continue to contribute to the richness and resources of the language as a whole, as they have done in the past'.

In Ceylon and Malaya the story is similar: the retention of English for such important purposes as higher education. In Malaya, the proclamation of September 1967 still leaves English as the medium of instruction in most senior schools and for virtually all university work, except of course for studies in Malayan and other oriental languages. In Ceylon, it is noteworthy that it is the medium for *science* teaching in the secondary schools, as well as still being used as the medium for all subjects at university level.

In the newly independent Commonwealth countries of Africa, English is still more important (and is increasing also in former French and Belgian territories: in the Congo, English is a compulsory foreign language and as such must be taught to all from the third year of grammar school). It is the official language of Ghana, where it is taught from the first year of primary school and is often the sole medium of instruction for all subjects from the second year of primary

15

school onwards. In Nigeria we have a similar position, but such African languages as Hausa and Yoruba are also widely used in the early years of schooling. But again we must note that 'English' does not necessarily mean 'British English', and in these countries too it seems possible that we shall see the emergence of new 'standard Englishes', sharing enough features with English elsewhere to make international use of the same language—English as a *lingua franca*—a constant reality, but with regular regional deviations. Just as it is usual today to speak of British English as distinct from American English, so we may well come to speak increasingly of other varieties such as Indian English or Ghanaian English.

But the mention of English as a *lingua franca* must remind us of a very much more radical deviant from English as it is known in English-speaking countries. Ever since the establishment of English trading-posts in China (there was one at Canton in 1664), the world has known the phenomenon of 'Pidgin English'. The name 'Pidgin' is an altered form of the word 'business', and this variety of English thus bears a name which is interestingly a direct description of the restricted purpose for which it was brought into existence. An American linguist, Robert A. Hall, has counted 1,500 different words in the Melanesian Pidgin of the present day and has shown how these words can be compounded to make a very large number of further words (as we do with *gas* and *stove* to make *gas-stove*). A great deal of complex and advanced communication is therefore possible in Pidgin, and there are a good many technical and medical books published in it—not to mention books of religious instruction such as the three-volumed work, *Yesus em i forman bilong yumi*. The title of this book, which may be translated 'Jesus is our leader', gives some indication of what Pidgin is like. The word *forman* is obviously 'foreman' with a generalised meaning; *bilong* is the sign of the

16

possessive ('which belongs to'); and *yumi* is a first person plural pronoun, 'we, us', connected ultimately with 'you and me'.

It may be worth mentioning in passing that this is not the only first person plural pronoun in Melanesian Pidgin. There is also *mifela*, derived from such expressions as 'me and the (other) fellow(s)'. In effect, this means that Pidgin is able to make a useful distinction not possible in ordinary English—the distinction between a 'we' which includes the hearer (as in 'You and I are both invited; shall *we* go?') and a 'we' which excludes the hearer (as in 'You wanted to see John and me; here *we* are'). This distinction is one which is made in the indigenous Melanesian languages and is carried over from these into Pidgin. It is one interesting illustration of the way in which a language may have in it a substratum of another. It also points to a reason (along with our need to speak of 'translating' from Pidgin to English) for regarding Pidgin as a different language from English, though closely related, rather than as one of the normal regional variants of English.

We have seen that a great many people—and a great many peoples—are involved in the use of English. Millions of men and women in four continents have it as their native language, and further millions in every part of the world use it as a second or foreign language. This must inevitably give us a sense of the importance of our language, but also it gives us something which is still more to the point: a sense of perspective about it and a readiness to see that English is not the prerogative or 'possession' of the English. It is the property of the Yorkshireman no more than the Californian, of the Londoner no more than the Tasmanian. Acknowledging this must—as a corollary—involve our questioning the propriety of claiming that the English of one area is more 'correct' than the English of another. Certainly, we must realise that there is no single 'correct'

English, and no single *standard* of correctness. It is therefore not for the American to tell us that English in Great Britain is 'clipped' or 'affected' and hence inferior to the English he speaks. Nor is it for the Englishman to say that Australian English is 'uneducated' and 'Cockney', or that American English is 'vague' and 'slangy'. In each of the major societies in which English is used, standards exist and—as we have seen—further standards are likely to become recognised. Such standards are determined by a particular society, in terms of that society's structure, and in terms of the purposes for which English is used in it.

Exercises and Topics for Discussion

1 (a) What is the difference between 'nationality' and 'race'? Which has the closer connexion with language? Consider the advantages and disadvantages of having one state per language.
   (b) Write on cases in recent history where there have been troubles over matters of language in relation to nationality.
2 What other languages were in use in the British Isles when Mulcaster wrote? Who used them and for what purposes?
3 Find out all you can about the British Council (or, if you are American, the USIA) and its work.
4 Pidgin was shown to be capable of a distinction not possible in English. Can you think of ways in which a dialect you know makes distinctions that cannot be made in Standard English? (Discuss the use of *gormless*, and *youse*, for example.) If you know a dialect which uses both *you* and *thou*, try to explain the distinction and suggest what, if anything, Standard English lacks in having only *you*.

5 You probably know some French or German and have experienced the temptation to let English intrude as you use it (perhaps by saying 'chew' for *tu* or 'shern' for *schön*). From your experience, set down some of the outstanding difficulties that a Frenchman (or German, as the case may be) is likely to have in learning English. The difficulties might be classified as (*a*) pronunciation, (*b*) vocabulary (especially words with several common meanings), (*c*) grammar, and (*d*) idiomatic expressions.

6 The letter which is reproduced below (in its entirety) was received from an Italian organisation by the editor of a British journal. Re-write it in what you would consider acceptable, idiomatic English, adding a commentary on the changes you make:

> Gentlemen:
>
> I am pleased to notice your address and I would intend to directly apply to cultural and public circles for diffusing your peculiar action in Italy, even through the newspapers of which I am a collaborator.
>
> That is I propose you to continually send me the contents of the issues of your periodical, enriched preferably with a brief account of each article.
>
> However, you could like to forward me the issues themselves as a documentation so I would meet any request of full details, or a possibility for translation of the best, according to Italian tastes, or propagating subscriptions.
>
> I do hope you would agree with my initiative, which has found the appreciation by the International Center for Comparison and Synthesis (ROME, Genoeses' Cloister —12, via Anicia), which groups a membership pertaining to the Italian highest cultural life.
>
> I remain, Dear Sirs,
> Very truly yours:
>
> P.S.—At your disposal for a cultural information service from my country, on an appointment to agree.

7 We spoke of a 'substratum' of another language making itself felt in Pidgin. A person who grows up speaking a dialect may subsequently use a form of Standard English which is modified by the dialect substratum in a somewhat similar way. Give and discuss examples in your own experience.

8 In September 1967, the Indian Minister for External Affairs (Mr M. C. Chagla) resigned from his post in order to emphasise his opposition to plans for abolishing the use of English in higher education. 'What,' he is reported to have asked, 'is the ultimate result if we hastily abolish English when we have no link language as a replacement?' Discuss India's dilemma in this respect.

2: *Range of Uses and Users*

THE uses to which English is put are as various as the peoples and societies that use it. We have already seen that one particular purpose—the conduct of 'business'—has actually called into being one extreme and remotely related form of English, Pidgin, and has given it its very name. Not all the purposes determine so clear-cut a form of language as Pidgin exhibits, but (as we shall see in some detail in a later chapter) every particular *use* of English is to some extent reflected in and determines the *form* of the language that is used for that particular purpose.

A sheep-farmer in Australia does not usually wish or need to use English for writing to *The Times* or reading a book on organic chemistry. An organic chemist in Chicago or Delhi does not usually wish or need to use his English for ordering a sheep-dipping or for entering wool-returns. To bring the examples a little nearer home and within our own experience, we may recollect having heard British sheep-farmers and British organic chemists speaking; if so, we shall be ready to acknowledge that there are considerable linguistic differences involved in the two occupations. Many of the words that a farmer uses are different from those of the chemist because his work is different.

It is differences of this kind that are probably largely responsible for the widespread belief that people in certain occupations have somehow 'less language' than in others. If an educated man (and we shall consider what this means presently) tries to talk about politics or drama with a farm-worker, he may well get the impression that the labourer

21

is short of language. But let us remember that many quite different factors may be contributing to this: the labourer may always be shy in front of strangers, or he may not be a talkative man in any circumstances; he may know little about politics or drama—and care still less. None of these necessarily points to his being in any meaningful sense ' short of language'. On the other hand, let the farm-worker turn the tables by trying to make the visitor talk about cattle-diseases or the parts of a plough, and it may well be the worker who turns away in disgust because ' some people can't understand plain English'. We are all in danger of being somewhat egocentric in our judgment of others, and our judgment of other people's language is no exception. In fact, no one has yet devised a satisfactory and reliable method of estimating how extensive anyone's command of a language is.

Yet there is a very real sense in which some people can be said to have a more generally useful command of English than others. Reference has just been made to an ' educated ' man—an expression which is more commonly used than defined. The farm-worker could talk about farming more competently than the ' educated ' man, and it would be reasonable to say that the worker was the better educated, so far as farming is concerned. In talking about politics, the ' educated ' man might be similarly surpassed by a politician; on physics, by a physicist. Perhaps the mark of the educated man is that he has a sufficiently wide and varied command of English to converse intelligently with *any* of these specialists to a certain degree. In this way, the physicist would show that he was also ' educated ' if he could hold a comparable discourse on politics with the politician. This, of course, is not all that is involved when we speak of an educated command of English—there are indices of several different kinds, including grammar and spelling, but we had better postpone discussion of these.

The earlier comparison of the prosperous Australian sheep-farmer and the Chicago chemist may have seemed somewhat artificial, not merely because it was (almost literally) far-fetched, but because a farmer's special language may well strike you as more 'provincial' than the chemist's. One reason for feeling this might perhaps be that in many people's view the chemist's field of interest has more prestige than the farmer's for a whole host of sociological and not very respectable reasons. Another (and more generally valid) basis for the feeling might be that the chemist's special language includes many elements from learned languages such as Latin and Greek: for example, *oxidize*, *precipitate, catalysis*. The language of science (and other branches of learning) is often, in fact, remarkably cosmopolitan, and so it naturally seems less 'provincial' than the homely names of farm animals. We find the same scientific words being used, slightly 'disguised', in several languages, and *oxidize* for instance is in French *oxyder*, in German *oxydieren*, and in Russian *oksidíroyat*.

But obviously we cannot press this too far. In these days of incubators, phosphates, and artificial insemination, we must beware of perpetuating the false nineteenth-century image of countryfolk who use only a few homely words.

Scientific and learned English is not merely international in using international words. English is frequently used internationally for these purposes, as was pointed out in the previous chapter. A scholar in Denmark or Czechoslovakia or even a vast country like Russia will today often write or at any rate publish in English, because his work will thereby reach a wider public. This does not mean that such a scholar has a native-like knowledge of English. In fact, the preface will usually acknowledge the help of someone who has corrected and checked the English or even done a good deal of translation. The scholar himself may be very poorly equipped to speak English or even to write

23

it, especially on any subject other than his own particular field of interest. Often he has only the ability to read (not even listen to) English material *solely concerned with his subject.*

This is what is today called having a 'restricted' or 'specialised' knowledge of English, and we have come to recognise increasingly not merely this limited degree of linguistic ability but also its potential value. Few people have the time that is required to master a 'full' knowledge of a foreign language and fewer still would be able to make much practical use of such a knowledge. Indeed, as has already been implied and as we shall see more clearly later, even as native speakers we vary greatly in the number and variety of fields of discourse in which we can feel at home.

By way of light relief, we may consider the following discussion of the specialised English of the legal profession— a burlesque, of course, but not *entirely* a joke:

> Legal phrases are rather long, strictly ungrammatical bits of English used by judges and barristers when they want to keep talking and give their brains a much-needed rest. They also use them to show that they've been in Court before and know the sort of things that barristers and judges do say, every quarter of an hour or so, to assure each other that they're all friends and have all been brought up the same way. No one would think of using any of them except a barrister or a judge talking the argot, and a witness who suddenly said 'In my humble submission' would be instantly and laughably shown up as some kind of imbecile.
>
> Here then are a few pieces of legal argot for aspiring advocates, not in any circumstances for use by the general public. Meaning, where a meaning can be traced, and the points at which they can be safely used, are indicated. . . .
>
> *'With the greatest respect . . .'*
>
> This, of course, means with no respect at all. 'With the greatest respect to the words which have just fallen from

your lordship, it is difficult to see how . . .' This means 'Did you sleep through *all* the evidence?' or 'They do you a very adequate hearing-aid on the National Health.' Note again the use of the word *fallen*. Words always *fall* from judges, sometimes like autumn leaves, occasionally like bricks. A short and untroubled judgment often used by second or third Lord Justices of Appeal: '*I agree with every word that has fallen from my lord and I have nothing to add.*'

'*With the greatest respect*' is as useful as '*In my humble submission*', which can be used at any juncture of any trial, and '*If your lordship pleases*', which can be used to start or finish a sentence. 'If your lordship pleases perhaps I might *mention* the case of . . .' Cases are always *mentioned*, lightly and hurriedly brought to the notice of the Court like a few inches of visible petticoat. Another useful time-filler which can be used after any question is '*I'm much obliged*'. Sometimes this can be less than apt. 'And as a result of this incident you sustained injuries?' 'Two black eyes.' 'I'm much obliged.' 'A broken rib.' 'I'm much obliged.' 'And a dislocated shoulder.' 'I'm *very* much obliged.' This form of examination in accident cases, though effortless, can be overdone. (*No Moaning at the Bar*, by Geoffrey Lincoln.)

The truth behind this burlesque, for our purpose, is that English in its entirety presents a vastly complicated picture to the native speaker, and is certainly too vast for the foreigner to master. The more widely that English has come to be used in the world, the more necessary it has become for the foreign learner to restrict himself to mastering sufficient for his particular purpose. Just as we have classes in this country teaching 'German for Science Students', there are schools on the continent of Europe which teach English for special purposes. Thus in Innsbruck, where the tourist industry is vital to the local economy, pupils can receive special instruction in a restricted form of English calculated to be adequate for serving the foreign tourist. And as a further reinforcement of what was said in the preceding chapter, it is worth pointing out that 'foreign tourist' in this connexion will mean 'a tourist who does not speak German', for English will be the language by which not only the British or American tourist can have his wants supplied but often also the Spanish or Swedish or Yugoslav tourist. To quote again from the Annual Report of the British Council for 1960-61:

> The airways pilot (to whom English is an international language of air communications), the NATO soldier or sailor (who learns English as a common military language), the African politician at the United Nations Assembly, the scientist at an international conference, the merchant, businessman and technician, all require English for their special professional use because it is a world language. The kind of English they need, and the level of proficiency they must have, depend on the uses to which they wish to put it.

One of the oddest of the restricted uses of English can be seen in foreign printing and publishing. There is a very common practice in the publishing houses abroad (especially in countries which are signatories to international copyright agreements) to make a brief and fairly stereotyped note in English on the preliminary pages. Often it is the printer's actual 'imprint' but more usually it refers to the copyright. A recent glance over the 'New Acquisitions' shelf in a library produced the following examples: A book wholly in German except for the words 'Copyright by Max Niemeyer Verlag' and 'Printed in Germany'; a magnificent volume published in Israel and entirely printed in the beautiful (but to us mysterious) Hebrew characters, except for the three words 'All rights reserved'; a book in Italian printed in Venice, but stating (in addition to 'Stampato in Italia') 'Printed in Italy' and 'Copyright by Neri Pozza'; a Brazilian novel had only one English word—in the hybrid phrase 'Copyright do autor'; and in a French book even this word appeared in an abbreviated form, '© 1956 by Editions Albin Michel'. Thus in the international language of the book trade, which still shows the older predominant influence of the Mediterranean in such usages as 8vo, 12mo, we now have in use a conventional symbol, ©, which tacitly acknowledges the predominance of English. Nor is this the only abbreviation current abroad which has its basis in English. Just as many of us use 'e.g.' without knowing the Latin expression in full, a Swedish envelope may have 'c/o' in the address, and the meaning of this is clear even to those who do not actually know the English words 'care of'.

We find another of the restricted forms of English in the field of international air transport, and of course this is a wider and more highly organised selection from 'full' English. The navigating crew of a TU-104 jet airliner arriving at Cairo from Moscow probably could not hold much general conversation in English, but as has already been said they 'call up' the control tower in English, and the Egyptian authorities reply in English with the permission and instructions for landing. International air control agreements allow some degree of latitude in the choice of language to be used in various parts of the world, but the commonest language adopted is undoubtedly English.

The restricted forms of English used by foreigners are not the only ways in which the influence of English makes itself felt internationally. In Mulcaster's time, when the prestige of English was low, many people felt the urgent need to enrich the language by adopting foreign words, and today English has many thousands of originally foreign words in its vocabulary: *ease* from French, for instance, and *area* from Latin. It is now the turn of English to supply words to other languages. In the Hausa language in Africa, for instance, you may find the word *sukurudireba*, though

27

it may take a moment or so to recognise this as our name for what is probably the most commonly used tool in the handyman's kit. A Muscovite watches a game of баскетбол, returns home by троллейбус and ascends to his flat by a лифт—these words being merely the Russian spellings, almost exactly symbol for symbol in the Cyrillic script, of *basket-ball*, *trolley-bus*, and *lift*. Polish, too, has adopted many English words—some of them curiously borrowed in the plural form but used as singulars in Polish; for example, *slums* and *komiks*.[1]

In some countries, great concern and disapproval have been expressed at the speed with which words are being adopted from the English language. T. Miyazawa (in *Sekai*, January 1966) is disturbed by the invasion of Japan by such words as *shyanpu-setto* (for ladies' hair), *takushi* 'taxi', *basu* 'bus', and *aisu kurimu* 'ice-cream', even if the latter may give people *sutamina* 'stamina'. One does not need much knowledge of German to understand most of the following dialogue which amusingly satirises the eagerness with which expressions are being taken over into German from English and especially from American English:

Kiki, sagt die eine, schau dir die Tinätscher-Dresses an, die würden gut zu unseren Släcks passen und unsern Sixapiel unterstreichen!

O keh, sagt Kiki, ich würde mir gern Schorts kaufen, wenn ich Monneh hätte.

Aber mit Schorts kannst du doch auf keine Paathie gehen, wirft die andere ein.

Warum nicht? Der Nju Luck mit Schorts wird bestimmt

[1] Among recent studies of the impact of English on other languages we have M. Benson, 'English Loan-Words in Russian', *The Slavic and East European Journal*, Berkeley, vol. 18, 1959, pp. 248-67; R. Filipović, *The Phonemic Analysis of English Loan-Words in Croatian*, Zagreb, 1960; R. W. Zandvoort, *English in the Netherlands*, Groningen, 1964; B. Carstensen, *Englische Einflüsse auf die deutsche Sprache nach 1945*, Heidelberg, 1965.

ap tu deit mit dem richtigen Meik ap dazu, wenn ein paar smarte Mänätscher die Sache in die Finger kriegen. Last not liest ist auch bald Kämpingzeit! Das wär ein Gäg!

Hm, ich kann mir jetst aber nix Neues leisten, ich will mir erst einen neuen Tschob suchen, in meinem Offis gefällt's mir nicht. Mit dem Tiemwörk klappt's nicht. Der Boss ist kein Tschentelmänn, denk dir, sein Hobbi ist Schopäng. Wenn ich dem was von der neuen Stardäst-Bänd in der Texasbar erzähle, guckt er bloss doof. Von Bibop, Dixiländ, Bluhs, Bugie Wugie und überhaupt von Tschäääs hat der altmodische Boy keine Ahnung, obwohl er Televischen daheim hat. Er kaut keinen Tschuing Gam, smaukt keine Kämmel, er kennt nicht mal die Monru, trinkt keinen Wiski, liest keine Bestseller, kauft keine Comik Bucks—und das will ein gebildeter Deutscher sein!

Kiki sieht auf die Uhr und sagt: Dämned, ich muss zum Läntsch, sonst schimpft Päps. Also, bis morgen: bai-bai!

Die beiden Girls machen shakehands und flitzen davon.

Der Chronist sagt zu sich: Deutscher Michel, go home mit deiner Muttersprache, sie ist nicht mehr up to date!

[Reprinted by permission of Eduard Wancura Verlag from *Des Deutschen Bürgers Plunderhorn*, by F. U. Gass, 1959.]

Reactions to the influence of English are not always so good-tempered. Some years ago, when the Cyprus trouble was at its height, there developed in Greece a very serious campaign against what was thought to be an unworthy and undignified pandering to the influence of English. Strong efforts were made to cut down the use of English, and even shops bearing English names were obliged to change them. One called 'Piccadilly' became 'Kypros'.

Nor does French opinion always welcome the impact of English. A French official in a speech not long ago expressed in the strongest terms his disapproval of the widespread use of such English words as *weekend, cocktail, pullover* (often shortened in French to *pull*, as *boxing* has been shortened to *boxe*), *shampooing, sweepstake*, and many others. So powerful was the tendency, he said, to ape the English language that whole phrases were becoming current that were directly modelled on English ones: for example, 'contacter quelqu'un', 'sous la condition que'. And the regular articles by Robert le Bidois in *Le Monde* on 'La Défence de la langue française' quite often concern defence against English. In January 1967, for example, we find him objecting to the many new words beginning with *mini*, such as 'minibus'.

But of course it is Titti Etiemble's satirical *Parlez-vous franglais?* (Paris 1964) that has most strikingly criticised the wholesale adoption of anglicisms. The example on his cover, 'Humph! Ce shériff manque de nerfs!', neatly exemplifies the way words, idioms and stereotyped exclamations alike are taken over, but it is tempting to give longer examples:

A peine sorti du teenage, l'ex-enfant-problème, l'ex-teenager français entre aux barracks . . . Lorsqu'il change son blue-jeans contre le (ou les) training slacks, et la tee shirt ou le pull contre le battle-dress . . . notre boy ne quitte son teen-gang que pour entrer dans un commando, s'il est un marine, ou bien un stick, pour peu qu'il se soit engagé dans les para-troops. Il reste donc fidèle à cette manière française de vivre que lui ont inculquée ses comics . . . (p. 93)

Tous les jours il remerciera Dieu: *God save our gracious queen!* d'avoir si bien lu ses comics. Tout ce dont il a besoin pour vivre heureux (*life must be fun*), ses lectures l'en ont pourvu. Du chewing-gum aux chiclets, des digests aux dinky-toys, des bobsleighs aux runabouts, des snow-cars aux scooter-balls, du suspense au happy end, des call-girls aux pull-overs, des starting-gates aux sleepings, tout lui fut prodigué à temps. Ainsi armé dans le struggle for life, il peut se dire comme un héros de Monty: 'Va, et n'aie pas peur: la victoire est dans nos pockets.' (p. 98)

Although the influence is primarily lexical, Etiemble shows

that accentuation, punctuation, grammar, and style are also affected:

> Quant à l'infinitif présent actif, il s'emploie sabireusement avec toutes sortes de sens, implicites : sur l'anglais *ready to wear*, la mode française a multiplié les expressions du genre : *prêt-à-porter* (où *porter* signifie *être porté*); *Venilia prêt-à-poser* (où *poser* signifie *être posé*). *Génie, la lassive qui lave sans bouillir* propose un infinitif plus intéressant encore puisqu'il signifie *qu'on ait besoin (qu-il soit nécessaire) de faire bouillir de linge*. Admirons ici l'extrême concision du sabir !
> (p. 192)
>
> Là-dessus, il me fallut subir : 'le Sporting Union agenais'. Pourquoi ce masculin? Manifestement, *Sporting Union* est formé sur *Sporting Club*. Si l'on dit *le Sporting Club*, à cause du genre de *Club*, il faut *la Sporting Union*, à cause du genre de *Union*. Mais *la Sporting Union agenaise* ne vaut guère mieux que *le Sporting Union agenais*. Moralité : parlez français. Vous n'aurez pas à vous demander quel est le pluriel de *cameramane*. *Quadrumane* et *mythomane* justifient un des pluriels que j'entendis ce soir-là : '*nos cameramanes*'; par infortune, au cour de cette émission précisément . . . on parla de *cameramènes*. (pp. 283-4)

For all his satire, Etiemble is not exaggerating unduly, as one can see from the following, perfectly 'straight' quotation from the first page in the sports section of a randomly purchased Liège newspaper, *La Wallonie*, 4 September 1966. It reports a football match between two Belgian teams, Seraing and Crossing:

> Le toss est favorable à Seraing. Le match, amorcé par Dos Santos, ne tarde pas à démarrer lorsque Tomasetig lancé par Toussaint rate probablement le premier but de la saison à la 30ᵉ seconde. Molenbeek réagit par ses avants de pointe et les locaux l'échappent belle en concédant corner. Quelques mauvaises passes sont à mettre à l'actif des Sérésiens tandis que

Nicolay est sifflé hors-jeu. Sur les gradins, le public s'énerve à cause des interventions de Spinoy et l'arbitre doit appeler le délégué au terrain pour calmer les excités. A la 20e minute, Seraing part à l'assaut, ouvre la marque par Warnotte, mais M. Deckx annule malgré les linesmen qui validaient le but. Un hand spectaculaire de Baresa laisse M. Deckx sans réaction : c'est la compensation. A la 25e minute, sur coup franc admirablement livré par Van der Waeren, Roosbeeck se met en évidence en arrêtant splendidement. A la 30e minute, Roosbeeck et De Jonghe unissent leurs efforts pour stopper une offensive adverse.

Compared with those of Robert le Bidois or Etiemble, protests on this subject have an even sharper and more anxious tone when they come from the French-speaking area of Canada, where it can easily seem that French is defenceless in the face of the Canadian and American English that encircle it. At a congress held in 1957 to look into ways of stemming the English advance, the Archbishop of Quebec and others spoke of the 'deep pessimism' felt at the way French was being 'threatened as never before'. A report of the congress pointed out that one of the troubles was that 'much of the technical literature used by specialists in Quebec originates in American and British universities. Its use does not predispose these specialists to think in French, much less express themselves properly in that language.' Technology, the cinema, radio and television were all tending to influence people 'to introduce English words into their native vocabulary', and French-speaking Canadians were urged 'to form groups similar to those in France which attempt to keep the language pure'. The specific references to technology and to scientific literature must remind us of what was said earlier about Swedish scientists and their tendency to use English when discussing these subjects.

Attempts, like these discussed in the last few pages, to

stem the flooding influence of the English language only serve to show further how widespread and insistent is the use of English in the world today. And we see in the protests themselves some significant glimpses of the reasons for the power of English. English has spread and is still spreading because of the predominance of the political and economic power of English-speaking countries, the leadership in scientific research enjoyed by British and American scholars, through the popularity of American entertainment, the forcefulness of commerce, and similar factors. If nothing else, such a list of factors helps us to see that 'England' is only one part—however important—of what 'English' denotes in the world.

There is something else worth reflecting upon. The French-Canadian conference aimed to keep French 'pure', and we often hear of linguistic purity as an ideal. Indeed, we often hear complaints that English is not 'pure', and charges may be levelled in the interests of 'purity' against someone who is noticed using an Americanism or some piece of technical jargon. In Mulcaster's time there was a great deal of heated discussion of the extent to which it was permissible and proper to import words into English from other languages. Many people took up just such disapproving attitudes as we have noted among Germans and Frenchmen today. Englishmen in the sixteenth century were prone to 'powder their talk' liberally with French, Italian and Latin words, and we are familiar with Shakespeare's satires upon linguistic excesses of this kind. One thinks of Holofernes, Sir Nathanial and Armado in *Love's Labour's Lost*, or of Mercutio's exasperated comments on 'the immortal passado, the punto reverso' of Tybalt in *Romeo and Juliet*:

The pox of such antic, lisping, affecting fantasticoes; these new tuners of accents! . . . these fashion-mongers, these

33

pardonnez-mois, who stand so much on the new form that they cannot sit at ease on the old bench? Oh, their *bons,* their *bons!*

Just as the German commentator of today can say ironically that his 'mother-tongue is no longer up to date' if it is not sprinkled with Anglicisms, so Thomas Wilson in 1553 was scornful about those who

> seeke so far for outlandish English, that they forget alto-gether their mothers language. And I dare sweare this, if some of their mothers were aliue, thei were not able to tell what they say . . . Some farre iourneyed gentlemen at their returne home, like as they loue to goe in forraine apparell, so thei wil pouder their talke with ouersea language. He that cometh lately out of Fraunce, will talke French English and neuer blush at the matter. An other chops in with English Italienated, and applieth the Italian phrase to our English speaking, the which is, as if an Oratour that professeth to vtter his mind in plaine Latine, would needs speake Poetrie, and farre fetched colours of straunge antiquitie . . . The vnlearned or foolish phantasticall, that smelles but of learn-ing (such fellowes as haue seen learned men in their daies) wil so Latin their tongues, that the simple can not but wonder at their talke, and thinke surely they speake by some reuelation.

Already, a decade before Shakespeare's birth, we spot Holofernes, Nathaniel, Costard and Dull in the wings. And similar attacks on the defilers of English continue in our own century. To show that French gives as good as she gets, Etiembe (*op. cit.*) quotes from George Moore and we may do the same (*Avowals,* London, 1924, p. 285): our basic education, says Moore, involves learning some French, even if it

> amounts to no more than a sufficiency of French words for the corruption of the English language. To many people it

34

sounds refined, even cultured, to drop stereotyped French into stereotyped English phrases. To use *badinage* for *banter*, and to think that there is a shade of difference, or I suppose I should say, a *nuance* of meaning . . . I am looking forward to reading in the newspapers a *précis* of a *résumé* of a *communique*. You see I omit the accent on the last *e*, and I wish you would tell me if the people who speak and write this jargon think that *résumé* is more refined than summary, abridgement, compendium. In society every woman is *très raffinée*. I once met an author who had written *small and petite*, and when I asked him why he did it, he said: *Petite* means dainty as well as small; I said: No, it doesn't, but if you wanted to say *dainty*, why didn't you say dainty?

We all enjoy laughing with the satirist on these occasions, but how valid is the underlying ideal of linguistic purity? Is it any more valid than the 'ideal' of racial purity? In the first place, it is worth noting that purity would seem to be *only* an ideal. That is to say, all languages seem to show the influence of other languages to some extent, even those (such as German) in which efforts are made to coin new words only from local resources. In the second place, we ought to consider whether, in objecting to the influence of another language, our *real* objection is to the culture of which this other language is the vehicle. If it is really American dancing and teen-age habits that the German commentator dislikes, it is little use taking a stand against the linguistic influence which is merely the *sign* of addiction to the habits.

On the other hand, if we welcome a particular cultural influence, can we effectively divorce this from the language in which it is couched? And if we can, what is achieved and is it worth the trouble? Let us take a simple example. At one time, we in this country badly needed to know all that we could from Italy about music. Today, the influence of Italy is seen *also* in the language we use when we are talking about music: *pizzicato*, *cello*, *trill*, *cadenza*, for example. Now we could have used the violoncello in England without adopting the Italian word for it; we could have referred to it as 'a biggish fiddle'; or we could have invented a name for it; *faddle*, let us say. But the gain would have been dubious—to say the least—while the inconvenience would have been great. Everyone would then have had to learn the new term—even those cultured Englishmen who were effecting our musical education, who needed to refer to these things most frequently, and to whom the Italian terms (and those only) were perfectly familiar.

Over the past millennium, English has adopted many thousands of words and expressions from many languages. It can in fact be argued that being receptive to foreign linguistic influence does not mean that a language is decadent and impure, its speakers weak and losing their identity: but rather that the members of the speech community are keenly alive to what is going on in the world and eager to keep pace with cultural developments elsewhere.

Exercises and Topics for Discussion

1 We would not expect to find Eskimos playing 'conkers' or (therefore) knowing the English word. Which fields of interest (and therefore uses of English) seem to you most 'international' and which most 'provincial'?

2 Write out a hundred English 'key words' and short phrases which you think would be most frequently required by someone (*a*) in the tourist industry, or (*b*) studying mathematics, or (*c*) interested in agriculture, or (*d*) visiting a trade fair.

3 Turn back to the passage quoted from a German news-paper and list the words that have been borrowed (sometimes in a strange disguise) from the English language. Which of them suggest that the speakers are young, adult, and female?

4 If a cello might have been known in English as 'a biggish fiddle', suggest English terms which might similarly replace *piano*, *pizzicato*, *trill*, *cadenza*, *concerto*, *sonata*, *trio*, *oratorio*, *opera*, *scherzo*.

5 With the help of a good dictionary, find out from what languages we have adopted the words used in the last paragraph of this chapter. Re-write the paragraph, trying to use as few originally foreign words as possible. Is your version an improvement? Consider our dependence on adopted words.

6 What, in your view, is implied by 'educated command of English'?

7 Suppose you were the author criticised at the end of the Moore quotation (p. 35); compose an argument, with examples, that you might use in reply.

3: *The Dress of Thought?*

IT may be profitable to take the discussion for a time away from the English language as such, and to consider the uses that are made of *any* living language. In a well-known passage in his *Lives of the English Poets*, Dr Johnson says that 'Language is the dress of thought', and it has become commonplace to quote this in support of the view that thought is behind all language and that language is primarily used to 'dress up' and send thoughts on their way: give *substance* to thoughts. 'Language', we are often told, 'exists for the expression of thoughts or ideas.'

There could be wide disagreement over what an idea or a thought exactly *is*, and therefore over the meaning of such a definition. But most of us would probably agree at any rate that the following quotation illustrates language being used 'for the expression of thoughts or ideas':

> The physicist Planck asserted that the energy of radiation is given out by a radiating body discontinuously, in definite fixed amounts or quanta, there being proportional to the frequency of the vibrations.

Most of us would equally agree that this statement of quantum theory represents a genuine, very important, and perhaps even very common use of language. We are not all physicists, but we all have to express 'thoughts or ideas' on this level from time to time:

> When the Grand Alliance had been formed, Louis recognised the impossibility of defeating his enemies on the Continent

38

in any decisive fashion and ordered his Marshals to stand mainly on the defensive.

After bending or welding, mild steel plate fittings must be normalized by heating them to a medium red, maintaining them at this temperature for fifteen minutes, then allowing them to cool in still air.

This novelist's concern is predominantly with the physical and mental growth of his characters, their subjection to accident, and to some extent their cyclic fluctuations of behaviour as circumstances come near to repeating themselves.

Some drugs, such as senega, act as stimulating expectorants because they increase the flow of blood which in turn increases the amount of the expectoration in the bronchial tubes and so aids its removal.

Genuine and important these observations are, without doubt, but are they what language is chiefly and primarily used for, what language 'exists for'? It may be illuminating at this point if we try to think back over a day's events and recall just how we have in fact been using our language. Calling someone to get up; morning greetings; singing to oneself in the bathroom; asking if breakfast is ready; grumbling about the weather or about where that other sock has disappeared to; teasing someone; appealing for help with a ticklish job. It would be stretching the meaning of 'thoughts or ideas' a very long way to make it cover all these, yet we can be fairly confident that they bulk large in the daily use of language by anyone—be he a Bertrand Russell or the local paperboy.

We may get some confirmation that this is so by further reflecting that these uses of language seem 'easier', seem to come more naturally, than the examples dealing with 'thoughts or ideas' which were quoted earlier. We can surely agree that all of us find it easier to ask for the sugar or grumble about our work than to discourse on expectorants, mild steel or Louis XIV. And we should realise that this is not merely because these particular subjects are beyond our competence: it would still be true if for 'expectorants' we substituted the name of our favourite hobby.

It would be a big mistake to dismiss the 'easy' uses of language as trivial and unimportant merely because they seem so ordinary. Indeed, the more ordinary they seem, the more obvious it should be that we start from them in considering the use of English or any other language. If they seem ordinary, it is this very fact that makes the use of English seem difficult when we are writing an essay or describing some complicated chemical experiment: difficult because unfamiliar and extraordinary. And again, at the risk of being repetitive and obvious, we must stress that it is not that the *subject* is 'unfamiliar and extraordinary'. We may have a perfectly clear understanding of the experiment and the essay may be on our favourite hobby. It is the use to which we are putting our language that is unfamiliar.

A paper-boy, a sixth-former, and a new graduate may be equally skilful in teasing, shouting instructions on the games-field, grumbling—or even swearing. They may be as skilful as each other or as Mr Graham Greene or Sir Bernard Lovell in any of these uses of language. But their skill will probably be unequal when it comes to drafting a letter, writing a report, or making a formal speech, because these last—for all their importance—are relatively rare and sophisticated uses of language. They might fairly be called 'exotic'—a term particularly apt for *written* language, in which we all need special training, which cannot be said to 'come naturally', and which has its own set of special rules and conventions. And if the word 'exotic' suggests 'glamorous', we are not being led perhaps so very far from the mark, since *glamour* itself was originally a variant form of

40

grammar which is derived from a Greek word connected with 'writing'.

However exotic or complicated the uses to which we have to put our language, we must all start from that common skill in the 'ordinary' and 'natural' uses of language which we share with Mr Graham Greene and the paper-boy. Moreover, since all the uses—exotic or ordinary—require to some extent different kinds of English, we improve our sensitivity to the occasion and our whole perspective over the range of English, if we increase our consciousness of the quite distinct uses of English that we hear or read daily.

'Language exists to express our thoughts.' We have seen some of the reasons for questioning this sweeping generalisation. There are several others. We are all aware that language is quite often used to *conceal* our thoughts. Voltaire is among those who have made this cynical observation: men, he said, 'n'emploient les paroles que pour déguiser leurs pensées'. Goldsmith has a similar comment: 'The true use of speech is not so much to express our wants as to conceal them.' The Danish philosopher Kierkegaard went one better even than this: people use language not merely to conceal their thoughts, he said, but to conceal the fact that they have no thoughts.

A. Ingraham in 1903[1] categorised the uses of language as follows:

   (i) to dissipate superfluous nervous energy;
  (ii) to direct motion in others, both men and animals;
 (iii) to communicate ideas;
 (iv) as a means of expression;
  (v) for the purposes of record;
 (vi) to set matter in motion (as in charms and incantations);
(vii) as an instrument of thinking;
(viii) to give delight merely as sound.

[1] *Swain School Lectures*, pp. 121-182.

To this imposing list, he added a further item, to the effect that language was also useful in keeping grammarians busy. But perhaps we should not treat this last as just a joke. It is worth studying language not merely because it is a useful tool in so many ways, but also because language is so fascinating in itself. In fact, it is man's most characteristic activity—the behaviour which most obviously and overtly distinguishes him from the rest of the animal world.

We shall return to scrutinise some of Ingraham's points presently, but perhaps it would be useful at this point to draw attention to the distinction between 'language' and 'a language'. Language in the abstract is our facility to talk to each other; it is the faculty of speech, which all human beings hold in common. On the other hand, a language is a particular code, a particular set of conventions which we operate through the possession of the faculty of speech; and a language is not held in common by all human beings but only by those who belong to a specific speech-community.

It is important to notice how things have been put in making this distinction. Language is our facility to talk to each other. The word 'talk' is used not merely to avoid a rather more technical and high-sounding word like 'communicate'; 'talk' is more precise and more relevant to the special nature of human language than 'communicate'. In the first place, all creatures—cat, sparrow, and bee—can be said to *communicate* with each other to some extent. They can attract each other's attention, warn of danger, woo their mates, and direct the way to food. We are still learning just how well animals can communicate with each other,[1] but there can be no doubt that animal communication is wholly rudimentary as compared with the complex

[1] There is an informative and entertaining essay on this subject by J. B. S. Haldane in the book, *Studies in Communication*, edited by Sir Ifor Evans (London 1955).

42

and subtle control of language possessed by even the least intelligent or least educated English tramp or Australian aboriginal. It is therefore appropriate to say that language involves 'talk' to emphasise that language is a peculiarly human activity.

In the second place, 'talk' is useful for the present purpose because it specifies the basic and most important way in which human beings communicate. As we have already seen in this chapter, it is far from being the only way. We use language when we write letters, draft notices, read books, or send messages by morse code. But all these are *derivative* from talk, and they are minor functions as compared with 'mere talk'.

The use of language primarily and predominantly involves making noises with our speech organs and receiving other people's speech noises through our ears. It is not a necessary condition of a language's existence that it should have a written form or indeed any form other than talk. All natural languages had a very long history as solely speech before they were ever written down or became associated with rules of spelling and punctuation. Many hundreds of languages exist in the world today which have never been written down yet. Most of the changes that affect languages in time and space (the differences between Chaucer's English and our own, for instance, or the differences between British and American English) are to be explained in terms of language as *spoken* and *heard*. Most of the difficulties we experience in using language in what we have called here its more 'exotic' ways (writing an essay, for example) arise from the fact that our chief competence in the use of language lies in talking it.

The primacy of *speech* in the consideration of language and the importance of understanding how speech is transmitted in sound are matters dealt with in Professor Gimson's Supplement. For the present, the vital point to grasp

43

is that although we can transmit language by highly 'unnatural' means such as the teleprinter, and can use language for highly sophisticated and intellectual purposes such as the statement of atomic theory, all languages are geared primarily to the fairly primitive needs of ordinary people and to the fairly primitive and physical conditions of tongue and ear. It is easy for literate people with some education to forget this and to think of language primarily in terms of its *written* manifestations.

The word 'primitive' has cropped up in the previous paragraph and perhaps we ought to dwell on it for a moment, since we have here a word that is often used illadvisedly in discussions of language. Many people think that 'primitive' is indeed a term to be applied to languages, though only to *some* languages, and not usually to the language they themselves speak. They might agree in calling 'primitive' those uses of language that concern greetings, grumbles, and commands, but they would probably insist that these were especially common in the socalled 'primitive languages'. These are misconceptions that we must quickly clear from our minds.

So far as we can tell, all human languages are equally complete and perfect as instruments of communication: that is, every language appears to be as well equipped as any other to say the things its speakers want to say. It may or may not be appropriate to talk about primitive peoples or cultures, but that is another matter. Certainly, not all groups of people are equally competent in nuclear physics or psychology or the cultivation of rice or the engraving of Benares brass. But this is not the fault of their language. The Eskimos, it is said, can speak about snow with far more precision and subtlety than we can in English, but this is not because the Eskimo language (one of those sometimes mis-called 'primitive') is inherently more precise and subtle than English. This example does not bring to light a defect

44

in English, a show of unexpected 'primitiveness'. The position is simply and obviously that the Eskimos and the English live in different environments. The English language would be just as rich in terms for different kinds of snow, presumably, if the environments in which English was habitually used made such distinctions important.

Similarly, we have no reason to doubt that the Eskimo language could be as precise and subtle on the subject of motor manufacture or cricket if these topics formed part of the Eskimos' life. For obvious historical reasons, Englishmen in the nineteenth century could not talk about motorcars with the minute discrimination which is possible today: cars were not a part of their culture. But they had a host of terms for horse-drawn vehicles which send us, puzzled, to a historical dictionary when we are reading Scott or Dickens. How many of us could distinguish between a chaise, a landau, a victoria, a brougham, a coupé, a gig, a diligence, a whisky, a calash, a tilbury, a carriole, a phaeton, and a clarence?

The discussion of 'primitiveness', incidentally, provides us with a good reason for sharply and absolutely distinguishing human language from animal communication, because there is no sign of any intermediate stage between the two. Whether we examine the earliest records of any language, or the present-day language of some small tribe in a far-away place, we come no nearer to finding a stage of human language more resembling animal communication and more 'primitive' than our own. In general, as has been said, any language is as good as any other to express what its speakers want to say. An East African finds Swahili as convenient, natural, and complete as an East Londoner finds English. In general, the Yorkshire Dalesman's dialect is neither more nor less primitive or ill-fitted to its speaker's wants than Cockney is for the Londoner's. We must always beware the temptation to adopt a naïve parochialism which

45

makes us feel that someone else's language is less pleasant or less effective an instrument than our own.

This is not to say that an individual necessarily sounds as pleasant or is as effective as he might be, when using his language, but we must not confuse a language with an individual's ability to use it. Nor are we saying that one language has *no* deficiencies as compared with another. The English words 'home' and 'gentleman' have no exact counterparts in French, for example. These are tiny details in which English may well be thought to have the advantage over French, but a large-scale comparison would not lead to the conclusion that English was the superior language, since it would reveal other details in which the converse was true. Some years ago, it came as something of a shock to us that we had no exact word for translating the name that General de Gaulle had given to his party—*Rassemblement du Peuple Français*. The BBC for some time used the word 'rally', and although this scarcely answers the purpose it is a rather better translation of 'rassemblement' than either of the alternatives offered by one well-known French-English dictionary, 'muster' and 'mob'.

The more we consider the question, then, the less reasonable does it seem to call any language 'inferior', let alone 'primitive'. The Sanskrit of the Rig-Veda four thousand years ago was as perfect an instrument for what its users wanted to say as its modern descendant, Hindi, or as English.

From what has been said, it must be clear that no one can make very positive statements about how language originated. There is no material in any language today or in the earliest records of ancient languages that shows us language in a new and emerging state. It is often said, of course, that language originated in cries of anger, fear, pain and pleasure, but the necessary evidence is entirely lacking: there are no remote tribes, no ancient records, providing evidence of a language with a larger proportion of such cries than we find in English. It is true that the absence of such evidence does not *disprove* the theory, but on other grounds too the theory is not very attractive. People of all races and languages (indeed, many animals too) make rather similar noises in reaction to pain or pleasure. The fact that such noises are similar on the lips of Frenchmen and Malayans, whose languages are utterly different, serves to emphasise the fundamental difference between these noises and language proper. We may say that the cries of pain or chortles of amusement are largely reflex actions, instinctive to a large extent, whereas language proper does not consist of instinctive signs but of signs which have to be *learnt* and which are wholly conventional.

This latter point, that the words in a language are *conventional*, is very important. There is no fixed or predictable relation between words and their meanings. That is to say, if you were idly turning the tuning control on your radio, and your ear caught what sounded like 'meel', there is nothing about these sounds themselves that could help you guess their meaning, and they are unlike a sound of merriment or annoyance in this respect. If you heard enough to know that *English* was being spoken, then you would interpret the sounds of 'meel' in terms of the English code of conventions and decide that a *meal* was being talked about. If you heard enough to know it was French, then the sounds would have to be interpreted in terms of the French code, which has *mille* with an entirely different meaning from the English word with roughly similar sound, *meal*. The sounds making up the English word *cry* mean 'edge' in Russian, and the plural of the same English word, *cries*, sounds like the German word which means 'circle'. We must not expect the *signs* of language to be direct *symbols* of what they mean, in the way that an 'x' symbolises a cross-roads or blue on a map symbolises the sea.

47

This of course is not to deny that all languages have some words which involve direct symbolism: these are the onomatopoeic, imitative or echoic words such as the English *cuckoo*, *splash*, and *whisper*. And even these are conventional to quite a large extent. The word *mutter* does not mean 'mutter' in German or French, even though these languages also have onomatopoeic words for 'muttering': *murren* and *marmotter*, respectively. If you throw a stone into the water, the sound you hear is by no means the same as when you say 'splash'. In any case, words like these, which show some degree of direct symbolism, constitute only a small and untypical minority in any language. Nevertheless, their existence is important in bearing witness to the desire that seems to be present in every linguistic community: for a language-sign to have as close and immediate relation to its meaning as possible.

Such a desire is reflected in the manipulation of onomatopoeic effects by poets, who group words—which individually may be purely 'conventional' signs—in a way that makes them seem directly representational in their sound. In the following lines, only one or two of the words that Tennyson uses are themselves echoic in origin, but their grouping makes them all onomatopoeic:

> The bare black cliff clang'd round him, as he based
> His feet on juts of slippery crag that rang
> Sharp-smitten with the dint of armed heels—
> And on a sudden, lo! the level lake,
> And the long glories of the winter moon.

The arrangement of sounds in these lines clearly contributes to the narrative: the sounds tell us something about the journey to the lake-side and about the peaceful beauty of the lake itself. In so doing, they *also* 'give delight merely as sound'—the eighth of Ingraham's linguistic functions.

But 'delight merely as sound' is not restricted to ono-matopoeia or to any of the other devices that we associate with the great poets or with 'literary beauty'. Mention has already been made of singing in the bathroom, and we may further heighten the contrast by quoting some material collected by Peter and Iona Opie, the authors of *The Lore and Language of School-Children*. No clearer examples of delight in sheer sound can be found than in the chants used by children at play. Here are some lines from a rhyme used when throwing a ball under one's leg at a wall:

> She sent for the *doctor*
> The doctor couldn't *come*
> Here comes the *ambulance*
> *Rum, Tum, Tum.*

The italicised words mark the points at which the ball passes under the leg. In the following, on the other hand, delight in sound is achieved along with 'word-play' proper:

. . . Shirley Sevenple, Shirley Eightple, Shirley Nineple, Shirley Temple.

Delight in sound for its own sake ranges from Cockney rhyming slang to the use of puns and word-play which are carefully selected for the purpose of giving pleasure and at the same time adding punch to what is being said. We find it in the laconic words of Senator Robert Kerr, outlining with shrewd verbal wit the role of John F. Kennedy when he was President:

This is how Bills become law: delayed, frayed, re-made, okayed, J.F.K.'d, and obeyed.

And we find it in ordinary, light conversation—though it

49

is doubtful whether the conversation that follows can exactly be called 'ordinary', or whether all conversations that accompany bridge-playing are so playful:

The players examine their hands. When they talk, they do not look at each other, but concentrate entirely on their cards.

FIRST MAN (*humming softly as he sorts*): Pom-pom-pom-pom, pom-pom-pom, pom-pom-pom-pom, pom-pom-pom, pom-pom-pom-pom . . .

SECOND MAN (*whistling through his teeth*): Ss, ss-ss-ss-ss, ss-ss-ss, ss-ss-ss, ss-ss-ss, ss-ss-ss-ss . . .

FIRST LADY: Bub-bub-bub-bub, bub-bub-bub-bub, bub-bub-bub, bub-bub-bub-bub—whose call?

SECOND LADY: Your callikins.

FIRST LADY (*still engrossed in her cards*): My little callikins, well, well, well—*my* little callikins. Let me see, then, let me see—I think—I think—I think-a-pink-a-pink—no bid.

SECOND LADY: Tch-tch-tch, tch-tch-tch, tch-tch, tch-tch, tch-tch-tch, tch-tch-tch—no bid.

FIRST MAN: One cloob.

SECOND MAN (*dropping into Irish*): Did ye say one cloob?

FIRST MAN (*dropping into Irish*): I did that.

SECOND MAN: *Er hat ein cloob gesagen.* (*Singing*) *Er hat ein cloob gesagen, er hat ein cloob* . . . One hearty-party.

FIRST LADY: Two diminx.

SECOND LADY: No bid, no bid.

FIRST MAN: No bid-a-bid-bid.

SECOND MAN: Two diminx, is it? Two naughty leetle diminx. This, I think, demands a certain amount of *considération.* (*Drums fingers on table*) Yes, yes, my friends, *beaucoup de considération.*

SECOND LADY (*after a pause*): Your *call*, partner.

SECOND MAN: I know it, I know it, I know it, I know it, I know it, indeed, indeed, I know it. (*Clacks tongue*) I know it, I know it, I double two diminx.

SECOND LADY: He doubles two diminx.

FIRST MAN: He doubles two diminx.
SECOND MAN: I double, I double, I double two diminx.
FIRST LADY: Very well, then, have at you. Two no trumpets.
FIRST MAN: Ha, ha!
SECOND MAN: Ho, ho!
FIRST LADY: He, he!
SECOND LADY: H'm, H'm!

They revert to their pet noises as they consider their hands.

(*Nine Sharp*, by Herbert Farjeon.)

Exercises and Topics for Discussion

1 The chapter began by referring to 'living' language. What is a *dead* language? Can Latin be called a 'dead' language when it continues to be used for example as the *lingua franca* and medium of instruction at the Pontifical Gregorian University in Rome?

2 Find out as accurately as possible the difference between the various carriages listed on p. 45, and supply a similar list of different types of motor vehicle in use today.

3 The following are among the commonest exclamations used in writing and having a conventional written form: *Oh, ah, eh, aha, oho, ugh, oo*. Bearing in mind that each may have more than one use (*Oh, well; Oh!; Oh?*), try to give an account of their use and 'meaning'.

4 An 'x' to denote a cross-roads was given as one example of a visual symbol to some extent directly representational. List as many others as you can, and explain in what respects they are representational.

5 'Croissant is the name we give to a crisp roll because it *is* a crisp roll.'
'Soup is the sucking noise that is made when it is eaten.'

'Biscuits are so called because of the sound they make when you break them.'

Examine these reactions in the light of the discussion of onomatopoeia and of echoic words such as *splash* and *mutter*.

6   Although all languages are in general equipped to express what their speakers want to say, this situation can remain so only if needs are supplied as they arise. Study the following proposals and comments, and (*a*) suggest how these specific needs might be met, (*b*) state and discuss any deficiencies in the language that you have encountered in your own experience, and, (*c*) consider whether there are any general principles that might be useful in coping with problems of this kind:

(i) 'Capable-of-undergoing-nuclear-fission'?

'It is unquestionable that "fissionable" is objectionable to the impressionable; but to the knowledgeable it is unexceptionable.'

'Fissionable is fashionable and surely reasonably admissible. Fissible is risible.' (Letters in *The Times*, 21 December 1953.)

(ii) Is 'know-how' respectable enough?

'I can think of no good reason . . . for the substitution of "expertise" for "know-how" in a recent leading article. "Know-how" has at least the virtue of a crystal clear meaning though expressed in an ugly form. "Expertise", on the other hand, has no widely accepted English definition except in its formal French sense of expert inquiry or valuation.

There is need for a concise and accurate English word to express this particular idea of expertness.' (*Daily Telegraph*, 5 December 1955.)

(iii) Should doctors 'vet' human patients?

' "To scrutinise" appears to supply the polite word

52

in place of the plebeian "to vet", with its faintly derogatory connotation.'

'I have been asked to "run the rule over", an expression quite as revolting. A better and frequent suggestion has been, "I want to be examined." It is difficult to suggest a word that will be dignified whilst satisfying those to whom dignity has little meaning. The best words I can offer are "investigation" and "inquisition". Either conveys the meaning admirably, but I fear neither would become popular; they are too pompous. I am afraid we shall have to continue vetting.'

'The word "sounded" suggested itself to me as a fair substitute for the detractory "vetted"; a word which has the felicity of being in the same genus as hale and hearty, unblemished and intact.'

(Letters in *The Sunday Times*, 11 December 1955.)

(iv) 'Vianaut'? 'Pupamotor'?

'About 300 suggestions for a new word to describe the driver of a motor vehicle have been received by the Automobile Association . . . The linguistic experiment started last month when Lord Brentford, chairman of the A.A., asked for a word to describe the driver of a motor vehicle of any kind from lorries to mopeds, so that "motorist" could be reserved for the driver of a private car. This distinction, the association thinks, is often necessary in reports of accidents and other incidents on the roads. . . . Many of the suggestions are compound words designed to be self-explanatory, while others fall back on the modern craze for initials to form a new noun. Hence autocarist, autovehiclest, autonaut, and chassimover. Less evident are doice (driver of internal combustion engine), licentiat (licensed internal combustion engine navigator trained in automobile tactics), and pupamotor (person using power-assisted means of travelling on roads). More

53

like basic English are motorman, wheelist, tractionist, trafficant, and roadent.' (*The Times*, 28 October 1961; reference might be made also to the leading article on the subject in *The Times* on 6 September 1961 and the correspondence columns of this and other papers around this time.)

(v) How high is a hippy at an okay scene?

If we are to prevent young people from joining the unfortunate 'junkies' and 'mainliners' who, starting by being 'sent' for 'kicks', soon know what it is to be 'cold turkey' and worse, we need to understand the language they use and acquire language precise enough to describe the effects, sinister as they may be. In the face of adjectives such as *hallucinogenic, psychotogenic, psychotomimetic, psycholytic, psychodysleptic*, and *psychedelic*, Sir Alan Herbert has recently commented on the latter word. As well as wondering why it should not 'on precedent . . . be psychodelic', he writes that

'there is, it seems, "a psychedelic revolution". I was stupidly baffled for a long time, but suddenly I remembered the Greek word *delos*—clear. The word must mean "making the soul clear". This does not match very well with descriptions I have read of "a trip" with LSD and other modern blessings. A better word might be psychechaotic. You "explore the consciousness" and you find swamp after swamp.' (*The Guardian*, 27 March 1967.)

54

4: *Language as Servant and Master*

We have seen something of what is involved in saying that language can 'give delight merely as sound'. We may now go back and look more closely at the rest of the list (page 41) which Ingraham gives of the uses of language. After what has been said about the primacy of 'ordinary' uses of language (as in greetings and grumbles), we can more readily understand why Ingraham heads his list with *dissipating superfluous nervous energy*. We may feel such 'superfluous nervous energy' when we hit our thumb instead of a carpet-tack, and although we may not agree that the burst of language which releases and dissipates the energy is the mark of a civilised man, a linguistic reaction—however violent—is arguably more civilised than some such physical alternative as throwing the hammer at the china cabinet. It is conceivable, perhaps, that people may some day be able to dispute without slanging each other with the rudest names they can conjure; but for the present we may be content to admit that, if hard words are regarded by both participants as a satisfactory substitute for hard blows, language is performing a useful service.

But outbursts of anger are not the only kind of nervous energy to be considered here. One thinks of the thrill of emotion experienced as one turns a corner and sees a beautiful sunset. Even if alone, we may find it difficult to repress an involuntary exclamation, 'Oh, how utterly lovely!' We may even add—'beneath our breath' or 'to ourselves', as we put it—'What a violent contrast that glowing cloud makes with the sombre brow of the hill!' In fact, it is a

55

common experience for many people to feel a special satisfaction according as they can release a flood of emotion by means of *precise* language, and by contrast to have a vaguely uncomfortable, even painful, pent-up feeling if they cannot find adequate words. 'Words fail me!' The wider and more flexible our range of language, therefore, the more readily and completely can we relieve our feelings when we are overcome by 'superfluous nervous energy'.

Ingraham's third and fourth points may at first blush seem to be one and the same. There is in fact, however, a worthwhile distinction to be made, even though one might prefer to reverse the order, since the former ('to communicate ideas') should be regarded as a special case of the latter ('means of expression'). 'I'm tired' or 'The paper's here' or 'I like chocolate creams' are hardly instances of communicating ideas, but they are good representatives of that important human characteristic of being able to express oneself through language. The non-linguistic alternatives to the three examples just given would be yawning (and perhaps going to sleep); pointing to the paper; and smacking one's lips and salivating freely at the mention of chocolates.

From this basic and elementary use of language, it is worth distinguishing the communication of ideas, since ideas are rather rare—and ability to communicate them effectively still rarer. It is in this range of linguistic usage that we need most practice and special training.

The seventh point made by Ingraham also deserves some comment: language as an instrument of thought. It is not always realised to how large a measure a language is tied to the thinking of its users, but this is a source of further complication when we try to be precise and scientific in our 'exotic' uses of English. The word 'democracy', meaning 'rule by the people', means something of which in our particular culture we strongly approve, and we tend to ignore the possibility that 'democracy' could connote any-thing but what is noble and right. But in the Nazi Germany of the thirties, where democracy was *not* an ideal, it meant something like 'rebellious lack of discipline'—and 'liberal' also had nasty connotations. Even in our own history, 'democracy' has not always been used approvingly. Lord Byron once wrote that democracy was 'an aristocracy of blackguards', and as recently as the middle of the last century, Sir Arthur Helps was able to speak—without im-plying a paradox—of having 'too affectionate a regard for the people to be a democrat'. There are unhappy signs that the 'permissive society' of the nineteen-sixties may be encouraging a reaction in which the word 'tolerance' may come to have a bad flavour.

In a country where there is a monarchy which is highly respected, the word corresponding to 'royal' will take on the meaning of 'noble', 'splendid', as well as the literal sense of 'relating to the monarch'. But in another country, which has just become a republic after a bitter struggle against an unpopular, tyrannous king, the corresponding word will still have the meaning 'relating to the monarch', but its additional connotations are more likely to be 'brutal' or even 'wicked' than 'noble' and 'splendid'. One would therefore have to be very careful in translating into the language of this second country something like 'They gave us a royal welcome.'

It has been pointed out that discussion of the colour problem in the world today is not helped by the words we use, because *black* and *white* have in many communities powerful connotations in addition to the literal denotation of colours. The word *black* in many communities denotes fear or even wickedness, and there is an equally widespread association of *white* with purity and goodness. These con-notations which accompany our words can dangerously affect our attitudes without our realising it. A comment in the *Unesco Courier* of February 1956 is worth quoting in this connexion:

> This complex emotional content of the word 'white' would become apparent to children of European origin if, for a period, they and their teacher used the rather more appropriate adjective 'pink' in classroom discussion of ethnic differences. The sense of superiority which comes to many people when they think of themselves as white . . . disappears when they think of themselves as pink.

The writer no doubt had in mind the social situation described as follows by E. M. Forster:

> The remark that did him most harm at the club was a silly aside to the effect that the so-called white races are really pinko-grey. He only said this to be cheery, he did not realise that 'white' has no more to do with a colour than *God Save the King* with a god, and that it is the height of impropriety to consider what it does connote. The pinko-grey male whom he addressed was subtly scandalized; his sense of insecurity was awoken, and he communicated it to the rest of the herd. (A *Passage to India*, 1924, chap. 7.)

Jeremy Bentham, nearly a century and a half ago, pointed out broader dangers which arise through the influence of language upon thought. Because many of our nouns refer to 'real things' like tables and shoes, having 'substance' (and classed grammatically as 'substantives'), we are in danger of thinking that nouns like 'liberty', 'crime' and the like are equally 'real' and 'substantial'. Bentham's line of thinking has been very much developed in the twentieth century by men like C. K. Ogden and the American linguist B. L. Whorf. A favourite example in demonstrating the domination of language has been the spectrum, which, in spite of its being a continuum, is broken by language into

58

discrete units like 'red', 'blue', 'yellow' which make it somewhat difficult for us to *see* (let alone talk about) intermediate shades for which our language does not provide us with names. And of course since a label like *red* in English does not correspond to a 'really' discrete unit, there is no guarantee that there is a colour-label in another language which exactly corresponds to our *red*. As Whorf pointed out:

> We dissect nature along lines laid down by our native languages. The categories and types that we isolate from the world of phenomena we do not find there because they stare every observer in the face; on the contrary, the world is presented in a kaleidoscopic flux of impressions which has to be organised by our minds—and this means largely by the linguistic systems in our minds. We cut nature up, organise it into concepts, and ascribe significance as we do, largely because we are parties to an agreement to organise it in this way—an agreement that holds throughout our speech community and is codified in the patterns of our language. (*The Technology Review*, vol. 42, 1939.)

But language does not only have this restrictive influence on thought: language also conditions our thinking in a positive and constructive way. In discussing a little earlier in this chapter how language released emotion, it was pointed out that a person might have a pent-up feeling if he could not find the words to describe an experience. This is very largely because we feel that we have not thoroughly apprehended something if we are unable to put it into words.

Not all of us depend to the same extent on words when we are thinking to ourselves, but it is certain that, in general, thinking and decision-making are vastly supported and facilitated by language, even though we may be using the language *silently*. Most of us can grasp and understand

59

distinctions better when we have the linguistic apparatus to chop it out of the flux and chaos of raw experience around us. It may be rather arbitrary to divide up the minutely graded dwelling places that we see around us into huts, cottages, bungalows, houses, mansions, and palaces: there is no hard and fast line between these in 'reality'. But even imposing this rough grid on what surrounds us is better than nothing; we are enabled to *see* the reality more clearly. Moreover, although it is not strictly to the present point, our cutting up of reality in this way helps us to *talk* about it to others, 'because', as Whorf says, 'we are parties to an agreement' to organise reality in this particular way in our speech community.

It is not very easy to demonstrate conclusively that language helps thought, but we can usually recognise the truth of it from our personal inner experience. Most of us can remember passing through stages like the following. Let us suppose we have attained, in early childhood, the distinction between 'round' and 'square'. Later on, 'round' is further broken down into 'circular' and 'oval', and it becomes easier to see this 'obvious' difference between shapes when we have acquired the relevant labels. But then we come to metaphorical extensions of the terms. We grope towards a criticism of *arguments* and learn to follow a line of reasoning; we learn to exercise doubt or be convinced according to how the argument goes. Some arguments may strike us as unsatisfactory, yet have nothing in common except their tendency to give us a vague lack of conviction and some discomfort. Then we hear someone discussing a line of argument and we catch the word 'circular' being used. At once everything lights up, and we know exactly what kind of argument is meant; the idea 'clicks', as we say. There is of course nothing about an argument which resembles the shape of a circle, and we may never have thought of 'circle' except in terms of

60

visual shapes. Yet in a flash we see the *analogy* that the *metaphor* presents, and thereafter we are able to spot this type of fallacious argument more speedily, now that we have this linguistic means of identifying it.

The importance of language in making distinctions is also seen in considering people who suffer from such conditions as ' nominal aphasia '. Professor Stephen Ullmann has told us of one psychologist's experiment with a patient who had completely forgotten the names of colours but who had retained perfectly good colour vision:

> Asked to choose from among a number of coloured threads those belonging to the same category, he found the task impossible and even meaningless. To him all the threads were different in colour. And so they were in actual fact, as far as their purely visual appearance was concerned. By losing the names, the verbal labels, the patient had also lost the principle of classification, the faculty of subordinating individual differences to some higher unity, the habit of introducing some man-made lines of division into the unbroken continuity of the natural scale of colours. Thanks to language, the spectrum had been divided up and had become articulate; with the loss of the verbal signposts, it had relapsed into chaos. (*Words and their Use*, p. 89.)

Leonard Bloomfield provided an everyday illustration of how indispensable our faculty of language is to us. After pointing out that a great deal of our thinking goes on by the use of words inaudibly, he continues:

> Our ability to estimate numbers without using speech is extremely limited, as anyone may see by glancing, say, at a row of books on a shelf. To say that two sets of objects ' have the same number' means that if we take one object from the first set and place it next to one object of the second set, and keep on doing this without using any object more than once, we shall have no unpaired objects left over. Now,

we cannot always do this. The objects may be too heavy to move, or they may be in different parts of the world, or they may exist at different times (as, say, a flock of sheep before and after a storm). Here language steps in. The numerals, *one*, *two*, *three*, *four*, and so on, are simply a series of words which we have learned to say in a fixed order, as substitutes for the above-described process. Using them, we can 'count' any set of objects by placing them into one-to-one correspondence (as mathematicians call it) with the number-words, saying *one* for one of the objects, *two* for another, *three* for the next, and so on, taking care to use each object only once, until all the objects of the set are exhausted. Suppose that when we had said *nineteen*, there were no more objects left. Thereafter, at any time or place, we can decide whether any set of objects has the same number as this first set, by merely repeating the counting process with the new set. Mathematics, the ideal use of language, consists merely of elaborations of this process. The use of numbers is the simplest and clearest case of the usefulness of talking to oneself, but there are many others. We think before we act. (*Language*, pp. 28-9.)

And, as Bloomfield's example shows, language plays a vital role in our ability to think.

There is one function of language that Ingraham does not make explicit but which is to some extent implied in his points numbered one, four, and eight. It is a function that has been very much discussed in recent years, especially in the light of observations made by the anthropologist Bronislaw Malinowski. He called this use of language 'phatic communion', and by this term he sought to distinguish that part of our speech behaviour which is given over to polite sociabilities, greetings, empty catch-phrases and the like, which we hear breezily passed around by people in the street or on buses or in casual café conversation : ' Nice again today', ' Oh it's you. How's things? ' ' Ah well, that's life', ' I'm pleased to meet you.' In what follows, we have a rather extreme instance of it:

'Have you had a busy day, dear?' Aunt Lin asked, opening her table napkin and arranging it across her plump lap.

This was a sentence that made sense but had no meaning. It was as much an overture to dinner as the spreading of her napkin and the exploratory movement of her right foot as she located the footstool which compensated for her short legs. She expected no answer; or rather, being unaware that she had asked the question, she did not listen to his answer. (*The Franchise Affair*, by Josephine Tey.)

It is a use of language that is easy to overlook in the serious study of language, but in fact it is very important, as we may see if we reflect upon what Malinowski has to say on the subject:

A mere phrase of politeness, in use as much among savage tribes as in a European drawing-room, fulfils a function to which the meaning of its words is almost completely irrelevant. Inquiries about health, comments on weather, affirmations of some supremely obvious state of things—all such are exchanged, not in order to inform, not in this case to connect people in action, certainly not in order to express any thought. It would be even incorrect, I think, to say that such words serve the purpose of establishing a common sentiment, for this is usually absent from such current phrases of intercourse; and where it purports to exist, as in expressions of sympathy, it is avowedly spurious on one side. What is the *raison d'être*, therefore of such phrases as 'How do you do?' 'Ah, here you are', 'Where do you come from?' 'Nice day today!'—all of which serve in one society or another as formulae of greeting or approach?

I think that, in discussing the function of Speech in mere sociabilities, we come to one of the bedrock aspects of man's nature in society. There is in all human beings the well-known tendency to congregate, to be together, to enjoy each other's company. Many instincts and innate trends, such as fear or pugnacity, all the types of social sentiments such as ambition, vanity, passion for power and wealth, are dependent upon and associated with the fundamental tendency which makes the mere presence of others a necessity for man. (Malinowski's Supplement to Ogden and Richards, *The Meaning of Meaning*, pp. 313-4.)

It is a matter of common experience that the person who does not speak (and who is on this account called 'unsociable') is liable to be somewhat distrusted, even feared or disliked. Walking along a country road at night, it is usual to break silence on passing someone, and the exchange of words is a mutual re-assurance. People vary from place to place (and of course from individual to individual) in their habits and feelings over this aspect of behaviour, but all of us should realise that there are some of our fellows who feel a very unpleasant tension in the presence of a stranger (as in a railway carriage) without some brief entry into 'phatic communion'.

When we consider how important and basic is this quite ordinary and unsophisticated use of language, it may be worth recalling what was said earlier (in Chapter 3) about the primacy of speech. Here obviously is a use of language which relates chiefly to speech, to spoken more than to written language, and one ought in particular to recall the earlier statement that 'all languages are geared primarily to the fairly primitive needs of ordinary people'. It is from such 'ordinariness' in the use of language that we all start; it is in these uses of language that we are all fairly equally competent. However much we may wish to cultivate a more refined and delicate use of language for argument and for precise writing, our language has at the same time to be kept going for these relatively crude and primitive purposes, and most of our *practice* in the use of language is in these crude and primitive situations.

Our ability to use English subtly or precisely is continually being interfered with by a constant, unremitting need which pulls our language in the opposite direction: by our need to use language simply and *imprecisely* for everyday purposes—such as phatic communion. 'Nice day again,' we say cheerfully, and we should find it intolerable if such utterances had to be given meteorological precision, with reference to temperature, wind-speed, cloud-height, and barometric pressure.

We sometimes rather thoughtlessly criticise an announcement or a government form which refers to 'male persons over the age of twenty-one years'. What ridiculous jargon, we think; why couldn't this pompous official have used the word 'man'! But the official may be forced into a jargon that he likes no more than we do, by the imprecision of the ordinary words that we may prefer. In the present instance, *man* may sound perfectly obvious as the right gloss upon 'male persons over the age of twenty-one years', but would the latter be equally our automatic interpretation if the word 'man' had been used? The word 'man' is applied regularly to hundreds of thousands of students, only a minority of whom have reached the age of twenty-one. We often use it of still younger males of sixteen or seventeen, and it can be applied to a school-boy of ten ('the team is a man short'). It may simply mean 'brave person', as when we tell a little boy of four to 'stop crying and be a man'. Or it may mean 'human being', without regard to sex, as in a phrase like 'not fit for man or beast'. It may even mean a wooden disc—as in the game of draughts.

This is the *ordinary* use of language which makes the *extraordinary* use of language (as in science or law) a constantly recurring difficulty, because—important as law and science may be—we cannot sacrifice the ordinary, everyday use of language merely in order to leave language permanently suitable for the 'loftier purposes'. And let us make no mistake: the imprecision of ordinary language is essential to the use and perpetuation of language of any kind. One simply must be able to make utterances of a general and imprecise kind: 'Quick—there's a man on the phone—long distance.' If one is not allowed a shorthand expression of this kind, it would cost the unfortunate 'person whose voice suggested that he was a male who had reached full maturity &c &c' a fair number of coins merely to have his call announced.

We can see, therefore, that language is rooted in the ordinary events of everyday and in ordinary men's usage. We *need* language to be imprecise because a great part of its convenience lies in its very adaptability to the making of generalisations and abstractions. When we talk airily of improving our language, it must be perfectly clear that we mean improving our language's *range*. It does not mean eradicating the lowlier uses of language as heard loosely used in greetings, grumbles and brief, sketchy observations. If we were to eradicate these, we should kill language itself in the process, since not only are these functions basically important but also language is kept alive and handed on by being used for these functions: they represent the basic, common uses of language. In other words, they give us most of our daily practice in language, and most of our motivation for using language.

For this double reason, we need to pay special attention to language in its most ordinary, everyday manifestations, when we are trying to make our control of language suitable for more 'exotic' purposes. Our most elevated rhetoric and our most subtle dialectic are rooted in ordinary usage which alone gives life to language, and which in countless ways conditions, affects, stimulates, rejuvenates the finer language that we need to use for a minority of purposes on a minority of occasions. Even the finest language cannot be a perfect and logical medium, since it is so closely related to language in its underlying 'primitive' functions, but

66

awareness of the latter should make it easier for us to make our language more careful and precise, when care and precision are called for, because they help us to see in what ways language is *not* normally careful and precise.

Just as learning about a man's imperfections helps us to sympathise with him, to come to terms and co-operate with him: so awareness of the inherent imperfections of language will fit us to make more effective use of the language. If a man knows that the steering of his car is in bad shape, he holds the wheel more carefully and avoids bumps in the road. So too, study of the points at which language is most liable to let us down can be a very useful safety precaution.

Exercises and Topics for Discussion

1 Whorf was quoted as saying, 'We dissect nature along lines laid down by our native languages.' Explain carefully and give examples. Where does the ankle end and the calf begin? Where does chest end and stomach begin? What distinguishes a branch from a twig? Consider the extent to which language makes arbitrary distinctions.

2 What do you think Bloomfield means by calling mathematics 'the ideal use of language'?

3 Try to recall experiences of your own in which your thinking has been (*a*) influenced, (*b*) assisted, by your language.

4 'Language is called the garment of thought; however, it should rather be, language is the flesh-garment, the body, of thought' (Carlyle, *Sartor Resartus*).
'He gave men speech, and speech created thought, Which is the measure of the universe' (Shelley, *Prometheus Unbound*).

Which of these now represents your view more nearly?
Are the two quotations incompatible?

5 (a) Give examples of English being used in each of Ingraham's eight ways (page 41) and in 'phatic communion'.

(b) Do the uses of language mentioned by Malinowski supplement or merely re-label those listed by Ingraham?

(c) Re-read the passage by Farjeon at the end of Chapter 3, and try to relate all the features of language to Ingraham's and Malinowski's categories.

6 Outline the aspects of a person's behaviour which would quality him in your view to be called 'sociable'.

7 We have noted that language is valuable in enabling us to make 'generalisations and abstractions'. Explore this idea further and discuss some of the different kinds of generalisation and abstraction that we find ourselves making habitually by means of English vocabulary.

5: *English and the Native Speaker*

'I SPEAK English, don't I? My cobbers understand me. Why the heck should you have to teach me English at all?' This quotation, given by Professor I. A. Gordon in his book on *The Teaching of English*, has a familiar ring for all its specifically antipodean flavour. The speaker is raising perfectly reasonable questions and deserves a careful and reasoned answer. It is one thing to teach a New Zealander French. Even this, of course, one may need to justify up to a point: he may have to be convinced that he ought to learn French. But at any rate he does not need to be convinced that there is something to be learnt. His knowledge of English, on the other hand, may well seem so complete and perfect that he feels he has nothing to learn.

The answer lies, as we should by now have seen, in the restricted nature of an individual's command of a language (the farm-labourer and the chemist may feel equally equipped for what they need to say), and in the many uses to which even a single individual may have to put his language. We are all equally well-equipped, perhaps, to utter greetings and grumbles: we are *not* equally equipped to write reports or to develop our thinking along unfamiliar lines. It is for this reason that, as well as the limitedly 'reasonable' complaint of the New Zealand boy, we can read equally 'reasonable' but utterly opposed complaints, such as the following which appeared in *The Times Educational Supplement* in 1960: 'The English language is a foreign language to most of our children.' Clearly this correspondent is thinking of the uses of language that do

69

not come naturally to us—what we have called the 'exotic' uses, which have to be carefully and deliberately learnt. Similarly, in 1958, Mr John Archbold, speaking as President of the National Union of Teachers, was quoted in *The Times* as saying that 'Far too many people today assume responsibility in local and national government without having progressed far beyond the language of their childhood and adolescence. How much more effective they would be if they had received a more intensive education in the use of their mother tongue!'

Being understood by one's 'cobbers' is simply not enough. In fact, the problem facing the native user of English is not confined to 'being understood', even outside the circle of one's 'cobbers'. True, this is a prime reason for extending our knowledge of our language, but it is not the only one. Language also has *social* complications which have to be understood: and no language involves more far-reaching social complications than English.

The newspaper report that we have just been considering went on to say that Mr Archbold 'told of a visiting inspector who called at a school where the local dialect was the daily mode of communication. He asked one boy to recite a poem. On rising to do so, the pupil looked at his teacher and asked: "Have we to swank a bit, Miss?"' Using English outside the circle of one's immediate friends is thus liable to be seen not merely as a broader, more general, less 'local' English, but as a 'swankier' English.

In Chapter 2, we noted that people were rather egocentric in their attitude to other people's language, and we questioned the validity of using 'pure' as a criterion of good English. As a wise and well-balanced American writer put it some years ago in the *Daily Telegraph*, language is 'very much a personal matter, and many people, objective in other areas of thought, are apt to be less rational about their tongue. In the matter of their language, they tend to be

70

highly ethnocentric and sensitive, to believe that only they use the language properly, and to resent the particular variations in use elsewhere.'

But talk of having 'to swank a bit' shows that we are concerned with more than personal and individual taste, with more than the variations according to individual or even region—except in so far as a particular place may be associated with 'swank'. We are confronted here with language as a status-symbol, with the existence of a certain amount of *agreement* about preferred usage, with awareness of some kind of standard, against which all deviations are measured.

The logic of 'My cobbers understand me' is no more relevant in this delicate social situation than the quickest way of gulping one's food is in the matter of table-manners. Our table-manners and the way we eat particular dishes are not determined primarily by desire to get the food into our mouths in the quickest and easiest way. If they were, the time-and-motion experts would very soon effect a revolution in our eating habits. No, our table-manners are part of our conforming to the social conventions of a community. So, too, in our choice of clothes: we do not think merely of keeping warm or cool, but of doing so within the conventions of our society. With our language habits also, then, we must always be sensitive to our environment and use the 'accepted' forms of English, just as we eat and dress in the 'accepted' ways.

Now, all of us at some time have experienced a certain amount of doubt with food and dress: the sudden alarm as to how one manipulates asparagus or what to wear at that wretched garden-party today. Yet the total system of conventions for eating or dressing is triflingly simple as compared with the delicate complexity of the conventions in language. It is not to be wondered at, therefore, that doubts can arise much more frequently (and letters can

71

appear in the press and questions be set in examinations) about the choice of linguistic forms. Of course, there is no problem while we are with our 'cobbers'. Even cabinet ministers have their opportunities for linguistic collar-loosening and for speaking without having to consider what it will look like in Hansard.

Outside the circle of our intimates, however, we begin to feel restraints of many kinds, and the further our activities carry us from the people and the background that we are used to, the more careful we have to be in our use of English. We become aware that there is such a thing as linguistic etiquette and linguistic tact. There are 'right' things to say or write, just as there are 'right' things to wear. And this is not only a matter of avoiding embarrassment to ourselves by committing a linguistic *faux-pas*. Linguistic tact also induces us not to embarrass others. If someone looking at your garden admires the 'broad-end-rums' (and obviously means it seriously) can you refer to them in the next breath as 'rhododendrons' without seeming to correct him?

A good deal of nonsense continues to be written about 'class-dialects' in England and elsewhere, and probably more harm than good is done by trying to 'do an Emily Post' and listing particular trivialities which are said to divide one 'class' from another. It is in fact beyond question that linguistic features which can be identified as the markers of real or fancied social classes are few in number, and that what we have are sharply declining in importance at the present time. The following paragraphs by Mr S. J. Sharpless largely represent facts and attitudes of a past age:

As children, we lived on the lower-class fringe of an upper-class suburb. . . . In the next street, by the railway, lived the rough children. Shrill, grubby, with torn clothes, they suffered one handicap in particular which, in my parents'

72

eyes, made them unsuitable for me to play with. Their speech was horribly uncouth. In the street on the other side, by the park, lived the posh children. They had pleasanter ways and were nicely dressed; best of all, they spoke with mild and expensive voices. But with these, too, I had nothing to do. We could not, without embarrassment, ask them home to tea in our small house.

So, at an early age, I ran into the phenomenon of class, and the speech differences bound up with it; and fenced in by solemn snobberies I learnt to walk the narrow way between two worlds, having, I suspected, less fun than either.

I think it worried my parents more than anything else that our speech would be corrupted by the aitchless community at our doorstep. We were constantly being pulled up for some real or fancied coarseness of enunciation or vulgar phrase. I soon found that speech, which distinguishes man from the animals, distinguishes Briton from Briton almost as sharply. The proposition about East is East and West is West applied to the London postal districts as well as to the hemispheres. I saw that learning to speak English with a genteel accent was more important to getting on in life than learning to speak French or German. It was years before I could discard this shabby obsession with vowels and consonants. (*The Observer*, 27 December 1953.)

But if language habits do not represent classes, a social stratification into something as bygone as 'aristocracy' and 'commons', they do still of course serve to identify social *groups*. This is something which seems fundamental in the use of language. As we saw in relation to political and national movements in Chapter 1, language is used as a badge or a barrier depending on which way we look at it. The new boy at school feels out of it at first because he does not know the right words for things, and awe-inspiring pundits of six or seven look down on him for not being aware that *racksy* means 'dilapidated', or *hairy* 'out first ball', or that something which sounds like 'K.V.'

means 'look out—a master's coming!' The miner takes a certain pride in being 'one up' on the visitor or novice who calls the *cage* a 'lift' or who thinks that men working in a warm seam are in their 'underpants' when anyone ought to know that the garments are called *hoggers*. The sailor cannot help feeling slightly superior towards the landlubber who calls the *companionway* the 'stairs'. The 'insider' is seldom displeased that his language distinguishes him from the 'outsider'.

Quite apart from specialised terms of this kind in groups, trades and professions, there are all kinds of standards of correctness at which most of us feel more or less obliged to aim, because we know that certain kinds of English invite irritation or downright condemnation. On the other hand, we know that other kinds (for instance, each year's crop of 'O.K. words') convey some kind of prestige and bear a welcome *cachet*.

In relation to the social aspects of language, it may well be suggested that English speakers fall into three categories: the *assured*, the *anxious*, and the *indifferent*. At one end of this scale, we have the people who have 'position' and 'status', and who therefore do not feel they need worry much about their use of English. Their education and occupation make them confident of speaking an unimpeach-able form of English: no fear of being criticised or cor-rected is likely to cross their minds, and this gives their speech that characteristically unselfconscious and easy flow which is often envied. Their nonchalant attitude to language was epitomised in the nineteenth century in the words of Bulwer Lytton: 'I am free to confess that I don't know grammar. Lady Blessington, do *you* know grammar?'

At the other end of the scale, we have an equally im-perturbable band, speaking with a similar degree of careless ease, because even if they are aware that their English is

74

condemned by others, they are supremely *indifferent* to the fact. The Mrs Mops of this world have active and efficient tongues in their heads, and if we happen not to like their way of saying things, well, we 'can lump it'. That is *their* attitude. Curiously enough, writers are inclined to represent the speech of both these extreme parties with *-in'* for *ing*. On the one hand, 'We're goin' huntin', my dear sir'; on the other, 'We're goin' racin', mate.'

In between, according to this view, we have a far less fortunate group, the *anxious* ('having, I suspected, less fun than either', as Mr Sharpless put it). These actively try to suppress what they believe to be bad English and assiduously cultivate what they hope to be good English. They live their lives (at any rate their public lives, in offices and the 'better' shops) in some degree of nervousness over their grammar, their pronunciation, and their choice of words; sensitive, and fearful of betraying themselves. Keeping up with the Joneses is measured not only in houses, furniture, refrigerators, cars, and clothes, but also in speech. In the autumn of 1961 the *Daily Express* printed an article called 'Bosses in Search of Boardroom Accents', describing speech training given to some men promoted from the shop-floor to executive posts. The managing director thought the training 'would give them confidence—they now worked with university men—earn them respect, and help them in the boardroom. The six new executives . . . found the idea amusing at first. But their wives egged them on.'

And the misfortune of the 'anxious' does not end with their inner anxiety. Their lot is also the open or veiled contempt of the 'assured' on one side of them (with jibes at 'suburban English'), and of the 'indifferent' on the other ('Cor, 'ark at 'er, goin' all lah-di-bloomin'-dah! ').

It is all to easy to raise an unworthy laugh at the anxious. The people thus uncomfortably stilted on linguistic high-heels so often form part of what is, in many ways, the most admirable section of any society: the ambitious, tense, inner-driven people, who are bent on 'going places and doing things'. The greater pity, then, if a disproportionate amount of their energy goes into what Mr Sharpless called 'this shabby obsession' with variant forms of English—especially if the net result is (as so often) merely to sound affected and ridiculous. 'Here', according to Bacon, 'is the first distemper of learning, when men study words and not matter. . . . It seems to me that Pygmalion's frenzy is a good emblem . . . of this vanity: for words are but the images of matter; and except they have life of reason and invention, to fall in love with them is all one as to fall in love with a picture.'

Well, we know what Bernard Shaw made of the Pygmalion story and what was more recently made of it in *My Fair Lady*. Studying the use of English is not directed towards producing a community of distraught Eliza Doolittles, and our aim must be not to increase the number of 'anxious' but the number of 'assured'. At the same time, we shall not achieve this by ignoring the fact that social and more especially (as we saw in the *Express* article) educational judgments are made on linguistic grounds. We shall achieve it rather by inquiring further into the facts, studying the nature of language in society, and the specific structure of English. A developed and mature awareness of our language and how it works around us is the surest protection against the malaise of 'anxiety' on the one hand and against the vacuity of 'indifference' on the other. The whole subject is taken up in more detail in Supplement II.

How then does English work? It seems reasonable to consider language as operating through three types of organisation, on two separate planes: *vocabulary* and *grammar* on one plane, *means of transmission* on the other plane. The part that usually seems most obvious, even most important, is the word-stock—also known as the *vocabulary* or *lexis*. We may think of this as our total collection of *names* for things: the names of actions, objects, qualities, and so on; words like *assume, box, taxation, finger, sharp, table, extraordinary*. The total vocabulary of English is immense and runs to about half a million items. None of us as individuals, of course, knows more than a fairly limited number of these, and uses even less, but obviously the greater our personal knowledge of vocabulary (the more words we recognise and the more we know how to use), the better we are able to enjoy our environment and describe our experience of it.

Words are so predominant in language, and a dictionary is so much regarded as the entire register of a language, that we are sometimes tempted to think that there is nothing else to consider. 'Man's word is God in man'—'Your words, they rob the Hybla bees.' But a language cannot work with words alone. A group of words like *arrive, girl, man, say* cannot tell us much until we have added a second dimension, grammar. Grammar contributes features like articles, prepositions, tense number, and the conventions of arrangement—which word goes before which. With grammar added, the four words we selected can be made to tell us something: 'The *man said* that the *girls* had *arrived.*'

Grammar has done three things here. It has arranged the words in a particular order, making clear who did the saying and who the arriving. It has contributed *tense* by the alteration of *say* to *said*, and *number* by the addition of *s* to *girl*. Thirdly, grammar has added some additional words: *the, that, the,* and *had*. This third point raises a difficulty. We have already described the first dimension of language as 'vocabulary', the stock of *words*: now, it is being suggested that grammar also consists in part of words. At first sight, it may be confusing to find the same word, 'words', applied to part of grammar as well as to the whole of the vocabulary. English has, in fact, two kinds of words, lexical words and grammatical words, and this basic distinction is important to learn—even if it is not very easy to apply in some cases. The distinction can perhaps best be seen (and the importance of the distinction for English most easily appreciated), if we contrast another language, Latin, in which 'grammatical words' are less numerous and play a much smaller part. The four words *arrive, girl, man, say*, would be in Latin (devoid of grammatical endings) *adveni-, puell-, vir*, and *dic-*. If we now add grammar, we shall still have in this case just four words, since *inflexion* alone is able to achieve what in English requires both inflexion and grammatical words: *vir dixit puellas advenisse*, 'The man said that the girls had arrived.'

The grammatical words which play so large a part in English grammar are for the most part sharply and obviously different from the lexical words, as one can see by comparing the two sets in our present example: *the, that, the, had*, and *man, say, girl, arrive*. A rough and ready difference which may seem most obvious is that grammatical words have 'less meaning', and in fact some grammarians have called them the 'empty' words as opposed to the 'full' words of vocabulary. But this is a rather misleading way of expressing the distinction. Although a word like *the* is not the name of something as *man* is, it is very far from being meaningless; there is a sharp difference in meaning between 'man is vile' and 'the man is vile', yet *the* is the sole vehicle of this difference of meaning. Moreover, grammatical words differ considerably among themselves as to the amount of meaning they have, even in the lexical sense (as we may see by comparing *the* and *should*, for example). Another name for the grammatical words has been 'little words'. Elizabeth Barrett Browning told her husband, 'You sometimes make a dust, a dark dust, by sweeping away your little words'—as well she might, in

78

view of such lines as 'Heine for songs; for kisses, how?'
But size is by no means a good criterion for distinguishing
the grammatical words of English, when we consider that
we have lexical words like *go*, *man*, *say*, *car*. Apart from
this, however, there is a good deal in what Mrs Browning
says: we certainly do create a good deal of obscurity when
we omit them. This is illustrated not only in the poetry of
Robert Browning but in the prose of telegrams and newspaper headlines. 'MacArthur Flies Back to Front' is an
example from war-time days which manages to be amusing
without being confusing, but 'Liverpool Tea Breaks Strike
Leader Under Fire' (1961) is only clear in a context of daily
news about a strike in Liverpool over tea-breaks. Otherwise
one might wonder what there was about Liverpool tea that
could break a strike-leader—or even why tea-breaks in
Liverpool should strike a leader already unfortunate enough
to be under a fire.

Grammatical words, then, (or 'function' words, as they
are also called in some books) are vital signals telling us
about the kind of connexion that is to be understood between lexical words. It is not that they have no meaning,
but that they have a special kind of meaning, sometimes
called 'grammatical meaning' or 'structural meaning'.
Another important characteristic is that they belong to a
relatively small and permanent set of words as compared
with the 'full words' of vocabulary. They do not come and
go with changing fashions and changing ideas. In different
occupations, in different places and at different periods, we
tend to use very different nouns and verbs; *totalitarianism*,
the *axis*, or *evacuee* may be very often on our lips for a
while; we may invent entirely new words like *vitaminise*
or *penicillin*; we may even adopt foreign words and bandy
them about freely and familiarly—*blitz* in the forties,
sputnik in the fifties, and *troika* made a frequent appearance early in the sixties. Vocabulary consists of *open* lists of

words. But we very rarely add to our stock of prepositions and pronouns, and it is equally rare for an odd one to go out of fashion. Grammatical words are in (relatively) *closed* lists. They remain constantly (and unobtrusively) at their station whether we are saying, 'The man said that the girls had arrived' or 'The dictator claimed that the democracies had deteriorated' or 'The beatnik found that the coffee-bar had closed.'

One may suggest an analogy in the goods and equipment of a store. On the one hand we have the articles for sale—dresses, hats, fur-coats; and on the other hand price-tickets, stands, coat-hangers, and measuring-tapes, which are used to handle the goods in which the shop deals. It is the stock that claims most of our attention; it changes from time to time; some parts of it are more in demand at one time, and other parts seem more important at another. But the things used by the shop-assistant—though often beneath our notice—are no less essential to handling the day-to-day business, and a hanger which supports a fur-coat one month may be used for a wedding-dress the next. So too we may think of vocabulary as the word-stock, and grammar as the set of devices for handling this word-stock.

When we have these two aspects of English clearly understood and distinguished, we can move on to consider the third. Language can exist only if there are means of sharing it with the rest of our community. That is to say, although we do quite frequently use language for *self*-communion (as we have seen), we are on such occasions using language in an entirely secondary way, imitating a normal situation in which we are talking or listening to someone else. A person has a vocabulary and grammar only because it has been transmitted to him by other people, to whom it was transmitted by other people—and so on, in an unbroken tradition. Our third type of organisation in language is necessarily therefore the *means* of *transmission*.

This needs to be seen as being on a different plane from the others for a number of reasons. For example, once a person has acquired a particular language, units such as sentences —joint products of grammar and vocabulary—can exist 'in him' independently of whether or not he decides to speak them or write them down. What is more, we can on occasion (some of us more than others) utter a sentence in a way that we know to be imperfect: with a stammer, a misordering, some repetition, or even the use of a wrong word. Often in such cases we not only know that we have transmitted the sentence wrongly but we know that our hearer has been able to make allowances and has grasped, despite the imperfections, the sentence we had intended.

The transmission of language is primarily effected through the use of our breath force as modified by organs in our throat and face to make noises, which we call our 'pronunciation'. How primary this means of transmission is we can see from the word *language* itself, which comes ultimately from the Latin word for 'tongue'—one of the speech organs which in many languages is taken as the type and symbol not only of all the physical organs of speech but also of speech itself. We have the same idea in English when we speak of 'a foreign tongue' or 'the tongues of men'.

But while pronunciation is primary, it is by no means the only method of transmission available to us. We can use our fingers and address someone by means of the deaf-mute alphabet, we can send messages by Morse code, and above all we can *write*. Important as these are, however, we must remember that they are secondary and are derived— whether immediately or ultimately—from language as spoken and heard. We shall look a little more closely at both the principal modes of transmission—speaking and writing—in the next chapter.

81

Exercises and Topics for Discussion

1 Mr Archbold was quoted as saying that people *today* assume responsibility in certain circumstances. Re-examine his statement and consider what is so special about the present time in this connexion. What different circumstances in the past may the speaker have had in mind?

2 How valid do you think the distinction is between the 'assured', the 'anxious', and the 'indifferent'? Write a short speech on the subject of Sunday football in the style which might be used by a speaker in each of these categories.

3 Explain and discuss the following expressions in the quotation from Mr Sharpless: 'mild and expensive voices'; 'aitchless community'; 'real or fancied coarseness'. Discuss the extent to which the situation today is different from that in Mr Sharpless's childhood.

4 (a) What might a landsman call a *bulkhead*, a *scupper*, a *galley*?
(b) Write out some words and expressions which you think could be reckoned 'insider' language with reference to (i) jazz, (ii) football, (iii) the theatre.

5 In a New Year resolution for 1959, *The Observer* ironically promised not to use a number of words including the following: *seminal, top, offbeat, beat, U, Angries*. Discuss the ways some of these 'O.K. words' have been used in recent years, and try to think of some words in similar currency at present.

6 Make two lists distinguishing what seem to you to be the words of vocabulary and the words of grammar in the closing paragraph of the chapter.

7 Re-consider the analogy of the shop (with its goods and equipment) and language (with its vocabulary and

grammar), and point out where the analogy breaks down.

8   Write opening paragraphs which you might expect to find beneath the following headlines:

(a) RUBBER BRIDGE AT MONTE CARLO: Fastest Players Win in Grand Prix (*The Times*, 6 April 1959).

(b) VIRGIN LANDS JOB FOR DISGRACED RED.

(c) NEWSPEAK MADE SIMPLIFAX (*The Times*, 28 March 1967).

9   'But their wives egged them on' (p. 75). What implications occur to you for English usage, from your own observations?

6: What is Standard English?

ALL the various kinds of English, which as we saw earlier are determined by differences in occupation, place, education and the like, display their variety in terms of the three dimensions of language: vocabulary, grammar, and transmission. Let us examine how this works out in the following examples of English by present-day writers.

1 Dickie: I'm on Mother's side. The old boy's so doddery now he can hardly finish the course at all. I timed him today. It took him seventy-five seconds dead from a flying start to reach the pulpit, and then he needed the whip coming round the bend . . .
Arthur: Doddery though Mr Jackson may seem now, I very much doubt if he failed in his pass mods when he was at Oxford.

2   Tonight the wind gnaws
           with teeth of glass,
           the jackdaw shivers
           in caged branches of iron,
           the stars have talons.

3 'What's the matter with your hand?'
   'I seem to have the most boring *thing*,' Vera replied. 'So unattractive.'
   'If it isn't better in the morning, we'll run you in to angel Dr Wingfield in the village. An absolute pie-man, charges two dollars a visit, and looks, I promise you, like Santa Claus.'
   'Heaven,' Vera declared.

4   Nah Jooab's middlin' thick like, bur 'e'd a 'ad to be a deeal
thicker net ta know ut ther wer summat wrang t'way
ut shoo wer preychin' on, an' so 'e late paper tummle
ontut' flooar an 'e sat theer an' gaped woll shoo stopped
fer breeath, an' then 'e sez, 'What the heck 'as ta agate
on, lass? Is ther summat up or summat?' An' that didnt
mend matters one iota. All it did wer ta start 'er off
ageean.
    'Just 'ark at 'im,' shoo sez. ''Ere's me, as thrang as
Throp's wife when shoo 'ung 'ersen wit' dishcleyat, an'
theer's 'im cahrd uv 'is backside! Coint see a job ut ther
is ta do! Wodnt dreeam o' doin' it if 'e cud . . .'
    'Nay!' bust in Jooab. 'Ahm nooan takkin' that
quitely. Thers monny a one war ner me an' full weel tha
knows it.'

5   At the end of the first act we went out with all the other
jerks for a cigarette. What a deal that was. You never
saw so many phonies in all your life, everybody smoking
their ears off and talking about the play so that everybody
could hear and know how sharp they were. Some dopey
movie actor was standing near us, having a cigarette. I
don't know his name, but he always plays the part of a
guy in a war movie that gets yellow before it's time to
go over the top. He was with some gorgeous blonde, and
the two of them were trying to be very blasé and all, like
as if they didn't even know people were looking at him.

6   I met ayont the cairney
            A lass wi' tousie hair
            Singin' till a bairnie
            That was nae langer there.

            Wunds and walds to swing
            Dinna sing sae sweet.
            The licht that bends owre a' thing
            Is less ta'en up wi't.

7   A thrush on the lawn kept looking with its small round

85

eye. Then he would make a dive to see if a worm was there. When he had eaten, he flew away but came back quickly, landing gracefully with a little curtsey. He stood listening. He hopped once, twice, three times. . . . Then listened again. He repeated this several times before he got his worm.

8 'Well,' says Ma, 'I kind o' had my face fixed fer chicken, but I guess we c'n manage. Here, Lump, you run down to Perkins' grocery and fetch up a few cans salmon an' any other vittles ye might think tech the spot.'

'Not me,' Lump says, 'Jedge tole me ef I got caught swipin' any more stuff out'n stores, he'd send me to state's prison sure 'nough.'

'That so, young Mister High-an'-Mighty !' snaps Pa Jukes. 'Well, lemme tell you one thing, you young whippersnapper, ef state's prison's good enough fer yer brother Timmy, it's plenty good enough fer you.'

9 My own nostalgia has risen in the memory of a camp by a rushing stream at the bottom of a gorge where the sun shines but a few hours each day. There the smoke of the camp was redolent with the scent of burning gum leaves; there was the splash of a lizard taking to the water, the twittering of birds in the trees, the laugh of the kookaburra, the call of the thrush, the crack of the coach-whip bird. The mimicry of the lyre bird echoed across the gully, while wonga pigeons and satin bower birds fed on berries in the neighbouring brush.

There are big differences between these nine passages. Some of the language we can 'place' at once. We can say that one is Scots; that another is a northern English dialect (even if we cannot be more precise); that another is to be 'placed' socially rather than regionally—a conversation between two rather fashionable people; that another is an American dialect; that another is American but is not so much dialectal as racy and slangy. The sources of the passages are here listed in random order, and you can probably pair off each passage with its source quite easily:

Christmas Landscape, a poem by Laurie Lee;
The Face of Australia, by C. F. Laseron;
The Catcher in the Rye, by J. D. Salinger;
The Winslow Boy, by T. Rattigan;
'Runnin' Repairs', by G. Vine, in the *Transactions of the Yorkshire Dialect Society*;
Empty Vessel, a poem by Hugh MacDiarmid;
Child's essay quoted by M. Langdon, in *Let the Children Write*;
The Pattern of Perfection, by Nancy Hale;
'The Jukes Family', by Frank Sullivan, in *The New Yorker*.

Let us consider first the differences in the *transmission* aspect. If we look at passages 1 and 3, we can find no sign of any difference in this respect, yet if we heard the four characters speaking, we would at once notice a sharp difference between on the one hand Arthur and Dickie (educated British), and on the other hand Vera and her companion (educated Americans). A difference in the primary kind of English transmission (pronunciation) does not necessitate a difference in the secondary kind (spelling), and in fact does not *usually* entail a difference. Thus passages 2, 5, 7, and 9 also use a spelling which is completely neutral as to pronunciation, though two of them are written by English people, one by an American, and one by an Australian. This kind of spelling is called English *orthography*, a word which means the *right* way of spelling.

Here, then, is the first sign of Standard English—a standard way of writing the language, which is accepted (with some slight variations) all over the world as the 'right way' to spell, no matter what the English it represents sounds like. Indeed, unless we have had special training in phonetics so that we can recognise sounds and write them in phonetic script, we have no other means of writing English than in terms of the conventions of English orthography. If, for example, we write *thought* as *thort*, we are not departing from the principles of English orthography: we are merely replacing one set of possibilities by another —instead of the *-ough-* as in *bought, ought, nought, thought*, we have the *-or-* of *port, sort, short, fort*. In other words, the spelling *thort* would not suggest the sound of the word 'thought' to a Frenchman or a Russian, but only to someone who knows English orthography. That English orthography has a clearly systematic basis is shown by the following witty note by Mr K. Clements in the *Daily Telegraph* (28 Sept. 1955), correcting a writer who had used the spelling 'gawmless': '"gawmless" is awften spelt "gormless" by Nawtherners. Orful, isn't it?'

The dominance of orthography over any more direct representation of pronunciation is also illustrated—paradoxically enough—in the eighth passage by the *departures* from orthography. The writer uses a number of non-standard spellings such as *fer, o', tole, jedge*, and these are enough for us to be able to give the writing a context of place and culture. If our experience of the dialect is great enough, we are then able to supply a dialect pronunciation to the whole passage, despite the fact that no attempt has been made to show this pronunciation in the spelling. For instance, *young, enough, brother, grocery, stores* and many other words are given in the ordinary orthography which is 'neutral' as to pronunciation.

Similarly, although the fourth passage shows a much more persistent attempt to show pronunciation in the spelling (and we find it far harder to read in consequence), there is still a fundamental connexion with orthography. Indeed, here too there are many words given in the standard spelling, as for example *thicker, know, gaped, stopped, matters, wife*. We must also notice that although some of the non-

standard spellings in both 4 and 8 indicate dialectal pronunciation (*jedge* in 8, and *takkin'* in 4, for example), many
of them indicate ordinary and universal pronunciation:
sez in 4 and *c'n* ('we c'n manage') in 8. In cases of this
kind, the convention seems to be that the non-standard
spelling suggests a lack of formal education by implying
an ignorance of orthography.

On the other hand, in passage 5 we have a convention
of a different kind. In Scots, there has actually developed
a partially independent orthography; basically, of course,
it is identical with the English orthography used the world
over, but there are regular deviations which are widely
known among Scotsmen. A Scot will have a 'right' spelling
for his form of 'so', 'light' and many other words, whereas
a Yorkshireman usually will not.

To a much lesser extent, American usage has developed
a separate orthography (*theater*, *leveled*, *defense*, etc), but
differences between British and American practice are so
slight that we may reasonably regard both these main
branches of English as using a single orthography. It is
interesting to notice that passages 1, 2, 3, and 5 do not
happen to show a single divergence in orthography, although two are British and two American. This may be
the point also for us to remember that there is some scope
for variation in spelling *within* both the American and
British habits: for instance, *judgment* and *judgement*,
connection and *connexion*, *tyre* and *tire* (the latter being
the usual American spelling but sufficiently common in
Britain to be given precedence in the *Concise Oxford
Dictionary*), *programme* and *program* (the latter again
being the chief American spelling but not uncommon in
Britain also, especially in the computational sense), and a
few others.

On the whole, then, variations in spelling are small, and
we may say that in this mode of transmission we have a

fairly clear and consistent 'standard'. But in the primary mode of transmission—pronunciation—the situation is very different. Indeed, the chief advantage of our unphonetic orthography lies precisely in the fact that it does not carry with it a commitment to a particular area's pronunciation. It is 'neutral' to the vast differences that can be *heard* in the varieties of English, and so it can be understood wherever English is spoken—however English is spoken.

There are great impediments to the general use of a standard in pronunciation comparable to that existing in spelling. One is the fact that pronunciation (the *primary* form of transmission, we remember) is learnt 'naturally' and unconsciously, whereas orthography is learnt deliberately and consciously. Large numbers of us, in fact, remain throughout our lives quite unconscious of what our speech sounds like when we speak, and it often comes as a shock when we first hear a recording of ourselves. It is not a voice we recognise at once, whereas our own handwriting is something that we almost always know. We begin the 'natural' learning of pronunciation long before we start learning to read or write, and in our early years we go on unconsciously imitating and practising the pronunciation of those around us for many more hours per day than we ever have to spend learning even our difficult English spelling. It is 'natural', therefore, that our speech-sounds should be those of our immediate circle; after all, as we have seen, speech operates as a means of holding a community together and to give a sense of 'belonging'. We learn quite early to recognise a 'stranger', someone who speaks with an accent of a different community—perhaps only a few miles away. And quite often, even if we don't habitually speak with our original local dialect, we may feel the need to retreat into it on occasion—as into our own home, when we want to be particularly private and personal, or when we want to declare our basic loyalties.

'Why do you speak Yorkshire?' she said softly.
'That! That's non Yorkshire, that's Derby.'
He looked back at her with that faint distant grin.
'Derby, then! Why do you speak Derby? You spoke
natural English at first.'
'Did Ah though? An' canna Ah change if Ah'm a mind
to 't? Nay, nay, let me talk Derby if it suits me. If yo'n nowt
against it.'
'It sounds a little affected,' said Hilda.
'Ay, 'appen so! An' up i' Tevershall yo'd sound
affected' . . .
'Still!' she said, as she took a little cheese. 'It would be
more natural if you spoke to us in normal English, not in
vernacular.'
He looked at her, feeling her devil of a will.
'Would it?' he said in the normal English. 'Would it?
Would anything that was said between you and me be quite
natural . . . ?' (D. H. Lawrence, *Lady Chatterley's Lover*.)

As Lawrence implies here, it seems quite natural in most
societies for people to recognise two distinct degrees of community: the immediate, local, and familiar community on
the one hand; and on the other, a wider and less familiar
community to which one also belongs and beyond which
begins the foreign world proper. Linguistically, these two
degrees are marked by a local dialect and a speech-form
which is not specifically regional and which may have an
additional prestige. It is to this latter, wider form of English
that Hilda is referring when she speaks of 'normal' English
as opposed to the 'vernacular'.

Most of us have an image of such a normal or standard
English in pronunciation, and very commonly in Great
Britain this is 'Received Pronunciation', often associated
with the public schools, Oxford, and the BBC. Indeed, a
pronunciation within this range has great prestige
throughout the world, and for English taught as a foreign
language it is more usually the ideal than any other pro-

nunciation. At the same time, it must be remembered that, so far as the English-speaking countries are concerned, this 'Received Pronunciation' approaches the status of a 'standard' almost only in England: educated Scots, Irishmen, Americans, Australians, and others have their own, different images of a standard form of English.

Even in England it is difficult to speak of a standard in pronunciation. For one thing, pronunciation is infinitely variable, so that even given the will to adopt a single pronunciation, it would be difficult to achieve. The word *dance* may be pronounced in a dozen ways even by people who do not think of themselves as dialect speakers: there is no sure way of any two people saying the same word with precisely the same sound. In this respect, pronunciation much more closely resembles handwriting than spelling. In spelling, there are absolute distinctions which can be learnt and imitated with complete precision: one can know at once whether a word is spelt in a 'standard' way or not. But two persons' handwriting and pronunciation may both be perfectly intelligible, yet have obvious differences without our being able to say which is 'better' or more 'standard'.

Moreover, while the easy and quick communications of modern times have mixed up and levelled dialectal distinctions to a great extent, and encouraged the spread of a 'neutral', 'normal' pronunciation, the accompanying sociological changes have reduced the prestige of Received Pronunciation. When Mr Robert Graves returned to Oxford in October 1961 to take up the Professorship of Poetry, *The Times* reported him as saying, 'Only the ordinary accent of the undergraduate has changed. In my day you very seldom heard anything but Oxford English; now there is a lot of north country and so on. In 1920 it was prophesied that the Oxford accent would overcome all others. But the regional speech proved stronger. A good thing.'

We have seen, then, that while there can be said to be *orthography*, a standard spelling, we can scarcely speak of an *orthoepy*—which would be the corresponding word for a universally recognised 'right pronunciation', if we had such a thing. It has long since ceased to be educationally fashionable to teach 'the art of right speaking and pronouncing English' (Simon Daines, *Orthoepia Anglicana*, 1640). We shall leave at this point the transmission side of English, which receives special treatment in Supplement I.

Although pronunciation is an obvious and immediately noticeable way in which two kinds of English may differ, it is not of course the only way. If we look back at the nine passages which open this chapter, we shall see that they differ very sharply in *vocabulary*. This is perhaps most noticeable in the specifically regional words in passages 4 and 6 (*thrang* and *cairney*, for example) which mark the passages as Yorkshire and Scots. In passage 5, words like *jerks, phonies, movie, guy* mark the passage regionally as American, but also stylistically—within American English—as *colloquial*. That is to say, 'movie' is *merely* American; 'jerk' is *additionally* slang, and as such is largely restricted to familiar, uninhibited, colloquial speech. Vocabulary can also show stylistic stratification without carrying any regional mark. In the American passage 5, we have *yellow* in the sense of 'cowardly' and in the Yorkshire speech of passage 4 we have *gaped* in the sense of 'stared'. Both are characteristic of the colloquial style, but in this style they can be used wherever English is spoken. Lexical differences of still another kind are to be found in the ninth passage. Words like *kookaburra* and *wonga pigeon* are part of the regional usage of Australia only because they represent things in the specifically Australian environment. Thus they mark Australian English very differently from the way in which words like *cairney* mark Scots or *thrang* the English of Yorkshire.

93

Most of the words we have considered so far proclaim their regional or stylistic status in isolation: *bairnie* is recognisably Scots and *kookaburra* Australian, *movie* American and *doddery* colloquial. But when *yellow* and *gaped* were mentioned in the preceding paragraph, a special note had to be added stating the sense in which each had been used. These words are not colloquial in themselves but only when they are used in a particular way. It is in fact usual to find that the status of a word is to be decided only from the way it is used on a particular occasion. There is nothing colloquial or slangy or American or British about 'old', 'boy', 'jerk' ('the car stopped with a jerk'), 'angel', 'smoking', 'ears'—so far as the words themselves are concerned. But when *angel* is used to describe a doctor it is colloquial, and when people are said to be 'smoking their ears off' this is slang; when a parson is referred to as an 'old boy', these words are being used in a way that is recognisably colloquial (and chiefly British); and when *jerk* is used in the sense of 'odd person', it is both slang and American.

It will be noticed that we are distinguishing between 'colloquial' (also called 'informal' and 'familiar') and 'slang'. There is, of course, some overlap; that is to say, it is unusual to find slang outside colloquial speech. But describing a usage as 'colloquial' means only that it tends not to be used on formal occasions, though perfectly polite and acceptable in informal conversation. A slang usage, on the other hand, is not generally introduced into informal conversation unless the speakers are on very intimate terms: slang embraces precisely those racy, daring and (at their best) fairly new expressions that have not been accepted by the majority of us as 'standard English'.[1] This is not to deny that the majority of us can keenly appreciate

[1] See further the useful and entertaining account of this subject in Eric Partridge, *Slang Today and Yesterday* (4th edn., London 1967).

94

the wit, vividness or purely bizarre quality that slang may have. It has been described as the ordinary man's poetry, and it is true that the imagery involved in slang is not so very different from that in poetry. On the one hand, we may call a girl a 'heart-throb' or speak of an arduous task that 'creased' us; on the other hand, we have a poetic image like 'the wind gnaws with teeth of glass' in passage 2. The following discussion is interesting in this connexion:

'But'—here Rosamond's face broke into a smile which suddenly revealed two dimples. She herself thought unfavourably of these dimples and smiled little in general society. 'But I shall not marry any Middlemarch young man.'

'So it seems, my love, for you have as good as refused the pick of them; and if there's better to be had, I'm sure there's no girl better deserves it.'

'Excuse me, mamma—I wish you would not say, " the pick of them ".'

'Why, what else are they?'

'I mean, mamma, it is rather a vulgar expression.'

'Very likely, my dear; I never was a good speaker. What should I say?'

'The best of them.'

'Why, that seems just as plain and common. If I had had time to think, I should have said, " the most superior young men ". But with your education you must know.'

'What must Rosy know, mother?' said Mr Fred, who had slid in unobserved through the half-open door while the ladies were bending over their work, and now going up to the fire stood with his back towards it, warming the soles of his slippers.

'Whether it's right to say " superior young men ",' said Mrs Vincy, ringing the bell.

'Oh, there are so many superior teas and sugars now. Superior is getting to be shopkeepers' slang.'

'Are you beginning to dislike slang, then?' said Rosamond, with mild gravity.

'Only the wrong sort. All choice of words is slang. It marks a class.'

'There is correct English: that is not slang.'

'I beg your pardon: correct English is the slang of prigs who write history and essays. And the strongest slang of all is the slang of poets.'

'You will say anything, Fred, to gain your point.'

'Well, tell me whether it is slang or poetry to call an ox a *leg-plaiter*.'

'Of course you can call it poetry if you like.'

'Aha, Miss Rosy, you don't know Homer from slang. I shall invent a new game; I shall write bits of slang and poetry on slips, and give them to you separate.'

Middlemarch, Bk. I, Ch. xi.

When we noted a little earlier that many words were not in themselves to be given restrictive labels such as 'American' or 'colloquial' but only in particular usages, this was equivalent to saying that there was some kind of neutral usage. Fred may claim, for the sake of argument, that 'correct English is the slang of prigs who write history and essays', but even he would not be able to identify the 'prigs' for whom words like 'thrush', 'lawn', 'round' in passage 7 were slang. And of course this applies equally to the majority of the words in the majority of the passages quoted in this chapter. Even those passages which have the most obvious stylistic marks of one kind or another contain for the most part perfectly ordinary words used in perfectly ordinary ways—as they might appear in private conversation, in a sermon, or in a history book. Words of which this can be said are clearly 'Standard English'. Some people would agree with Fred Vincy to the extent of calling highly technical jargon a sort of slang, but this is a point we can discuss later (see especially Chapter 10). In general, we can say that there is far greater agreement in the English-speaking world about standard vocabulary than about standard pronunciation, though with vocabulary too the image of 'standardness' varies to some extent as between the major communities (particularly Britain and America), and even as between individuals.

Finally, let us look at *grammar* in relation to the various kinds of English presented in the nine passages. In number 4, we find numerous features which—although they may seem expected and ordinary in the context of Yorkshire dialect—would be very surprising, and possibly incomprehensible, in any of the other passages. For example, 'shoo wer preychin' on', begins with two features of purely regional grammar: *shoo* is a northern dialect form of 'she', and in the same area *wer* is often used for standard English 'was'. On the other hand, *'e sez* (which differs from Standard English grammatically in having a present tense form instead of a past) cannot be said to represent specifically Yorkshire dialect grammar. Any of us has experience enough to be aware that 'he says' or 'says he' can be heard *anywhere* in this usage, on the lips of people who have had little education. It is not dialectal so much as uneducated or (to use another common term) 'sub-standard' grammar.

In passage 8, *out'n* for Standard English 'out of' is a feature of dialect grammar in the southern states of America, but *Not me*, used by the same speaker, is neither dialectal nor sub-standard but *colloquial* grammar, used everywhere. And of course the same applies to features like the contracted forms of negatives and verbs (such as *won't, isn't, we'll*) which are to be found in passages 1, 3, 4, 5 and 8. These are colloquial grammatical forms which occur in everyone's speech except sometimes when we are being very formal; they are usually avoided in print—except in representations of spoken English. This is why we find the contractions in passage 1, for instance, but not in 7 or 9. Another feature of colloquial grammar which would be

97

avoided in careful, formal writing is to have the plural pronoun *they* referring to an indefinite pronoun like *everybody*: 'everybody smoking their ears off' in passage 5 is in harmony with the rest of the colloquial features in these informal reminiscences.

Grammatical differences between colloquial English and formal, 'literary' English can be further seen in comparing passage 9 with most of the others. For example, we have 'the sun shines but a few hours'—a form of expression uncommon in colloquial English where we would more usually find 'the sun only shines a few hours' or (from a somewhat more careful speaker) 'the sun shines only a few hours'. We may also notice the formal grammatical patterning in passage 9: 'there was the splash of a lizard taking to the water, the twittering of birds in the trees'—two complex nominal groups with close correspondence of form: *splash* balanced against *twittering*, *lizard* against *birds*, and *taking to the water* against *in the trees*. This pair is followed by a list of three further items expressed with identical grammatical structure: 'the laugh of the kookaburra, the call of the thrush, the crack of the coach-whip bird'. Careful balancing of this kind is a characteristic of some kinds of formal, literary English. By contrast, the writer of passage 3 (equally carefully, of course) imitates the careless ease of the informal grammar found in light conversation: 'So unattractive.' 'An absolute pie-man, charges two dollars a visit.'

As we see from these nine passages, the greater part of English grammar is common to all dialects, educational levels and styles: such grammar is clearly within the range of what can be called standard English. But we see also that there are some grammatical features which distinguish one dialect from another within Great Britain, or which distinguish British from American usage, or which distinguish formal from colloquial and colloquial from uneducated usage. There is one other thing that is important for us to see. The major regional distinctions (between British and American usage in particular) do not over-ride others. That is to say, passages 1 and 3 (although British and American) have features in common, because they are both colloquial, and are together in contrast with passage 9—not, of course, because this is Australian in origin, but because it is formal.

It is reasonable to make the term 'Standard English' cover not only the grammar that is common to *all* kinds of English but also the grammar used in the speech and writing of educated people: in other words, we should exclude grammar which is peculiar to dialectal or uneducated use. In effect, this means the usage of the 'wider community' which we discussed earlier in this chapter, the usage that bears least restrictive (such as regional) mark, the usage that has widest acceptability. Since, however, one of the marks of the 'educated' is that they use this kind of English, we are undoubtedly involved in some circularity here, as has long been recognised. As an American scholar put it in the late nineteenth century: 'If pressed to say definitely what good American English is, I should say, it is the English of those who are believed by the greater number of Americans to know what good English is' (R. O. Williams, *Our Dictionaries*). To learn what determines that belief, we should be led to inquire into the workings of that delicate structure, society itself. But Williams's statement reminds us afresh that there are standards, not *a* standard. In grammar, as with vocabulary and transmission, the image of a standard varies to some degree along with the limits of the 'wider communities': in British English, I *have gotten* is dialectal and hence non-standard, but in American English the same form has the status of standard grammar.

Standard English is, as Lawrence's Hilda put it, 'normal English'; that kind of English which draws least attention to itself over the widest area and through the widest range of usage. As we have seen, this norm is a complex function of vocabulary, grammar, and transmission, most clearly established in one of the means of transmission (spelling), and least clearly established in the other means of transmission (pronunciation). This latter point draws attention to one important factor in the notion of a standard: it is particularly associated with English in a *written* form, and we find that there are sharper restrictions in every way upon the English that is written (and especially *printed*) than upon English that is spoken. In fact, the standards of Standard English are determined and preserved, to no small extent, by the great printing houses.

We have seen that Standard English is basically an ideal, a mode of expression that we seek when we wish to communicate beyond our immediate community with members of the wider community of the nation as a whole, or with members of the still wider community, English-speakers as a whole. As an ideal, it cannot be perfectly realised, and we must expect that members of different 'wider communities' (Britain, America, Nigeria, for example) may produce different realisations. In fact, however, the remarkable thing is the very high degree of unanimity, the small amount of divergence. Any of us can read a newspaper printed in Leeds or San Francisco or Delhi without difficulty and often even without realising that there are differences at all.

Exercises and Topics for Discussion

1 Point out features in the usage of passage 1 which would suggest that the speakers were of different generations, and features in passage 3 which suggest the sex of Vera's companion.

2 Re-write passage 4 in educated (standard) colloquial English.

3 Passage 5 represents the *colloquial* style of an *American* who shows some *education*. List the points of usage which justify in turn each part of this statement.

4 Re-write passage 9 as it might have occurred in the direct speech of a novel, where the style might be less precise and polished but at the same time rather more personal and expansive.

5 Explain in detail the distinctions *vocabulary*, *grammar*, and *transmission*, drawing all your illustrations from passages 7 and 8.

6 How does Lawrence indicate the dialect to which Hilda objects? How does he convey by contrast the 'normal English'?

7 In the light of your own experience, discuss the views on dialect expressed by Hilda and Mellors.

8 Continue Fred Vincy's argument, giving some examples of what he might see as 'shopkeepers' slang' today and of the 'slang' used by poets. Re-examine in this connexion the passages quoted on pages 38 and 39, and attempt to justify (or refute) his concept of 'the slang of prigs who write history and essays'.

9 Give other examples, like 'judg(e)ment', of permissible variants within standard English spelling. Can you think of analogous variation in *pronunciation* within the educated speech of your society?

10 Illustrate the differences between formal and informal educated usage by listing examples of differences in (*a*) grammar and (*b*) vocabulary.

11 There are fields of usage (for example, scientific writing) in which there are almost no differences between British and American English. Give examples of ways in which these two forms of English show greater difference: (*a*) in ordinary narrative prose, (*b*) in in-

structions for car maintenance, (c) in educated collo-quial usage, and (d) in slang.

12 Without necessarily knowing anything about Swedish, comment on the statement in *The Scotsman* (16 Sept. 1963) that Swedish speakers in Finland 'speak and write a far better Swedish than that found in Sweden'.

7: *Nonsense and Learning*

IN *She Stoops to Conquer*, Tony Lumpkin sings a song which begins

> Let school-masters puzzle their brain
> With grammar, and nonsense, and learning.

There are probably many people who would agree in associating 'learning' and 'grammar' with nonsense, so far as English is concerned, since it is so often claimed that English has no grammar to learn. Yet, oddly enough, one of the comments made on Tony's song is, 'I loves to hear him sing, because he never gives us nothing that's low'—a remark which illustrates at least one grammatical feature which teachers feel obliged to make us learn. And we saw in Chapter 5 that the words *man, say, girl, arrive* could not convey much until a good deal of grammar was added to them.

How much grammar English has and what grammatical categories are involved in it can, in fact, be readily seen by observing the speech of any young child who is still in the process of learning it. Let us take for example, the following authentic remark of a five-year old: 'Eric and me has just buyed lots of fings.' This sort of thing warms and charms the heart—of a parent at any rate—precisely in the extent to which the child has *not* learnt the allegedly non-existent grammar of English. In fact, even this brief utterance shows that the child has already mastered a vast amount of grammar. He has arranged the main sentence-elements perfectly:

the subject 'Eric and me' placed before the verb 'has buyed', and the object 'lots of fings' at the end. A different arrangement would indeed have made nonsense. His other word-order patterns are just as secure: he says 'has just buyed' and not 'just has buyed' or 'buyed just has'; he says 'lots of fings' and not 'fings lots of'. He says 'Eric and me' and not 'me and Eric', and unless this is accidental it marks an even more subtle grasp of good English than the other points mentioned so far. He seems also to have grasped the ways of English *aspectual* expression, having selected a perfective verb-form, *has buyed*, along with *just*, where 'just bought' would be less idiomatic. No doubt he would have made the matching selections 'Eric and me *always* buy' or '*Last week* Eric and me bought' with the same sureness of touch.

The child has also mastered the *inflexion* of regular verbs: he knows that *has* is to be used with a particular verb-form which in the case of many verbs ending in a voiced sound (*love, play, swallow*, for example) has /d/ added, and so he says 'has buyed'. He seems to have little idea of *concord* yet, being apparently under the impression that 'has buyed' can be used whether the subject is singular ('Eric') or plural ('Eric and me'). No doubt he will soon learn this convention and will notice too that, although he has heard many people say things like 'Eric and me' in response to a question, or after a verb ('They saw Robin and me'), far fewer will be heard saying *me* in front of a verb. And of course he will also learn that, although *has* accompanies a verb ending in /d/ in many cases, this verb *buy* has an irregular form in this relationship, a form that has to be memorised separately. So it will not be long before he is saying 'Eric and I have just bought lots of things', like the rest of us.

This discussion has by no means exhausted the grammatical competence shown by the five-year-old in this single
104

utterance. The 'rightness' of *has buyed* should suggest, for example, that he understands *voice* distinctions as well— the difference between, 'has buyed' and 'is buyed', 'I've forgotten' and 'I'm forgotten'. What the discussion has attempted to show is grammar-learning from the child's point of view. We have spoken of his learning that '*has* is used with a verb ending in /d/', rather than of his learning that 'past participles end in /d/'. The latter is an alternative way of stating the fact, but it is essentially a grammarian's way: an attempt to find some abstraction to which a great many disparate facts of language can be referred. The facts themselves may be, from one point of view, 'loved, swallowed, played, eaten, bought, put, found, had &c.'; from another point of view, 'the form of the verb that enters into construction with a part of the verb *to be* in making a passive' (and it will be realised that 'a part of the verb to be' is itself an abstraction of *am, are, is, was* . . .). For these and other statements, 'past participle' is a convenient shorthand expression, and because most of us have to make abstractions of this kind from time to time, we find it useful to have at our finger-tips a grasp of simple and widely understood grammatical terminology. It is not just grammarians who need to be able to use such terms, any more than it is just engineers who need to be able to use such a word as 'thread', instead of attempting a vague (and inaccurate) description of 'little grooves running parallel to each other at a slight angle from the diameter of a bar in such a way that one piece of metal can encircle the bar and move across it'. But 'thread' is an abstraction that we learn to make, of course, long after we have been screwing things together as we made Meccano models, and in the same way we learn to fit *has* and *played* together long before we have heard of a 'past participle'.

What the child learns is a series of activities which constitute patterns, and he learns that disregard of these patterns makes nonsense. How we recognise the distinctions that we later call 'parts of speech' can perhaps be demonstrated best by seeing these patterns imposed upon nonsense. First, let us consider the following:

1 croatation ungleshably polanians pleakful ruggling plome rit will the in be the.

Although we recognise individual grammatical words as 'English' here, and some individual lexical words which *might* be English (inasmuch as *pleakful*, for example, is in various ways more English than, say, *lufkaelp*), there is no recognisable relationship between the 'words'. They seem to form only a random, shapeless list. Now, consider them re-arranged as follows:

2 plome the pleakful croatation will be ruggling polanians ungleshably in the rit.

It is at once obvious that the second arrangement is less nonsensical than the first, and this is because every 'word' now falls into a *pattern* that is recognisably English. We do not know what *rit* means, yet if we were to replace it by a word that we do know, we should choose one like *nest* or *bag* or *office* or *terror*: we should not be satisfied with 'in the politely' or 'in the of' or 'in the beautify' or 'in the then'. What is it that *rit* has in common with *nest* and *office* that it does not have in common with *beautify* or *then*? Clearly, one answer is that *rit* is a noun, and we must now see that we have recognised *rit* as a noun not because it is 'the name of a person, place or thing' but because it is used in (2) in the framework where words like *office* but not *then* frequently appear. We cannot know that *rit* is the name of a person, place or thing in (1) and even in (2) we do not know what exactly *rit* is the name of. Our familiarity

106

with the patterns displayed in (2) can be shown by extending this little exercise and replacing the words which we do not know by others that we do know.

	a		b	c			d
(2)	plome	the	pleakful	croatation	will	be	ruggling
(3)	then	the	artful	delegation	will	be	muddling
(4)	suddenly	the	fine	horse	will	be	facing
(5)	probably	the	young	publisher	will	be	reading

	e	f	g
(2)	polanians	ungleshably	in the rit
(3)	politicians	unpardonably	in the street
(4)	picnickers	shyly	in the field
(5)	manuscripts	through	in the evening

There are two quite different kinds of grammatical identity here. The vertical sets *a* to *g* each comprise items grammatically identical (*a* and *f* adverbs; *b* adjectives; *c*, *e* and *g* nouns; and *d* present participles of verbs), and the horizontal structures are grammatically identical too. But there is a vital connexion between the two kinds of identity: *fine*, for example, is grammatically the same as *artful* only because they appear in the same 'horizontal' structure 'the *b c*' in the same position, *b*. If we replaced *pleakful* by *fine* in the arrangement (1), we could not assign it to a vertical set, since arrangement (1) does not display horizontal structures: it might be a verb ('the croatation will *fine* polanians'—when they offend) or equally a noun ('the pleakful *fine* will plome the polanians ungleshably'). There are two other points that we should not miss here. The horizontal arrangements (2) to (5) are structural, but it must be noted that they display not just *a* structure but *structures*. That is to say, we do not—as we have seen—need to consider the whole of (2) to decide that *rit* is a noun: the little sub-structure '(in) the rit' is enough for that. Similarly if we re-arranged the ending of (1) to read 'will the in be the

107

rit', we should have enough structural guidance to conclude that *in* is a noun too. The all-important notion that English has structures within structures is one that we shall develop further presently.

The other point is this. Arrangement (3) is closer in form to (2) than is (4) or (5), and this draws attention to the fact that there is a 'grammar' within the word as well as between words. Such words as *croatation* and *delegation* have their noun character suggested by their form alone, even before we see them identified as nouns by their use in a structure. Moreover, the correspondence between the noun *delegation* and a related verb *delegate* would lead us to postulate a verb *croatate*, just as the relationship of *unpardonably* to *pardon* would lead us to interpret the 'internal grammar' of *ungleshably* as concerning an act which cannot be *gleshed*. This grammar within the word is something which will be taken up again in Chapters 8 and 11.

Comparison of arrangement (2) with arrangement (1) gives us not only some idea of the kind of grammar our language has but also some insight into how we learn it. We meet words in structures, and the structures help us to interpret the words grammatically: that is, a structure tells us with what other words in our past experience we should link a new word that we come across. It gives us the necessary information to use the word correctly, when we follow up our observation by imitation. Thus in response to (3) one might say doubtfully 'I've never seen an artful delegation', just as one might say (still more doubtfully) in response to (2) 'How ruggled will the polanians be?' If this question receives serious attention, we silently store a little more information that we have learnt about the use of 'ruggle'. The question may on the other hand be rejected as incomprehensible, as the corresponding one would be in response to (4): 'How faced will the picnickers be?' But here too the attempt is not wasted; it leaves us with positive information and we know a little more than we did about the verb *face*.

It is useful to distinguish two stages of learning through which we must pass. The first stage aims at *comprehensibility* and the second at *conformity*. The child who said 'Eric and me has just buyed lots of fings' has completed the comprehensibility stage for this particular utterance but has not yet completed the conformity stage. We need to keep the two stages clear in our minds because it is likely that it is the conformity stage that gives most trouble for the native-born user of English. That is to say, ordinary social needs usually compel us to make ourselves comprehensible quite early and we should not be misled into thinking that the adjustments necessary for full conformity are made in order to achieve comprehensibility.

We may recall the comment on Tony's song which was quoted earlier: 'I loves to hear him sing, because he never gives us nothing that's low.' In the lack of accepted concord between *I* and *loves*, and in the double negative, we notice the speaker's failure to conform with standard grammar, but of course we do not in the least fail to understand what he says. If therefore we say a double negative is wrong because 'two negatives make a positive', we are guilty of a misstatement because we allege that the grammar offends in the matter of comprehensibility. And this, as we have just seen, is patent nonsense—one of the instances of nonsense that perhaps Tony had in mind when he associated grammar-teaching with nonsense. If a boy says 'I haven't done no homework', the teacher is yet to be born who will reply (without sarcasm) 'Oh good, I'm glad you've done it'. The two negatives here do not make a positive: they make a quite emphatic negative, but they make an unsatisfactory English utterance because the usage does not conform with educated conventions. To say in French *le grand maison* instead of *la grande maison* is a grammatical error, but not because it fails to be comprehensible: any Frenchman will understand us when we make this slip, but he may shudder nevertheless because we are failing to conform with conventions by which he sets great store.

So far as the majority of the grammatical features of English are concerned, there is no disagreement (as we saw in Chapter 6) among the members of the English-speaking world about what is right and what is wrong. It is natural in every speech community for members to reach harmony about their grammatical conventions, so that most of us have no difficulty in adopting without deviation the forms used by our relatives, neighbours and immediate friends. The community on Tristan de Cunha seem to constitute just such a closely knit speech unit, as we in Britain were able to note during the period of their evacuation in the early sixties. But as soon as a speech community becomes so large that daily contact becomes impossible and we have to speak of an 'immediate' and of a 'wider' speech community (as of course we do in relation to speakers of English), differences begin to appear. Most of the 'problems' of English grammar crop up because of a clash between the very definite grammatical conventions of our social circle and the equally definite but often very different conventions of the wider circle of the nation as a whole.

When we say that 'I don't want no cake' is wrong, we mean that it is wrong in relation to the wider community: wrong in being unacceptable to the nation-wide (indeed world-wide) community of educated English speakers. Within a narrower circle of—say—some lads in Bethnal Green or Everton, this is regular and acceptable in its grammar, obeying strict conventions which would exclude 'I no do want not cake' as unacceptable and unidiomatic to *any* native speaker of English. It is not that 'I don't want no cake' has *no* grammar. A man who goes to be interviewed

110

for a job as a clerk wearing an open-neck shirt is wrongly dressed for the occasion, but no one would say that he is not wearing clothes. Most of us are fairly easily convinced that, although none of our close friends thinks we are objectionable when we have an open-neck shirt, a potential employer most certainly would if we were thus dressed at an interview. In just the same way, we come to be aware of which grammatical conventions pass muster among our friends and which need adjustment when we are in touch with a wider circle.

An appeal to our sense of conformity, convention and fashion will often make sense to us where talk of 'this is meaningless' or 'don't you know that two negatives make a positive' would not. There is more convention than logic in matters of dress, and the same applies to language. And the conventions of language are nearly as changeable as those of dress. In Charles Dickens's time, it was correct for the young clerk to say 'He don't look well', just as it was correct for him to wear a frock coat and top hat. It is convention that makes 'they have forgotten it' acceptable where 'they have forgot it' is not acceptable. It is not that one form is more 'logical' or even more 'grammatical' than the other: the two differ simply in following different conventions, as we can see if we compare our usage in 'they have got it' which has the very participial form of which we disapprove in 'they have forgot it'. Logic might insist that we fall in with the Americans in saying both *forgotten* and *gotten* or that we fall in with some dialects in saying both *they have forgot* and *they have got* (which might arguably entail our saying also *they have spoke*, and *they have wrote*). Pure reason might equally suggest that if it is a cold day I may go for an interview in a roll-neck sweater, whereas if it is hot I may go with an open neck. But the conventions of human behaviour are not all determined by logic and reason, and language is part of human behaviour.

111

It is true that there is a kind of logic or reasoning which is very powerful in grammar: we call it *analogy*. After hearing *love~loved*, *rub~rubbed*, *play~played*, and learning this correspondence, we may conclude without necessarily ever hearing the forms of the verb *swallow* that the past tense is *swallowed*. This is a logical, rational conclusion —and of course in this as in most cases it turns out to be right: indeed, as we look at the *history* of a language, we find that it is such conclusions that *make* them right. We hear corresponding sets like *poor~poorer*, *small~smaller*, *big~bigger*, and we can logically supply *great* with a corresponding *greater*, without necessarily hearing it in use. We hear dozens of utterances like 'I lit the gas', 'I like the book', 'The man saw me', 'The book pleased him', and we become so familiar with this kind of ordering and this kind of form-selection, that we may invent logically the remark 'I saw him' or 'He pleased me', without ever having heard those particular utterances before.

All this is perfectly normal in the grammatical processes, but we cannot go far before we find forms which resist our logic. Some of our inventions turn out to be unacceptable and nearly all of us have to learn that the logic breaks down with *gooder*, for example. We find that there are special forms which either belong to some smaller, less compelling pattern (as with *bind~bound*, *find~found*) or to no pattern at all (as with *go~went*). There was an instance of unacceptable analogy in the five-year-old's speech quoted earlier: 'Eric and me has just *buyed* lots of fings.'

Forms like *I seen him* persist in sub-standard speech partly because they respond to the analogy of other forms which are accepted throughout the English-speaking world. With most verbs, the past tense form and the past participle are identical; that is to say, we have:

<pre>
I loved ~ I have loved
I had   ~ I have had
I found ~ I have found
I sat   ~ I have sat
I clung ~ I have clung
</pre>

So there arises a natural tendency to apply this pattern to all verbs and to say *I done~I have done*, *I wrote~I have wrote*, and

<pre>
either I saw   ~ I have saw   or I seen ~ I have seen
        I drank ~ I have drank or I drunk ~ I have drunk
        I swam ~ I have swam or I swum ~ I have swum
        I sank ~ I have sank or I sunk ~ I have sunk
</pre>

Most examples of this kind do not, of course, give us much trouble because the educated community is in agreement on the forms that are to be regarded as acceptable— and we very soon learn the terms of that agreement. With some, there is no such agreement, and *I have shaved* exists in educated use alongside *I have shaven*: so too *I have sewed/sewn*, *I have showed/shown*, *I have knitted/knit*, and a good few others. In the case of the verb *to wake*, we may find *I have waked* or *woken* or *woke*.

On points like these, where there is divided usage, we find a good deal of controversy, and much energy is fruitlessly expended in attempting to prove that one or other is 'correct'. Two issues which are particularly notorious in this way are illustrated in the sentences 'I am sure we will succeed' and 'It is me', some people being strongly of the opinion that 'It is I' is the only acceptable form and that only 'we shall succeed' is correct when we want to indicate the future. A fuller discussion of such issues and the attitudes they promote must be left for Supplement II, but it should be made clear here that disputed points of

113

this kind are small in number and that their importance has been exaggerated beyond all measure by the distorted judgment of those whose feelings run high on the subject. It is surely time we acquired a sense of proportion about them and rid ourselves of the idea that *they* are what English grammar is about. The very fact that usage is divided, that we are all aware that some say one thing and some another in these disputed areas, should itself make it obvious that it is impossible to call one 'correct' and the other 'incorrect'. One might as well argue about whether *begin to work* is more correct than *start to work* or whether a plain tie is more correct than a striped one, cotton underwear more correct than nylon.

It was Swift's Lilliputians who displayed the absurd intolerance of disputing which end to open an egg, and it was Goldsmith's contemporaries (as Mr Warburg explains) who are largely responsible for promoting similar disputes in matters of usage—disputes which in no small measure contribute to the association of 'grammar' with 'nonsense'. But there is another good reason for the association. Tony Lumpkin's song went on to say that the schoolmasters' brains were puzzling over 'Their *Qui*'s and their *Quae*'s and their *Quod*'s', and much of our feeling that English grammar is somehow unreal results from the way in which grammarians have traditionally looked at English only through the lattice of categories set up in *Latin* grammar. And the extent to which we have remained unconvinced that English has a grammar like Latin is probably the basis of the popular fallacy that English has no grammar at all.

English, as we have seen, is certainly not without grammar, but this does not mean that it has the same grammar as Latin—or any other language for that matter. Just as the vocabulary of every language is distinct and peculiar, so is the grammar of a language. There is so common a failure to grasp this point, that one must be pardoned for offering some elementary explanation of it.

In English we have three verb expressions which we can distinguish as 'simple present', 'continuous present' and 'emphatic present' and exemplify in 'I play ~ I am playing ~ I *do* play', 'I work ~ I am working ~ I *do* work'. In some languages there is only a single verb form corresponding to these sets of three: for example, in French, we have *je joue* and *je travaille*; in Russian, *ya igráyu* and *ya rabótayu*. The first thing that we should note is this: the fact that the French and Russians do not possess three separate verb forms does not mean that they cannot express these distinctions. They most certainly can, but it is not done, as in English, by a change in the verb form. Americans, after all, do not possess special fish knives and forks as people do in Great Britain, but this does not mean that Americans cannot eat fish.

The second thing to note is that, in making these distinctions by other means than a change in the verb, the Frenchman feels no obligation to give three different names to the verb he uses when he makes them. 'Je travaille chaque jour', he may say where we might use the simple present, 'I work each day'; 'je travaille en ce moment', he might say on the other hand, where we should be more likely to use our continuous form 'I'm working at present'. Thirdly, we might hear the Frenchman say, 'Je travaille— je vous l'assure', where we could use our emphatic present, 'I *do* work'. In English, the three verb-forms need three labels, but naturally the Frenchman does not call *je travaille* 'simple present' in the first case, 'continuous present' in the second, and 'emphatic present' in the third; he does not need three labels for a single verb-form, merely because English has to use three different verb-forms.

This sounds obvious, yet until very recently it has been common to talk about English as though it made its distinctions in precisely the same way as Latin does. There are grammars still in print today which give one label to *came* in 'I came yesterday' ('indicative') and another label to the same form in 'If I came tomorrow, would you see me?' ('subjunctive'). Similarly, we find a sentence such as 'I gave the dog a bone' described as containing one noun in the 'accusative' (*bone*) and the other in the 'dative' (*dog*). On the other hand, in 'I gave the dog away', *dog* would be called 'accusative'—the same form having two labels— while in the sentence 'I gave a bone to the dog', *to the dog* would be called 'dative'—two different expressions (*the dog* and *to the dog*) thus having the same label.

Just as the Frenchman would regard it as nonsense having to learn to call *je travaille* 'simple' in one sentence and 'continuous' in another (and very difficult indeed to learn if he did not know English), so the Englishman is puzzled at the apparently arbitrary distinctions he is supposed to learn in this kind of grammatical description. It may be argued, of course, that it is only arbitrary to the ignorant. To the person who knows that Latin distinguishes *dedi canem* from *dedi cani* by a difference of case, it is supposed to be obvious that any translation of those words into any language whatever must make a distinction of case, and that therefore *dog* switches from dative to accusative in the sentence, 'I gave the dog a bone' and 'I gave the dog away'. Yet a recording of the two, from which the last syllable was cut, would sound identical: 'I gave the dog a —'.

Alternatively, it may be (and still frequently is) argued that, although we have no 'dog-em' and 'dog-i' correspondence with the Latin accusative and dative, we nevertheless express the same distinctions in English as are expressed in Latin by means of cases, and that it may therefore be a convenience to keep to the same terminology. A common terminology may after all be a help if we learn Latin or

116

some other foreign language. But, as we have seen, it is a commonplace for a particular distinction to be achieved in utterly different ways in two languages. Latin distinguishes subject, direct object, indirect object by case-differences (differences in the inflexion of the word) and arrangement is not very important. English also distinguishes subject, direct object, and indirect object, but it does so largely by arrangement. Take the pair of sentences 'I offered my only son the army (as a career)' and 'I offered the army my only son'. It is nonsense to say that in the first we know that *my only son* is the indirect object because it is dative: we know it *only* because of its position in the sentence. But in a Latin translation, we should know that it was the indirect object *only* because it was dative. Using Latin categories thus involves inventing distinctions for English *and* ignoring the distinctions that English makes.

Nor is this kind of procedure merely pointless: it can be positively misleading. If a French boy were in fact taught to call *je travaille* 'simple' in one sentence and 'continuous' in another, merely on account of the general context, he would naturally be predisposed to think that the 'simple-continuous' distinction in English was to be achieved similarly, and he would say things like, 'Do not disturb me: I work.' An English boy who learns to call *dog* 'accusative' or 'dative' according to the general context is hindered from understanding that in Latin the accusatives and datives that are supposed to correspond are quite differently distinguished.

We may go further and claim that, even where English has inflexional differences (I ~ me, he ~ him, and so on), these should not be referred to as 'nominative' and 'accusative'. True, in these instances, we certainly can talk of *cases*, and we need two labels for the two forms. But to call them 'nominative' and 'accusative' would be to suggest that these labels would have the same application

117

as they have in Latin or German or Russian grammar, where there are not two but four or five forms to distinguish and where 'nominative' and 'accusative' form a set along with additional labels such as 'dative', 'ablative', 'prepositional', and the like. Obviously, the meaning of 'accusative' in a two-term system, nominative/accusative, must be different from the meaning of 'accusative' in a four- or five-term system.

Let us consider an analogy. A train leaves Waterloo Station for Southampton: its passengers must be in one of two categories—first or second class. When they are 'translated' to the *Queen Elizabeth*, they must be redistributed into three categories: first class, cabin, or tourist. The two sets of categories have one label in common, 'first class', but this does not mean that a person who travelled *first* on the train is travelling *first* on the ship. A given person may feel that for his taste and his income, the proper equivalent of *first* on the train is *cabin* on the ship. The identity of the *label* 'first' is not much help: in the one case it operates in a two-term system, in the other in a three-term system.

So too if we call *him* an 'accusative' in expressions like 'I obey him', 'I am like him', 'I sat on him', the term 'accusative' may actually hinder us when we translate into another language which has an accusative along with several other cases and in which the word for *obey* takes the dative, the word for *like* the genitive, and the word for *on* the ablative—as they do in Latin.

To sum up, then, English has a very definite and complex grammar with some variation (such as we have in pronunciation and vocabulary) according to the social groups in which we mix, and with a small area of what we may fairly call *free variation*, where opinion may differ as to the preferable form. In examining and discussing our language, we need to observe carefully *all* the distinctions but *only* the distinctions which are made in our own grammar, and to be on our guard against phantom distinctions that are 'wished on' English merely because they exist in the grammar of other languages.

Exercises and Topics for Discussion

1 Explain and illustrate the process of 'analogy', not restricting yourself to matters of language.

2 We can say 'a round table' and 'he rounded the bend', but *pleakful* is likely to have only one grammatical function by reason of the affix *-ful*. What other affixes are there which seem to restrict words to particular grammatical functions?

3 'How ruggled will the polanians be?' Attempt other comments on and expansions of arrangement (2), p. 106.

4 In arrangements (2)—(5), it will be seen that while columns *b* and *c* are fixed in relation to each other, as *c* is in relation to *d*, columns *a*, *f*, and *g* permit some mobility. How much and with what effect?

5 Try to write definitions of noun, adjective and adverb, with reference only to the positions that they can take up in relation to other words. (If your definition leaves you equating *railway* and *new* because both can occur between *the* and *station*, you haven't gone far enough!)

6 A good many grammatical words like *through* and *in* can be either adverbs or prepositions. How can one tell? How many utterances can you think of in which there is a similarity of position as in 'He ran up a hill' and 'He ran up a bill'?

7 'Comprehensibility and conformity.' How many of the favourite grammatical shibboleths (such as the 'dangling participle' or *due to* and *owing to*) concern the one and how many the other? With which of the shibbo-

119

leths may we be in error even in thinking that *conformity* is at issue?

8 Which categories from Latin grammar have no relevance for English and which categories are equally necessary for describing both English and Latin?

8: Words, Words, Words

W HEN all things began, the Word already was. The Word dwelt with God, and what God was, the Word was.' Reading this opening of St John's Gospel (in the *New English Bible* version), we cannot help feeling struck by the mystical significance that words as such have had in many civilisations and also by the fact that, so important does the *word* seem to us, that we frequently use it by a kind of synecdoche for language itself. As we have seen, vocabulary —the set of *names* for things—is only one component of language but, by reason of this mystical quality that names have, vocabulary tends to overshadow all else in our consideration of language.

In his book on *The Religion of Ancient Egypt and Babylonia*, A. H. Sayce observed how the *name* ' was the essence of the person or thing to which it was attached', and although speakers of English might deny any such belief today a great deal of it in fact survives. Most parents ponder with enormous seriousness before deciding what to call a baby. Some people are even inclined to take an instant dislike to a person on account of his name, before ever meeting him, and this is no doubt why actors and actresses seek to adopt a stage-name which will in itself be pleasing to the public. 'The very names of things belov'd are dear', as Robert Bridges said; we may speak of a person's name having been ' stained'; we may carve a sweetheart's name on a tree, and both Spenser and Landor have written of the irony of writing a lover's name on the sand, the irony deriving of course not from the writing but from the imperman-

121

ent medium which will allow the name to be obliterated:

> Well I remember how you smiled
>   To see me write your name upon
> The soft sea-sand—'Oh! what a child!
>   You think you're writing upon stone!'
>
> I have since written what no tide
>   Shall ever wash away, what men
> Unborn shall read o'er ocean wide
>   And find Ianthe's name again.

By finding Ianthe's name, Landor implies that something of the 'real' Ianthe will be found: such is the feeling that somehow a name is the embodiment of the person or thing named.

Not long ago, the BBC discontinued 'Children's Hour' and partially substituted first 'Junior Time' and later 'Story Time'. Whatever change in the orientation of the programme accompanying the change of name, many people felt that the prime object was to avoid the word 'children' because—according to one view—'Children no longer like to be called children'. Towards the end of 1961 there was a heated correspondence in *The Times* on the subject, and although in the words of one writer, the name was 'not the only loss', it was clearly the change of *name* which excited most of the correspondents. Only a minority seemed to be as linguistically mature as Juliet:

> What's Montague? It is nor hand, nor foot,
> Nor arm, nor face, nor any other part
> Belonging to a man. Oh, be some other name!
> What's in a name? that which we call a rose
> By any other name would smell as sweet;
> So Romeo would, were he not Romeo call'd,
> Retain that dear perfection which he owes
> Without that title: Romeo, doff thy name;

And for that name, *which is no part of thee,*
Take all myself.

Thus, while one writer did indeed ask, 'What does the name matter after all?', most felt that it mattered a great deal, and one correspondent put it like this: 'Words with similar meanings have not similar values, and when a word is a name, it exerts an influence, and *becomes a person.* Children's Hour "gave to airy nothing a local habitation and a name". It was evocative. But Junior Time is a nonentity, evoking nothing. An influence has been disintegrated.'

In the early months of 1967, a chancery suit opened in London to decide whether the Spanish wine trade should be protected by forbidding the use of the word 'sherry' for wines other than those of the Jerez district. The word 'champagne' was restricted by a court decision in 1960. In protecting us from libel and slander, and in forbidding the use of obscene language, the law acknowledges the power of a word to carry with it the force of a physical act or the offensive physical presence of the thing named. We may smile at what we call Victorian pruderies when we read of people who would not use the word 'leg', speaking instead of a 'limb'—even if it were a 'table-limb'. We may be amazed to learn that in 1907 the performance of a Synge play in Dublin broke up in disorder because the word 'shift' was uttered. But in fact we today are only a *little* less liable to feel the extreme power of words: the principal change has been in the particular words which exercise such power so far as we today are concerned.

In the British Isles within the last thirty years men have been called in to cure such ailments as styes by means of verbal incantations and charms: perhaps they still are in some areas. Moreover, there are many who believe that much of the modern doctor's curative powers lies in the words he uses. The learned medical scientist, Sir Clifford Allbutt, once wrote that sick people attach great importance to learning the name of their complaint and that they 'feel that if they can get hold of the name of a disease they thus penetrate nearer to its essence, and obtain some greater measure of control over it'.

One consequence of the identification of the name with its 'referent' (what is named) is the comparably strong feeling that the particular name that we are used to is just 'right' for the particular referent. 'Children's Hour' is so 'right' that the referent cannot possibly be the same if the name is 'Junior Time'; a rose could not possibly smell as sweet if it were called a 'blunk'. Words, as Locke said in *An Essay Concerning Humane Understanding* (1689), 'come to excite in Men certain *Ideas*, so constantly and readily, that they are apt to suppose a natural connexion between them'. It is quite likely that many English speakers —especially dog-lovers—think it quite absurd and inappropriate that in other countries *dogs* can be called *chiens*, *Hunde*, or *sobaky*: and it is equally likely that the French, Germans and Russians feel the same about our word. 'Look at them, sir,' says old Rowley in Huxley's novel *Crome Yellow*, pointing at a number of swine wallowing in the mud, 'rightly is they called pigs'.

We need to be aware that 'word-magic' of this kind does indeed exist and that we are liable to be dangerously misled through being mesmerised by a word or through mistaking a word for its referent. It is no use pretending that such tendencies do not exist naturally in all of us. But this should make us more, not less, critical as we listen to political or religious argument and when we read advertisements or 'smear' campaigns in the popular press. As Lord Home said during the Berlin crisis of 1961, 'It is really no good looking upon the word *negotiation* as an incantation that can be repeated and will resolve everything.' It should stimulate us

124

to inquire more objectively into what is implied in a name or an attitude to a name. Often, for example, we find that the high feeling about a word on 'aesthetic' grounds turns out to be a disguised and possibly unconscious anti-American attitude. This could be seen in the correspondence about 'Junior Time'. On another recent controversy, one man announced in the press that he would be against a decimal *currency* (the 'thing') if it involved calling any coin a *cent* (the 'name'), because such a word would be un-British. Any degree of linguistic neurosis which puts a higher value on a word than on its referent deserves urgent and careful treatment.

But we must not underestimate the high value that words have for their own sake. Discussing the 'circumlocution syndrome' in the United States, where with that charming self-denigration it is often felt there is more than a fair share, a *Newsweek* article (8 June 1964) has this to say:

> She and her husband—a successful *mortical surgeon*—live in a *planned community*. Their place is not just a furnished apartment: it's a *garden apartment* containing *oversized rooms* furnished with *quality appointments*, and done in *decorator colors*. They prefer, however, to drive a *pre-owned car*. Like most *young moderns*, she suffers mildly from *hair fatigue, problem skin, irregularity*, and *over-acidity*, but she has licked her *figure problem* and is again down to *graduation-day size*. Someday, of course, she and her husband will become *senior citizens* and retire to a *leisure village*. 'I'm no *over-achiever*', she likes to say. 'All I want from life is to become a happy, *fully-realized person*.'

This young lady may well have her wish, for she already fully realizes that the first rule of current U.S. linguistic practice is never to call a spade a spade—euphemistically speaking, it's an agricultural implement. . . . At the United Nations, meanwhile, the U.S. and the Soviet Union are again struggling to influence the backward nations—but not calling them such; they're now referred to as less-privileged, less-developed, emerging, developing, have-not, catch-up, needy, low-income. Politically, nations are unaligned or uncommitted or positive neutralist. And Atlanta Negro leader Jim Forman calls civil-rights demonstrations 'creative conflict'. The law is equally ingenious. A Chicago police official once referred to police dogs as 'crowd engineers'.

Alice had no idea what latitude was, or longitude either, but she thought they were nice grand words to say. Each of us has opinions about the niceness or grandness or ugliness of words (*winsome, potentiality, slime,* for example), but we must be clear about two things. First, our opinion is likely to be a private, personal one, with no guarantee that it is generally held. Secondly, our opinion is likely to be based not on the word itself, but on the associations that the word and its referent have for us. If the associations are primarily with the *word* (we first heard it in a moving address or we always remember it as a favourite with some absurdly garrulous neighbour or we were once teased because we did not know its meaning), then, whatever our opinion is, it is not likely to be shared by others. If the association is more with the word's use and its referent (it is applied to charming behaviour or is used chiefly in learned discourse or refers to something unpleasant), then our opinion of the word is likely to be generally shared. There might well be a large measure of agreement, therefore, that *winsome* is a 'nice' word, that *potentiality* is 'grand', and *slime* 'nasty'.

With many words, it is by no means so easy to gauge the general opinion. Irritated or scornful comments from our friends often help us to realise the reactions to particular words, and so too do letters in the press. One gathers that words which are relatively specialised and technical will be howled down as 'jargon' when they are used too obtrusively outside a technical context. One gathers that words which are relatively new or which are used in a new sense or which are chiefly used in a different speech-community are also likely to evoke disapproval. The sensitive user of English is always storing hints and information on these lines as best he can, so that he may select words with the greatest possible *linguistic tact*, having regard to the particular audience and context of situation.

It is not, of course, always possible to be wholly 'tactful' by everyone's standards, since—as already explained—the basis of the standard in a particular case may be so arbitrary and because many of the most outspoken critics of words so perversely ignore commonly established usage. Consider the following extracts from letters to the press:

1 In these days of scientific as opposed to cultural education we need specially to be on our guard against debasement of language. Witness the horrible jargon 'break-down' (of figures). . . . (*Radio Times*, 17 August 1961.)

2 Is it not time someone protested against the very frequent use of two of the most vulgar words? They are guts and job. Many parents are skinning themselves alive to send their sons to Eton and Oxford, or similar places of culture. Yet if, when the finished product comes down, he has occasion to refer to courage he calls it guts, and if he is looking for work he calls it a job. Exalted personages are said to be doing a very good job. (*Daily Telegraph*, 11 August 1955.)

3 Sir George Chetwode has just given us a healthy venting of his pet abominations, 'Ashes' and 'Aussies'. May I give a top priority to 'Transportation' and recommend the boycotting of all travel agencies that make use of this vile word? (*Ibid.*, 7 July 1956.)

4 'Lay-by' . . . is a combination of verb and preposition of rather obscure meaning. It is indeed a dreadful term to use for something for which the simple, well-established

127

word 'siding' is available, and would be readily intelligible to all. One wonders who is responsible for the atrocity. (Ibid., 10 August 1955.)

There was a fresh outburst of correspondence on *lay-by* more recently, from which we may give some extracts:

5 'Siding' is a much more palatable word than the hideous hybrid 'Lay By'. (*The Times*, 28 June 1960.)

6 This is an ugly and an ungrammatical monstrosity. What is wrong with 'pull up'? (*Ibid.*, 1 July 1960.)

7 Vehicles do not lay but lie therein. It is hard to tell whether 'by' is a preposition governing some assumed noun or an adverb. Would it therefore not be better to call it a 'lie bay'? (*Ibid.*, 4 July 1960.)

Amidst this highly charged talk of 'atrocity' and 'abomination', 'ugly', 'monstrous', 'hideous', 'vulgar', 'horrible', 'vile', 'dreadful' usage, it is a pleasant contrast to read the eminently sensible and urbane comment by the writer, John Moore. It is only rarely that letters in the press show such a mature awareness of the nature of language and such a tolerance and sense of perspective:

8 People make words, and pedants can't stop them; otherwise our language would be as dull as ditchwater and as dead as the dodo. So I applaud 'lay by', which perhaps for the tired lorry-driver has some lullaby-baby echoes in it. He did not, however, invent the word; bargees were using it for a 'slack' where they could tie up long ago as the 1870s—as your indignant correspondents could have discovered if they had looked it up in the O.E.D. (*The Times*, 5 July 1960.)

Moore's letter was of little avail, however. Almost exactly three years later (9 July 1963), the same column of the same paper carried a plea to 'substitute the ungrammatical "lay-
128

by " for the correct " lie-by " '. Ironically, the correspondent seems to have meant the converse of what he wrote.

Since we wish our words to *communicate* something, we need to watch that an unfortunate choice will not trivially distract attention from what we are communicating to the mere words we are using. Moreover, since the cultivation of an understanding tolerance of other people's habits is prominent among the ideals of education, our sense of linguistic tact will not urge us not to use words that may offend or irritate. By the same token, linguistic tact will prevent us from falling into the hysteria which might cause us to condemn other people's words as 'hideous' or 'vile'.

It is certainly a rather sterile pursuit to attack what we know (or what dictionaries could tell us) are thoroughly established words. Despite strong opinion to the contrary, it is futile to try to stop words from being used in a sense different from that in which they were used at some earlier period. Such an 'etymological fallacy' betrays, in any case, a lamentable ignorance of the nature of language. We are still occasionally told that it is incorrect to use *tremendous* in the sense of 'huge' because the word 'really' means 'that which causes trembling', the 'really' deriving its force from the fact that *tremendous* comes from the gerundive of the Latin verbe *tremere*, 'to tremble'. If such pedantic considerations are taken as the basis of 'correctness', then the 'correct' meaning of *style* is 'a pointed instrument' and the 'correct' meaning of *like*, 'a body'. One could not speak of *arriving* at King's Cross, because King's Cross has no shore, and the word's derivation shows that at one time it meant 'to come to the shore'.

We have been told in a recent interesting book that 'The word detergent means simply something which cleans; soap is therefore a detergent. The experts, when they came to name newly discovered substances which were made from quite different materials, called them soapless detergent.

129

Since ordinary people will not bother with such fine distinctions, we now talk of soap and detergents as though they were different things.'[1] In a way, this is an admirable little account of how we came to use *detergent* in the way we do, but it is marred by the author's inadequate knowledge of English and of linguistic processes. It is obviously untrue that *detergent* 'means simply somethings which cleans': everyone knows that *detergent* has a much more specialised meaning than that; the author is confusing etymology and meaning. In the second place—and as corollary—we do not talk of soap and detergent 'as though they were different things': everyone knows that they *are* different things. The writer would have discovered the failure in his linguistic logic if he had applied his standard to 'soap' as well as to 'detergent', and looked up this word in one of our etymological dictionaries, that of W. W. Skeat, for example, which was compiled in the closing years of the nineteenth century. If 'detergent means simply something which cleans', *soap* 'means simply', it would appear, 'grease or tallow', from which (as every O Level chemistry examiner knows) soap is made.

The pedantic urge to reduce every word to what (in some naïve sense) it 'really means' is to ignore the fact that words of course change their meaning. But it also ignores the less fully explored fact that words which are near-synonyms have importantly differed ranges and classes of nuance according to whether they are relatively old or new in the language. What applies rather trivially to *soap* and *detergent* applies also and with rather greater interest to *pottery* and *ceramics* and a host of others—even, no doubt, to *fatherly* and *paternal*.

Change of meaning is a commonplace, and indeed it would appear to be fundamental in living language. One

[1] L. Hunter, *The Boys' Book of How Things are Made* (London 1959), p. 109.

reason for the futility of objecting to a modern meaning lies in the fact that almost every word we use today has a slightly different meaning from the one it had a century ago: and a century ago it had a slightly different meaning from the one it had a century before that. Or rather *meanings*. For it is natural for a word to have more than one, and we can even say that, the commoner the word, the more meanings it has: and this is a further reason for seeing the search for *a* 'correct' or 'basic' meaning as futile. In *Studies in Words*, C. S. Lewis explained the steps by which even an apparently 'simple' word like *sad* has radically changed its meaning over the years. It once meant 'full to the brim', 'well-fed'; one could be thoroughly 'sad' with food and drink (*sated*, *satiated*, *satisfied*, and *saturated* are etymologically related to it). From this it came to mean 'solid' as well; a good spear could be 'sad', and one could sleep 'sadly'. This idea of *solidness* was then metaphorically applied to human character, and a person who was reliable and firm could be called 'sad'. It is now easy to see how the chief modern sense could come into existence; a well-fed person may feel solid, heavy, and dull, and thus be sober-faced on that account: we must not forget the slang use of the expression *fed-up* which offers something of a semantic parallel. Alternatively, a person who is reliable and firm is a serious person, and serious is the opposite of light-hearted and gay.

In the face of so universal a natural process, one may as well sit on the shore and order back the advancing tide as attempt to turn back the tide of semantic change. The conclusion is obvious (and has been accepted by dictionary-makers for generations): the only practical and reasonable standard of a word's acceptability at all or in a particular sense is usage. If *lay-by* is in use among lorry-drivers, Ministry of Transport and local government officials, that is enough: the word can be recorded in our dictionaries

131

with the meaning that is current among those who use the word. If *guts* is used for 'courage', but with some contextual restriction, the lexicographer will still record this sense, but will add a note on the particular restriction he has noticed ('informal' or 'colloquial' perhaps). In either case, he will be accurately and objectively representing the usage as he observes it: he will not be sitting as a magistrate, frowning upon the 'ugly', 'atrocious' or 'vile'.

As pointed out earlier, ugliness or vulgarity is often attributed to a word because of the ugliness or vulgarity of its referent or of the associations the word has for us. A word is a string of sounds and few such strings can in themselves reasonably be called ugly—or beautiful. Nor, except for a few echoic words like *cuckoo* (as we saw in Chapter 3), have words any 'sort of resemblance to the ideas for which they stand', as Burke pointed out in his essay *On the Sublime and the Beautiful* over two hundred years ago. Yet such is the associative power of the human mind, that words and parts of a word can become so highly charged by reason of their collocations as to make them work in a very ugly and dangerous fashion indeed. One of the important recommendations of the Royal Commission on Mental Health in 1957 was the dropping of the term 'certify'—and the very fact that this recommendation ranked as important is an indication of how much 'word-magic' survives. Strikes have been caused through the injudicious use by management of the word *exploit* ('We must exploit to the full our resources in materials and manpower'), because of the role this word has played in the collocations of anti-capitalist argument. According to *The Guardian* in February 1958, 'restrictive practice' had become so highly charged that a Ministry of Labour inquiry on the subject had to use the euphemism 'the efficient use of manpower'. During the years of controversy over the Central African Federation, *federation* itself became a 'dirty word' among many Africans, particularly in Nyasaland, and in March 1959 *The Times* reported the Duke of Montrose as having said in the House of Lords that the 'fact had to be accepted that this word "federation" would have to be changed for something else'.

And of course there are plenty of more trivial examples. Many people have associated the verb *get* so strongly with classroom condemnation that they go to absurd and pathetic lengths to avoid it when they put pen to paper. A correspondent to *The Times* in April 1961 began with the words 'How stupid can the English become!' and recent candidates for GCE have shown that the dogma about what has been called 'the three-letter word' still persists; one wrote: 'The car came to receive us.'

Ludwig Wittgenstein's oft-quoted dictum, 'the meaning of a word is its use', has obvious connexion with what has been said here. Less obviously, perhaps, it should be applied to the way in which we learn to use words. We hear them in context—in collocation with other words that we have met before (if this condition does not hold, we have not begun to 'break the code': it is a foreign language). It is partly on account of this that a word like *sad* has changed its meaning from 'full'. The process can be seen at work in the version of 'All people that on earth do dwell' attributed to a child at Sunday school:

> We are his flock, he doth us feed;
> And for his sheep he doth a steak.

The unfamiliar inverted word-order 'doth us take' has presented a puzzle and has been rationalised in terms of the collocated *feed* of the preceding line. When the French word *crevice* (modern *écrevisse*) was introduced into Middle English, its connexion with 'sea food' caused people to *metanalyse* the final syllable as *-fish* ('crayfish'), and the

133

school boy who translated the same word, *écrevisse*, as a 'lady typist' was performing an analogous wrong interpretation or metanalysis. So too after learning something of the use of *conduct* and *decent*, *direction* and *animate*, *guide* and *definite*, *lead* and *variable*, and comparing the use of these with the use of *misconduct* and *indecent*, *misdirection* and *inanimate*, *misguide* and *indefinite*, *mislead* and *invariable*, we learn to attribute constant functions to the word-fractions *mis-* and *in-*. But we continue to make 'errors' because we cannot always identify the particular morpheme (as linguists call a minimum stretch of meaningful language). We either see too many (as when we wonder whether Louis XIV's *mistress* is a wrong kind of tress) or we see too few, as when a child suddenly becomes aware that what he has been reading for years as 'mizzled' (and to which he has given the meaning 'miserably deceived') is in fact *misled*.

Errors in identification can be more serious. In face of the correspondence *decent ~ indecent*, *animate ~ inanimate*, *definite ~ indefinite*, *variable ~ invariable*, some people have been in danger of misinterpreting the word *inflammable*, seeing in it one part obviously connected with *flame*, the final part obviously the 'same' morpheme as in *workable*, *tolerable*, *curable*, and the initial negative morpheme of *intolerable*, *incurable*. Increasingly in the past few years, therefore, manufacturers have used the form *flammable*, with which no misinterpretation is possible.

An American wit, David McCord, has for some years amused us by pretending that many other words can be analysed into a prefix and a meaningful remainder—as though *mistress* consisted of two morphemes, *mis* and *tress*:

> I know a little man both ept and ert
> And intro? extro? No, he's just a vert.

134

Shevelled and couth and kempt, pecunious, ane;
His image trudes upon the ceptive brain.[1]

Our willingness to perform comic analyses of words in
this way and to invent correlatives like *backispiece* beside
frontispiece or *outcidentals* beside *incidentals* is a reflection
of the way in which we learn words as wholes and then
analyse them, grammatically so to speak, to make sense in
relation to our experience with other words. This matter of
'the grammar of the word' itself is something of which
we caught a glimpse in Chapter 7 and which we shall need
to discuss again in Chapter 11, but it may be interesting
here to link this with what was said earlier about the bases
for judging words in such terms as 'ugliness'. We said
that *slime* might be generally agreed to have nasty associations. This is not entirely and simply because the referent
of *slime* is nasty, but, in addition, because the initial consonant cluster very often occurs in words which have unpleasant meanings: it is almost as though *sl-* had itself the
status of a morpheme. Consider, for example, *slack, slag,
slander, slang, slap, slash, slaughter, slave, sleazy, sleet,
slick, slobber, slouch, sly* and many others. There are so
many that (despite *sleep* and a few more which do not share
the stigma) we do not need Humpty Dumpty's explanation
of *slithy* to connect it with slippery unpleasantness. Similarly, we abstract from *wriggle, sparkle, gabble,* etc. enough
to associate *-le* with 'little actions oft repeated', and to have
some idea of the meaning of a 'new' word such as *ruggle,*
which we met in Chapter 7.

It is in fact by analogy in this way that many new words
come into use, whether they are 'portmanteaus' like
brunch, 'back-formations' like *liaise* (from *liaison*) or
'metanalyses' (like *crayfish*). A recent Air India advertisement used neologisms, playfully coined for the occasion, like

[1] Quoted in B. F. Huppé, J. Kaminsky, *Logic and Language* (New York
1957), p. 96.

relaximost, appetingling and *Air-Indiassuredly*. A snackbar may call itself a *coffeetearia* and a service station a *lubritorium*. A literary periodical may allow a nonce-word like *pompetent* in describing a competent, though pompous, expert in something.

In 1962, a *New Statesman* competition offered prizes 'for three words, with dictionary definitions, expressive of well-known but hitherto wordless states or plights', and it was interesting to see how naturally and creatively the blend principle seemed to be used by the word-coining entrants. The present writer was asked to adjudicate and his report shows that he was tempted to try his hand on the same lines. Although many of the words had a topical relevance now difficult to revive, some quotation from the report may not be out of place. In noting the glimpse that the entries gave of the competitors' personal experience, he gave as examples:

The nostalgic memories of Whitsun holidays (dieselment, carstipation, inautomobilization). Delight in the simple teleside pleasures of home, enjoying rich telefusion in complete telassitude, until utterly teevitiated. A tolerant, grimond-bearit attitude to the unemployed politician trying to turn an honest vote (volvotism, to travel orpfully is actually to arrive[1]), but a tendency to be unkind to the government, as can be seen in the macmilaise and inselwyncy of antivotion at this period of the macmillennium. The interest, as one might expect, in the hire mathematics of finance (credidentials, supercredemptory), but a less lloydable, takeitorleavis attitude to litter-ature. The touching little problems of daily life: frusturinated by inconvenience; buscillation—dodging between bus stops in rush hour; brastration—when a lady cuts a poor figure . . . Almost every competitor had lexecuted *one* masterpiece . . . and we select for the three-guinea

[1] An excruciating reference to the stir made in March 1962 when the Liberal candidate won the Orpington by election.

award the following entry in which the winspiration was maintained in three words which Nuttall our pottering in Chambers had hitherto revealed:

Argentility: Council-house tenants' obsession with silver tea services, kept in readiness for distinguished visitors.

Proletentiousness: A tendency, especially in modern literary and artistic circles, to boast of real or imagined working-class origin.

Telephoria: Belief, induced by commentators and news readers, that essentially all is right with the world.

(*New Statesman*, 22 June 1962)

Often—as we saw in Chapter 3—words are coined because an acute need is felt, but a common objection to coinages and adoptions is that they are synonyms for perfectly good words already in the language. It is rare, however, to find perfect and complete synonyms. The most one can usually say is that there are contexts which will admit a choice of two or even three possible words without noticeable difference of meaning. For example, 'the rainfall in April was exceptional' or 'the rainfall in April was abnormal'. These examples may give us grounds for saying that 'exceptional' and 'abnormal' are synonymous *in certain contexts*—but we do certainly need to add that qualification. Applied to people, these adjectives are by no means synonymous, as we may see by comparing 'My son is exceptional' and 'My son is abnormal'.

Like synonyms, perfect and complete antonyms are fairly rare. It is true that languages seem to offer fairly 'naturally' a large measure of polarisation, but it is usual to find the antonymous polarity restricted to certain contexts. Thus *thick* is only one antonym of *thin* ('a thin slice' ~ 'a thick slice'); another is *fat* ('a thin man' ~ 'a fat man'). The opposite of *peculiar* in 'It is a custom peculiar to some countries' is *common*; but the opposite of 'he has peculiar tastes' is not 'he has common tastes' but 'he has average tastes'.

There is one other important factor which interferes with the simple opposition of antonyms. In dealing with grammar (as we shall see in Chapter 11), it is often useful to see some contrasts in terms of 'marked' and 'unmarked' members. Thus *love* and *loved* are in contrast as 'present' and 'past', but only the latter is actually 'marked' as such; *love* is 'unmarked' and as such may be much more widely used than merely as a present in contrast with *loved*. In 'Penguins live in the Antarctic', *live* is so to speak 'tense-less', since the statement is true not merely for the present but for the past and (presumably) the future. Similarly in vocabulary, *man ~ woman*, *lion ~ lioness* are in contrast, with the second member of each pair morphologically 'marked', and we find that we can frequently use the first member (the unmarked one) to subsume the second but not vice versa. 'There is a lion in this cage' does not exclude the possibility that it may be a lioness, but 'There is a lioness is this cage' is specific. So too we may speak of 'man or beast' and not exclude women: 'so long as men can breathe or eyes can see'.

The notion can obviously be extended to pairs in which there is no actual *morphological* marking by morphemes like *-ed* or *-ess*. Although *horse* in some contexts may be in contrast with *mare*, *horse* can often be used to include mares, as *geese* can to include ganders. In this respect, *horse* and *goose* may be thought of as 'unmarked' members of a contrast. So too with many adjectives. We may agree that *old* and *young* are antonyms, as are *light* and *heavy*, *big* and *small*, *short* and *tall*. But in each of these pairs, one member is 'unmarked', as can be seen in the fact that we can ask 'How old is the baby?' or 'How tall is your fence?' without implying that the one is old or the other tall. It is the lack of antonymous mark which enables us also to say 'It is three feet *high*' and the like.

Here again, in fact, we find ourselves able to speak about

a word's value only when we have it in a context, in actual use. It is a fatuous exercise to give synonyms or antonyms for words in isolation and it is impossible to answer the question 'What does the word *love* mean?' in isolation. The word is used 'correctly' but quite differently in 'I love my wife', 'Brotherly love', 'I love ice cream', 'Love all mankind!' and 'The score is love—all'. If therefore we cannot say what the meaning of a word is until it is put into an adequate context, we should beware of thinking that the meaning resides in the word itself: it is rather spread over the word and the neighbouring words, because only the latter identify the 'semantic field', the group of relevant associations, in which we have contrasting words by which to measure the one used. In one semantic field, for instance, *rose* operates in contrast with *tulip* and *dahlia*; in another, it is in contrast with *red* and *purple*. That use of *put out* which is in the semantic field of 'fire' allows *extinguish* as a synonym; but in the field of broadcasting we would not say that the BBC had extinguished the news item that we have just heard on the radio. And in still another field, one does not extinguish the cat before going to bed.

The semantic field is rather like the system of terms in grammar that was discussed in Chapter 7. *Rose* in the system of colours is in contrast with the other colour terms and its value is determined not so much positively as negatively: what other colour terms are there and how much do *they* cover. 'He is a captain' does not mean very much until we know the semantic field in which *captain* operates (the merchant service, the navy, the army) and what the terms of the relevant rank system are. Just as we know the value of 'dative' used of a given language only when we know what other cases there are, so we know what 'captain' means only when we know whether his subordinate is called the 'mate' or 'first officer' (merchant service), 'commander' (navy), 'lieutenant' (army).

This is what is meant by saying that knowing the meaning of a word is knowing how to *use* it, and it must lead us to take warning in one important respect. Vocabulary is the 'open end' of language: we spend our lives enlarging our knowledge of words. The more we can do to enlarge that knowledge, the more we can attain the satisfaction of knowing precisely what we are enjoying (as we saw in Chapters 4 and 5) and of being able to share that knowledge with those around us. But words are to be thought of rather as tools than as medals and ornaments. We would think a man ridiculous who bought an electric typewriter only for show and kept it on display in his drawing-room. Enlarged vocabulary is equally a ridiculous acquisition without the corresponding knowledge of how the words we have learnt are in fact used and of where they serve a useful purpose.

Exercises and Topics for Discussion

1   Study again the second of the numbered extracts in this chapter. What does the writer mean by 'vulgar'? Might he himself be open to the charge of vulgarity for using the expression 'skinning themselves alive'? Is it true that *guts* tends to be used as a complete synonym for *courage*? Write a rejoinder to this letter.

2   Go through the files of a local or national newspaper, scanning the correspondence columns; collect and annotate the comments you find on words and their use. (You may find it useful in this connexion to re-read Question 6 at the end of Chapter 3.)

3   If you have access to back issues of *The Times*, look up the correspondence series called 'A Word for it' (late April 1963), 'Naming a Chair' (mid January 1964), and 'Old Word, New Life' (mid-March 1965).

(a) How do you explain the use of *under-nasalized, monumentalized, concertized, secretized*? (Note also the use of *containerisation* in Metro-Cammell advertising, June 1967.)

(b) Adjudicate between *escalate* 'is indispensable' and *escalate* is 'an appalling word', the 'horrible' *donate* being 'no less detestable'.

(c) A University Chair of Transportation may suggest nineteenth-century penal laws while a University Transport Department suggests an area where vehicles are kept; it is equally easy to see objections to a Chair of Reinforced Concrete. Suggest other possibly misleading professorial titles and suggest also how each such new field of study might be named without unwanted overtones.

4   Discuss the following criticism of the word *growth*:

> If implements that could be made to last a lifetime have to be replaced with increasing frequency, that is growth. If serviceable goods are discarded sooner through quicker fashion changes, that is growth. If teenagers are persuaded to consume more gin and cigarettes, that is growth. (*The Times*, 15 January 1964.)

5   Sir Harold Nicolson (*Observer*, 18 August 1957) speaks about 'toying with such words as *bottleneck, targets* and *ceilings*, which are dangerous indeed'. In what respects do you think there may be dangers in the way these words have been used in recent years? What other words might be considered dangerous?

6   Look through the words beginning with *squ-* listed in a dictionary. Do any groups of words suggest a semantic constant analogous to that of *sl-*?

7   Write and classify examples so as to show the contemporary range of meaning, usage and semantic field of

141

the following words: *law, blue, English, word, nativity, inaugurate, wit.*

8 What instances of 'word-magic' have you come upon in your own experience? (Do not overlook the use of certain favourite word-elements in the names of patent medicines.)

9 'The President of the Probate, Divorce and Admiralty Division, discussing the use of the words "adultery" and "misconduct" in divorce cases, said that in the High Court today "it is such a pity that plain English is not used about these matters . . . I mean that, so far as I know, ever since the tablets of stone were translated into English in the English version of the Bible, 'adultery' has been the word, not 'misconduct' or 'intimacy', or any other paraphrase of it."' (*The Times*, 15 October 1959.)

Why do you think the President dislikes words like 'intimacy' in place of 'adultery'? Is there any analogy in the use of 'trade recession' for 'slump'? Are there other analogies that occur to you?

10 Explain the formation of the 'new words' in the *New Statesman* passage, pp. 136f.

9: *What do you Read, my Lord?*

HAMLET'S response to this question was the title of the previous chapter, and the time has now come to look at some of the types of books *about* words. A few years ago, great importance was attached in a law-suit to the use made by the appellant of the swear-word 'bloody'. The appellant was reported in *The Times* (28 September 1957) as having said that he 'had looked the word up in *the dictionary*, and it was a colloquialism not even a slang expression'. This quotation reminds us that everyone regards 'the dictionary' as the primary book about words. But it reminds us also of the almost biblical authority that is attributed to 'the dictionary', and finally the appellant's use of *the* with the singular reminds us of the tendency to think that there is only one dictionary, which is apparently published in a variety of editions like the works of Shakespeare. Corresponding to these implications in the expression '*the* dictionary' is the widespread belief that the dictionary-maker or lexicographer is vested with a special prerogative: that he ascends the mountain of his deliberations and comes down with the tablets enshrining the Word and its Correct Meaning, Correct Spelling, Correct Pronunciation.

All this of course is naïvety of a deplorable kind. There are many dictionaries, old and new, big and small, good and poor. And there are more dictionary-makers than dictionaries, partly because few of us today have the stupendous energy of a Dr Johnson, partly because in any case modern lexicographers know that only a poor dictionary could be made by one man's efforts alone: every

143

dictionary must be the result of collaboration of specialists in many fields. The dictionary-maker also knows that the smaller the dictionary he publishes the less trustworthy it will be, because he will have had to make so many more misleading and oversimplified statements. This means that our best dictionary is beyond question the *New* (or *Oxford*) *English Dictionary*, published in thirteen volumes (including the Supplement), work for which was begun in 1857 and whose volume V-Z appeared in 1928, followed by the Supplement in 1933. Scholars refer to it with the initials N.E.D. or O.E.D.

This is the most 'authoritative' dictionary that exists for English, but it must be carefully understood on what basis this authority rests. Sir James Murray and his colleagues examined millions of quotations illustrating the *use* of the words to be defined, and abstracted from the way any word was used a statement of how it was used—that is, the meaning. The process adopted was exactly the one that we should use if we encountered in our reading a word that we had never met before. Let us assume that we find the word *clop* in the following contexts while we are reading:

1. 'Do get me a clop,' she said, smacking her lips, but her brother, with a scornful glance up at the branches, said that there were none ripe yet.
2. A girl with clop-yellow hair came towards them.
3. The Malayan terrorists smuggled arms to the dockside under crates of clops.

By this time, we should be ready to conclude that a 'clop' (noun) was 'the name of an edible yellow fruit grown in South-East Asia; a commodity in the export trade of Malaya'. And if there were no further evidence in the shape of textual references, this would be as much as we could say or would need to say. We have done our best to give the full and correct 'meaning' from the evidence at our disposal. If, of course, we have been slip-shod and have not noticed other references to *clop* in the particular book which might have helped to define *clop* more closely; or if we have been too lazy or too short-sighted and have not had many other books searched for references to the word, then the 'authority' of our dictionary is small. But the *N.E.D.* was carefully planned, thousands of books were read by devoted helpers, and the quotations were scrupulously examined for every possible ray of light that could be cast on the use of English words, and so the authority of this dictionary is very high indeed.

No one can form an adequate impression of the great Oxford Dictionary from a mere description: there is no substitute for actually handling and using this 'greatest scientific achievement in lexicography so far completed', as it has been described by Professor C. L. Wrenn.[1] There are few public libraries without a copy, and its size makes it easy to find. Meanwhile, however, we may faintly taste its quality in the course of explaining how it deals with a single entry. The noun *temper* gets practically the whole of a large three-column page to itself (the verb gets another page, and there are several further pages dealing with related or derived words like *temperament*, *temperance* and so on). The entry begins by giving an indication of the modern pronunciation, and the various spellings are listed; we are told that from the fourteenth to the sixteenth centuries, *tempre* was common, that in the fifteenth the second syllable was spelt in a variety of ways but that the present-day spelling became established from the sixteenth century onwards. Not even spelling, we note, is a matter for dogma: 'right' or 'wrong' must be judged on the evidence of what *occurs*. We are then given an etymological note, telling us that the noun is derived from the verb: and if we wish to follow this up by turning to the verb entry, we find that

[1] *The English Language* (London 1949), p. 100.

there was a verb *temprian* in Old English (*alias* 'Anglo-Saxon'), that this is related to the verb *tamper* and to the Latin *temperare*, which meant 'to mingle in due proportion', or 'regulate'. After this introduction, the entry proceeds to deal with the ways the noun *temper* has been used since the Middle Ages. This account of usage is in four main sections (always denoted in this dictionary with roman numerals) and fourteen subsidiary sections (in arabic numerals), several of which are subdivided (a, b, . . .). An obelisk (†) at the head of any subsection indicates that the usage to be described has become obsolete, and so it is easy to run through any entry to take note only of modern uses. In the present case, there are nine subsections not marked as obsolete. The first reads:

> **2.** Proportionate arrangement of parts; regulation, adjustment; hence, means or medium, a middle course; a compromise; a settlement. *arch.*

As though to emphasise that the lexicographer does not speak with the voice of oracular infallibility, there follows a selection of the quotations from which the definition has been abstracted, beginning with one dated 1523. The most recent is one from Macaulay in 1855, and as we read it we can decide for ourselves whether or not the lexicographer has decided rightly in saying that this meaning of the word is archaic ('*arch.*'):

> He would probably have preferred a temper between the two rival systems, a hierarchy in which the chief spiritual functionaries should have been something more than moderators and something less than prelates.

It is worth noticing that the citation is continued beyond *systems*, at which point many a man might have felt that his definition was adequately illustrated. It would not have

146

been, of course: *temper* might have meant 'war', if so much was all we knew about Macaulay's use of it; the crucial part is 'something more than moderators and something less than prelates'. We see, therefore, that the quotations are not mere illustrations: they provide the raw material of the evidence and we can thereby evaluate the definition. Other separate uses of the noun *temper* distinguished in the N.E.D. include:

3. Mental balance or composure, esp. under provocation of any kind; moderation in or command over the emotions, esp. anger; calmness, equanimity: now usually in the phrases *to keep* or *lose* (one's) *temper, to be out of temper* . . .

5. The particular degree of hardness and elasticity or resiliency imparted to steel by tempering . . .

(There are two sets of citations for this, distinguishing literal from figurative use.)

9. Mental constitution; habitual disposition . . .

10. Actual state or attitude of the mind or feelings; frame of mind; inclination, humour . . .

One of the citations is from *Robinson Crusoe*: 'He brought me an Account of the Temper he found them in.' This tenth use has a subdivision:

b. IN GOOD-TEMPER, ILL-TEMPER, *bad temper* (the latter leading to sense 11) . . .

11.=*Ill-temper*: Heat of mind or passion, showing itself by outbursts of irritation or anger upon slight provocation; explosive ill-humour.

The first quotation to support the latter definition is dated 1828 and the authority is the American lexicographer, Noah

147

Webster. But despite the apparently American origin and the patently colloquial origin of this sense, the N.E.D. editor does not assume the 'holier than thou' attitude of the pedant, but proceeds in the usual way to plot the word's progress in this sense through the nineteenth century and into our own. The lexicographer knows words (and loves his fellow-men) too well to let himself fall into such word-hysteria as we saw illustrated in the previous chapter.

Does this mean, then, that the lexicographer never passes judgment, never says 'This is wrong'? Of course not. He is always having to exercise judgment: he must carefully weigh his textual authority not merely to gauge the meaning but also to decide whether a particular sense chiefly occurs in colloquial (or formal or legal or dialectal) usage. And if he finds a quotation in his material which is clearly out of step with the rest, he may well judge that its author simply did not know the 'correct' (that is, commonly accepted) use of the word. Take for instance the N.E.D. entry for *trenchant*. The last adjectival use given, 'Capable of being cut', is flatly branded 'erroneous', though the author of the only citation is Charles Lamb. It should by now be obvious, however, that this is 'erroneous' not because 'trenchant' *ought* not to be used in this sense but because it *was* not: Lamb had 'erred and strayed' from the path of usage. If his original error had been followed by the rest of us, it would *ipso facto* have ceased to be an error: *communis error facit ius*, or as Pierre-Claude La Chaussée put it in 1747, 'Quand tout le monde a tort, tout le monde a raison.' When the expression 'a foregone conclusion' is used in *Othello*, it means 'an experience previously undergone'; but through misunderstanding long ago, the expression is now used for a 'decision or opinion already formed before the case is argued or the full evidence known', as we are told in the N.E.D. entry for *foregone*. Needless to say, the N.E.D. does not call our modern use 'erroneous'.

148

The N.E.D. is the great repository of the English vocabulary. If we are puzzled by *gomeral* in Stevenson's *Kidnapped* or by the phrase *a uberty of optimism* which appears in a twentieth-century journal, our desk-dictionary may not help us, since it is impossible to do justice to the immense vocabulary of English in one volume. (Neither *gomeral* nor *uberty* is in the *Concise Oxford Dictionary*, for example.) We must go to the N.E.D. If we want to see the connexion between the many different uses or meanings of *table*, we must study the eleven closely-printed columns on the subject in the N.E.D. So too if we want to know how *unctuous*, with all its nasty connotations, can possibly be the adjective corresponding to the noun used with deep solemnity in expressions like 'administer extreme unction'; or if we want to know how *Tory*, which once 'signified the most despicable Savages among the Wild Irish', could so rise in public esteem as to become a label that Sir Winston Churchill was to bear with pride: the N.E.D. can tell us.

But of course the N.E.D. is too bulky for ordinary use and ordinary everyday needs. For practical purposes, we need a shorter, more compact dictionary, which will ignore for the most part words or uses of words that do not occur in the modern language, and (not least) which will include more recent usage. Thanks largely to the N.E.D. itself (which sets the standard for objectivity even where it is not more closely imitated), English is equipped with a finer range of just such practical dictionaries than any other language. The most obviously related to the N.E.D. is the excellent Clarendon Press series, ranging from the *Shorter Oxford English Dictionary* as revised by Dr C. T. Onions (2,500 three-column pages, printed in one volume for less than £7[1] or two volumes for slightly more), through the famous *Concise Oxford Dictionary* (originally the work of

[1] This and other prices mentioned in this chapter are those current at the time of going to press.

149

the Fowler brothers but now in a revised edition—1964—of over 1,550 pages, at twenty-five shillings), and the *Pocket Oxford Dictionary* (a very sound volume of over a thousand small pages, which sells at fifteen shillings), to the *Little Oxford Dictionary* for a still more modest pocket (in both senses), a volume of 640 very small pages for 8s 6d. The reader for whom English is not the native language is magnificently catered for with the series of dictionaries by A. S. Hornby and others, published by the Oxford University Press.

Outside the Oxford family, one might mention the following, all of which are roughly comparable in scale with the *Concise* just mentioned, and all of which can be confidently recommended: *Cassell's English Dictionary* (1,350 pp., 36s), *Chambers' Twentieth Century Dictionary* (1,400 pp., 27s), *Collins New English Dictionary* (1,300 pp., 25s) —and, of course, this is merely to give a selection of the excellent dictionaries on the market and of British origin. As we should by now expect, the entries in all of them are written according to actual usage as the lexicographer sees it, and not (as is sometimes popularly believed) according to what the lexicographer decrees that usage *ought to be*.

Most British dictionaries have useful appendices, listing foreign names, explaining foreign phrases, common abbreviations, scientific symbols, weights and measures, and the like. Some even give guidance on formal modes of address. Thus in *Collins* (which also has plates, maps, and 'encyclopedic' data) we can learn that to address the wife of an Earl's eldest son, we should proceed 'as if the courtesy title were an actual peerage'.

Many people, however, prefer to select the dictionary they are going to buy from the impressive American range, though these dictionaries are in general more expensive than British ones. One of the attractions is that whereas British dictionaries generally restrict themselves to the language itself, the American tradition is to include 'encyclopedic' entries dealing with people of importance, places, mythological characters, and the like. The entry on 'coverlet' will be followed by one on 'Coverley, Sir Roger'; one learns not only about grubs but also about Grub Street; the nature of guano as well as the location, government and population of Guadeloupe; cereals and Ceres herself. American dictionaries also provide useful diagrams (illustrating and naming the parts of an out-board motor, for example), a service that has become rare in British dictionaries. They make the provision of 'synonyms' a special feature too. Not least important, while British dictionaries tend to concentrate on British English without much attention to American English usage, the modern American dictionary is fairly dutiful in recording the forms and meanings of both sides of the Atlantic, and indeed those of English as a *world* language.

There are a good many other criteria by which we should judge the usefulness of a dictionary. One is its date—or the date when it was last thoroughly revised. Just because vocabulary is the 'open end' of language, it is always changing, as we have seen: new words are added and new senses for existing ones. If our one-volume desk dictionary is more than twenty years old, it is time to treat ourselves to another, or it will constantly let us down in failing to record the modern vocabulary: neither *maser* nor *laser* will be in, for example, nor will *rand*, the unit of South African currency.

The best known American dictionaries are doubtless those which trace their ancestry back to the great lexicographer of the new republic, Noah Webster, and outstanding among these is the Merriam-Webster *New International Dictionary of the English Language*, with a new two-volume edition in 1962. A shortened version, with a special orientation towards the student's needs—the *New Collegiate*

151

Dictionary—sells at three guineas (1,200 pp.); among its appendices can be found a 'vocabulary of rhymes'. Also bearing Webster's name, there is the *New World Dictionary* (1,700 pp.; about £2 10s). Among other outstanding American dictionaries, we must mention the great *Funk and Wagnall Standard Dictionary of the English Language,* in two magnificent volumes running to a total of about 3,000 large pages, with photographs and illustrations in colour as well as in line and half-tone; and *The Random House Dictionary* (1966), edited in 2,000 imposing pages by Jess Stein. Then there is the *American College Dictionary* (over 1,400 pp.), which was published by Harper and Random House of New York and which sells in Britain at under £3. It was edited by one of America's leading lexicographers, Clarence L. Barnhart, who has to his credit a large number of other dictionaries and reference-books such as the *Thorndike-Barnhart High School Dictionary,* published by Scott Foresman, the *World Book Encyclopedia Dictionary,* published by Doubleday (1963, nearly 2,300 pp.). In these works, Barnhart is pursuing lines established in collaboration with the late E. L. Thorndike who, with Irving Lorge, did important work finding out what are the commonest English words in use and in which meanings they are most commonly used—matters of obvious importance for the lexicographer.

Let us now compare some of the dictionaries mentioned, and we can do this by taking as specimens their definitions of the noun *temper* which we have already seen handled by the N.E.D.

Shorter Oxford English Dictionary:

I. 1. The due or proportionate mixture or combination of elements or qualities; the condition or state resulting from such combination; proper or fit condition. Now *rare* or *Obs.* **2.** Proportionate arrangement of parts;

regulation, adjustment; hence, mean or medium, a middle course; a compromise; a settlement. *arch.* 1523. **3.** Mental balance or composure, esp. under provocation of any kind; moderation in or command over the emotions, esp. anger; calmness, equanimity; now usu. in phr. *to keep* or *lose (one's) t., to be out of t.* 1603.

(There follow citations from Burke, Steele and Dickens.)

II. †1. =Temperament II. – 1759. **†b.** Of things immaterial : Character, quality – 1651. **2.** The particular degree of hardness and elasticity or resiliency imparted to steel by tempering 1470. **†3.** =Climate *sb.* 3, Temperament II. 2 – 1705. **4.** The relative condition of a body in respect of warmth or coldness – 1884. **†5.** Bodily habit, constitution, or condition – 1707. **6.** Mental constitution; habitual disposition 1595. **7.** Actual state of the mind or feelings; inclination, humour 1628. **8.**=*ill-temper*: Heat of mind or passion; explosive ill-humour 1828.

(There follow citations from Shakespeare, Macaulay, and others.)

III. Concr. senses. **a.** *Sugar-making.* A solution containing lime or some alkaline substance serving to neutralise the acid in the raw cane-juice and clarify it 1657. **b.** An alloy of tin and copper 1875.

Concise Oxford Dictionary:

1. Mixture, esp. suitable combination of ingredients (*of* mortar &c.); resulting condition or consistence. **2.** Condition of metal as to hardness & elasticity. **3.** Habitual or temporary disposition of mind, as *was of a saturnine, frigid, fiery, placid ~ , persons of congenial ~ , found him in a good ~* (not irritable or angry), *in a bad ~* (peevish, angry); irritation, anger, as *fit of ~ , what a ~ he is in!, naughty ~ !; show ~ ,* be petulant; *lose* one's *~ ,* become angry; *keep, control,* one's *~,* not lose it; *out of ~ ,* angry.

Pocket Oxford Dictionary:
Degree of hardness & elasticity in steel &c. (of the *finest t.*); composure under provocation &c. (*keep, lose,* one's *t.; out of t.*, angry or irritable); disposition or mood (*has a fiery, placid, t.; is in a good, bad, forgiving,* &c. *t.*, ready to be pleased, offended, mollified, &c.), fit of anger, anger (*is in a t.; show t.*, behave petulantly).

Little Oxford Dictionary:
degree of hardness & elasticity in steel, &c.; composure under provocation, &c.; disposition or mood; anger.

Cassell's English Dictionary:
Disposition of mind, esp. as regards the passions or emotions; composure, self-command; anger, irritation, passion; the state of a metal as regards hardness and elasticity; condition or consistency (of a plastic mixture as mortar).

Chambers' Twentieth Century Dictionary
due mixture or balance of different or contrary qualities : state of a metal as to hardness, &c. : constitution of the body : temperament : disposition : habitual or actual frame of mind : mood : composure : self-control : uncontrolled anger : a fit of ill-humour or rage : lime or other substance used to neutralise the acidity of cane-juice.

Collins New English Dictionary:
due proportion; consistency required and achieved by tempering; (*Fig.*) balanced attitude of mind; composure; anger; irritation.

Webster's New Collegiate Dictionary:
1. State of being tempered; specif.: **a.** Of a compound substance, due or just mixture of different qualities; as, the *temper* of mortar. **b.** The state of a metal or other substance, esp. as to its hardness or toughness. Temper in steel is indicated either by its carbon content or its color in tempering. **2.** *Obs.* Constitution of body; temperament.

154

3. Disposition or frame of mind, esp. as to the passions and affections; as, a fiery *temper*. **4.** Equanimity; composure. *Archaic*, exc. in the phrases, *to keep* or *lose one's temper*. **5.** Heat of mind or passion, proneness to anger. **6.** *Obs.* Mean; medium. **7.** A substance added to or mixed with something else to modify its properties. – **Syn.** See MOOD: DISPOSITION. [By permission. From Webster's New Collegiate Dictionary, copyright 1961 by G. and C. Merriam Co., Publishers of the Merriam-Webster Dictionaries.]

Webster's New World Dictionary:
1. The state of being tempered; specifically, *a*) [*Archaic*], properly proportioned mixture. *b*) the state of a metal with regard to the degree of hardness and resiliency. 2. frame of mind; disposition; mood: as, in a bad *temper*. 3. calmness of mind; composure: now used only in the phrases *lose one's temper*, *keep one's temper*. 4. a tendency to become angry readily: as, she has a *temper*. 5. anger; rage: as, he went into a *temper*. 6. something used to temper a mixture, etc. 7. [*Archaic*], mean; middle course. 8. [*Obs*], *a*) character; quality. *b*) bodily constitution. – **Syn.** see **disposition, mood.**

American College Dictionary:
1. the particular state of mind or feelings. **2.** habit of mind, esp. with respect to irritability or patience, outbursts of anger, or the like. **3.** heat of mind or passion, shown in outbursts of anger, resentment, etc. **4.** calm disposition or state of mind: *to lose one's temper*. **5.** a substance added to something to modify its properties or qualities. **6.** the particular degree of hardness and elasticity imparted to steel, etc., by tempering. **7.** *Archaic*, a middle course; compromise. **8.** *Obs*. the constitution or character of a substance. [From *The American College Dictionary*, © 1947, 1966 Random House, Inc., New York. Used by permission.]

At the end of the entry, we are told that synonyms for *temper* in sense 2 are given in the entry for *disposition*, and in order to see how synonymy is treated in a good representative dictionary, we may follow the directive on this occasion. We find:

> DISPOSITION, TEMPER, TEMPERAMENT refer to the aspects and habits of mind which one displays over a length of time. DISPOSITION is the natural or prevailing aspect of one's mind as shown in behavior and in relationships with others; *a happy disposition, a selfish disposition*. TEMPER sometimes denotes the essential quality of one's nature: *a temper of iron*; usually it has to do with propensity toward anger: *an even temper, a quick or hot temper*. TEMPERAMENT suggests the delicate balance of one's emotions, the disturbance of which determines one's moods: *an artistic temperament, an unstable temperament*.

We have concentrated in this chapter on dictionaries which seek to describe the standard use of the whole vocabulary of English, but of course there is a wealth of *specialised* dictionaries as well. For expert guidance on pronunciation, there is the world-famous *English Pronouncing Dictionary* by Daniel Jones (with a new edition in 1967, revised by A. C. Gimson). If one's interest is in the history of a word's form and meaning, one goes to an *etymological* dictionary, such as *The Oxford Dictionary of English Etymology* edited by C. T. Onions (Oxford 1966), or Eric Partridge's *Origins* (4th edn, London 1966). If our interest lies in the endings of words (and it may be a grammarian's interest in finding the words which use the verb-forming suffix *-ify*, or a poet's interest in finding words that rhyme with *night*), we can turn to the extraordinary *Rhyming Dictionary*, first published by John Walker in 1775. It is not in fact strictly a *rhyming* dictionary, since it will not direct us to *write* as one of the words rhyming with *night*; it is a dictionary arranged alphabetically according to the spelling of the

156

words in *reverse*, and so *replica* is near the beginning and *buzz* is near the end of the volume. Again, there are specialised dictionaries dealing with slang (for example H. Wentworth and S. B. Flexner, *Dictionary of American Slang*, London 1960, and Eric Partridge's *Dictionary of Slang and Unconventional English*, sixth edn, 1967), the language of medicine, the theatre, and many other fields.

All these books about words have one thing in common: the entries are arranged alphabetically, that is, according to the spelling. From one point of view, this is very convenient: we know exactly where to find all about a word, provided only that we know the word to begin with, and have a reasonably good idea how to spell it. But, as we saw in considering the *American College Dictionary's* treatment of synonyms, there is a relation between *temper* and *disposition* which does not show in the spelling, and the alphabetic arrangement enforces their separation. Similarly, the dictionary must treat *kingly*, *regal*, and *royal* on widely separated pages, though *kingly* may be treated on the same page as the totally unrelated *kinetic* or *kink*, *regal* on the same page as *refuse* or *regard*. Yet, as we saw in Chapter 8, words seem to be connected in our minds according to the collocations and associations they share—according to their 'semantic field'. Thus *larceny* is in the same semantic field as (and its meaning is to be stated in relation to) *theft*, *robbery*, *burglary*, *pilfering*, *swindling*, and so on; one of the meanings of *petty* is that it is frequently collocated with *larceny*. Yet in our dictionary, *larceny* may follow *larboard* (through the trivial connection of sound and spelling) and none of the more 'deeply' connected words may be within sight. *Measles* will be near *measure*, but *pneumonia* will be near *plywood*.

Careful lexicographers see that they avoid circular definitions, whereby a *fort* might be defined as a small castle and *castle* as a large fort, but since words in the same semantic

157

field are in fact mutually defining, it is impossible to achieve thoroughly satisfactory definition by treating each word in isolation on the alphabetised pages. One notable achievement in mutual definition is the Duden principle. The firm of Harrap publishes a book called *The English Duden* (adapted from an originally German work, Duden's *Bildwörterbuch*) which seeks to contextualise any word which is susceptible to visual explanation. If we look up *square sail* in the alphabetised index, we are given a reference to a page of numbered diagrams facing a page of correspondingly numbered words: we not only see what a square sail is but see this in relation to the necessary associated words such as *staysail*, *spanker* and *mizzen*. On the other hand, *square root* in the index will lead us to a page illustrating and explaining the fundamental operations in mathematics, from decimals to logarithms and differential co-efficients.

Often our principal problem is not to find the exact meaning of a word but to find the exact word for a meaning which is floating, so to speak, in our heads. A dictionary is not much help, any more than a telephone directory would be if we had a number on a piece of paper and wanted to find out whose it was. Let us imagine that we are in the middle of writing something and are suddenly stuck for the 'right' word: we know it has to do with *growing smaller*, but this is as far as we can get, though we have the irritating feeling that the word is on 'the tip of the tongue'. What we want now is not an alphabetically arranged dictionary but something more like a *classified* telephone directory in which all house-painters (for example) are brought together, whether they are called Abbot or Young. A word-book of precisely this kind exists and is known as *Roget's Thesaurus*, originally compiled by Peter Mark Roget, F.R.S. (1779-1869) and first published in 1852. Roget was the son of a Huguenot minister and his name is still pronounced as French. Primarily a scientist and a medical specialist, he wrote a tract with the title *Tentamen Physicum de Chemicae Affinitatis Legibus* before he was twenty, became a Professor of Physiology, was one of the founders of the University of London and an original member of the University's Senate. Like many eminent scientists in his time (and ours), this remarkable man had a profound interest in language also. He ventured upon a practical application of the accumulated reflections of such men as Wilkins, Hume, and Horne Tooke on semantics and linguistic philosophy. For him, ' the filiation of words presents a network analogous to the natural filiation of plants and animals'. The enormous network that he postulated is nothing less than a categorisation of the universe. For example, 'Periodicity' and its correlative 'Irregularity' constitute polarised sub-classes of the sub-class 'Recurrence' of the sub-class 'Time' of the class 'Abstract Relations'—and therefore all words used in connexion with periodicity and irregularity must be brought together: *beat, pulse, rhythm, revolution, steady, cyclical,* etc., on the one hand; *fitful, casual, flickering, uncertainty, capricious, desultory,* etc., on the other. It will be obvious that the word *temper* will be found in *Roget*, not in one place as in a dictionary, but in several places according to the various 'filiations' into which it enters. In the same way, Abbot & Co. may appear at several points in the classified directory—not merely among the 'House-Painters' but probably among the 'Builders', and perhaps also among the 'Undertakers' and the 'Joiners'.

Roget's Thesaurus has been through various editions; one version today is published by Longmans, Green, and there is another in the Everyman Library. With the *Thesaurus* to hand, we can now speedily settle our problem over the word for 'growing smaller'. We can either turn directly to the sections dealing with relative size or be guided to them by looking up any common associated word in the index. We find a whole set of words in the required field of meaning: *lessen, reduce, condense, contract, attenuate, dwarf, wane, diminish, decrease, shrink, dwindle*, and several others. The *Thesaurus* does not give definitions of the individual words and if we come upon one in the list that is unfamiliar, we must turn to a good dictionary to inquire into its precise use. But since our 'passive' knowledge of words is always so much greater than our 'active' use of words, it is often enough merely to see a word in a list to know that it is just right for our needs.

It is clear, then, that there are many books which we *ought* to consult about 'words, words, words', books which can enlarge our experience by making us see our world in greater detail and which can help us to communicate our experience of it to others with greater precision, at the same time providing us with the necessary assurance of what others are likely to understand by our words and with the equally necessary protection against pedantic word-hysteria.

Exercises and Topics for Discussion

1 Look up the words *draft* and *draught* in the N.E.D. Try to explain the connexion between the many ways in which they have been and are used. Why are they spelt differently? Do you think it would be just as appropriate to have had three or four spellings—or a single one?

2 With the help of the N.E.D., explain why we can use the same word in 'train the soldiers' and 'catch the train'; 'he is *patient*' and 'he is a *patient*'; 'he has

a long-playing *record*' and 'he has the long-jump *record*'.

3 Study and compare the treatments of *temper* quoted from the various dictionaries (except the N.E.D.), and consider the following questions:

(a) Which dictionary gives unnecessary information from from your point of view?

(b) Some lexicographers seem to seek the most abstract and embracing statement while others prefer the narrower, more specific statement. Quote instances of the two types and consider which is preferable.

(c) On what principles do these dictionaries appear to work in deciding the order for presenting the different meanings? Write what seems to you a good treatment of *temper*, deciding on (and justifying) your order of presentation.

4 Is your dictionary up to date? First, consider the following utterance: 'She was absolutely livid because I said her boy-friend looked rather anthropoid.' Second, without looking up any word in the dictionary, write a paraphrase of this remark, taking care to find substitutes for both *livid* and *anthropoid*. Thirdly, read what your dictionary says about these words. Fourthly, check with your friends to make sure that your understanding of the words (as shown in your paraphrase) is similar to theirs.

5 A distinction has been drawn between 'grammatical words' and 'lexical words'. Using any good and fairly full dictionary, compare the entries for *make, may, the,* and *thin*. Is the lexicographical method of description equally effective for all four? In what ways does the presentation of 'definition' differ between the four?

6 In trying to keep up to date by including new words, dictionaries at each revision have to be relieved of some

meanings of words (and some words themselves) which have become obsolete. Take any four consecutive pages of a one-volume dictionary and consider carefully how much material you might recommend to be discarded for this reason.

7 Using *Roget*, consider the range of substitutes for the following words and phrases in the contexts in which they occurred in Question 4 above: *up to date, consider, absolutely, looked, remark, check (with), friends, make sure, understanding.*

10: Looking at English in Use

WE have seen something of what is involved in grammatical and lexical distinctions. Let us now look at the way distinctions of these kinds actually manifest themselves in the English we are liable to come upon any day within a single linguistic community, inspecting varieties of English with a somewhat different focus from that in Chapter 6.

Rather more than a century ago, Thomas Wade started off on the road to becoming one of the outstanding Chinese scholars of his time. He sought out the best-qualified man he could find and said, 'Please teach me Chinese.' We may imagine his dismay at the reply: 'Which Chinese is it you want to learn, sir? There is the Chinese of the ancient Classics, the Chinese of official documents, the Chinese used in writing letters, and there is the spoken Chinese, of which there are many dialects. Now which Chinese is it that you want to learn?'

Now, of course, Chinese is a notoriously extreme case, but as we have seen, the situation with English is certainly analogous. We are all aware of the distinctiveness of the regional dialects, but we less generally acknowledge the comparable distinctiveness—both in spoken and written English—of other kinds of 'dialect' which are comparably self-consistent and (with a different concept of speech 'community') comparably justified. The incomplete recognition of these makes us too liable to join in the intolerant and ill-informed tirades upon jargon—a wholly pejorative word often applied to a perfectly respectable 'trade dialect' which

163

has its own rules and the users of which have their own rights. We become susceptible also to the great deal of nonsense which is written about incorrectness and impropriety of expression, insisting mistakenly that a given form is either 'correct' or 'incorrect' in all styles and circumstances.

We have seen that the word 'English'—like 'Chinese' —is an abstraction, conveniently summarising a wide range of different, partly self-contained forms of communication. Only the individual forms themselves have an 'actual existence' as English, but they all have enough in common to justify the application of the generic term 'English' to all of them. One may compare the word 'dog'. Everyone can tell the difference between a dog and a cat, but there is an immense range of animals which share the designation 'dog', and one cannot point to one dog that has all the features present in all dogs: there is no actual embodiment of 'dogginess'. Nor can we say (if the analogy may be pressed a little further) that one dog is 'doggier' than another: a feature that is 'correct' in one variety of dog is 'incorrect' in another.

So it is with English, and in Chapter 6 we attempted to show something of the total range of English, and singled out from that range some features and forms which we said could be called 'Standard English'. The object now is to look at the corresponding range that exists within educated usage itself and especially at the forms of English that characterise the various *uses* of Standard English. No attempt can be made, however, to discuss all the varieties even within this relatively narrow band which is loosely called 'Standard'. But it is worth emphasising that the few, very distinctive varieties exemplified in this chapter could easily have come from the lips and pens of people who, for ordinary purposes, would seem to be using as uniform a type of English as it is possible to find. The distinctive

164

features revealed are no less real for that, and may be all the more noteworthy.

Let us consider first an example of religious English, written within the past few years:

1 Eternal God, Who dost call all men into unity with Thy Son, Jesus Christ our Lord, we pray Thee to pour Thy spirit upon the students of all nations, that they may consecrate themselves to Thy service; that being joined together by their common faith and obedience, they may come more perfectly to love and understand one another, that the world may know that Thou didst send Thy Son to be the Saviour and the Lord of all men; through the same Jesus Christ our Lord Who with Thee and the Holy Spirit liveth and reigneth one God world without end. Amen. (Prayer published for the Universal Day of Prayer for Students, 15 February 1953.)

Even the opening two words embody a construction which is almost entirely restricted to religious usage—adjective plus noun in direct address. One may compare the epistolary formula, 'Dear (Sir)', and beyond that there is little except some colloquial expressions like 'old man'. We notice that in religious English the noun in direct address may be post-modified by a relative clause, a feature which is a common and living one in this kind of English but virtually unknown outside it.

Perhaps the most obvious characteristic is the use of the distinctive second person pronoun and the equally distinctive second and third person singular verb forms. What is more, the pronoun has separate subject and object forms, a feature absent from the usual second person pronoun: something more is involved than a straightforward one-for-one correspondence such as we find between *lives* and *liveth*; *you* corresponds to *thou* or *thee* according to rules which do not affect you. Such special pronoun and verb forms are

165

all but absent from other varieties of Standard English, though some continue to crop up in poetry from time to time. And some, of course, continue to flourish in several regional dialects. Of them all perhaps the third person inflexion in -*eth* is the most restricted. About two hundred years ago, the grammarian John Ash tells us that the termination is 'used in the *grave* and *formal* Style; but *s* . . . in the *free* and *familiar* Style'. From this time there has been a severe limiting of the functions grave enough to require the -*eth* forms and a corresponding extension of the occasions on which -*s* would not sound too flippant. Even today, however, the special pronoun and verb forms are not merely optional in religious usage; if we were to repeat the last part of the prayer, replacing *Thee* by *You*, and *liveth and reigneth* by *lives and reigns*, it would sound to most people intolerably impertinent and irreverent, perhaps even profane. It is a matter of common observation that forms which are thoroughly to be expected in one variety of English give us a sensation of shock when they are introduced into a variety in which they are not expected.

There are several other features that one might mention even in this short passage. There is the special use of *through* in 'through . . . Jesus Christ' which we nevertheless accept so readily in religious discourse. And there are lexical words which, if not actually confined to religious use (*saviour, consecrate, amen*), are used in other kinds of English chiefly when it is desirable to convey the echo or suggestion of devotion piety or high seriousness. But we must turn our attention to other varieties.

The English of laws and regulations is an easy butt, and passages like the following can be cited as almost beyond the reach of ridicule and derision:

2   In the Nuts (Unground) (Other than Groundnuts) Order, the expression nuts shall have reference to such nuts,

other than groundnuts, as would, but for this Amending Order, not qualify as nuts (Unground) (Other than Groundnuts) by reason of their being nuts (Unground). (Quoted in the *Daily Telegraph*, 3 April 1956.)

For the purposes of this Part of this Schedule a person over pensionable age, not being an insured person, shall be treated as an employed person if he would be an insured person were he under pensionable age and would be an employed person were he an insured person.

(National Insurance Act, 1964, 1st Schedule, Part II.)

Yet even this style of writing has its justification undiminished by the fact that some specimens of writing in this style may be bad or unnecessarily clumsy. Any of us with the smallest experience of drawing up regulations even for a small society or club must find it easy to sympathise with the lawyer.

Contrary to popular belief, there are few lawyers who contrive obscurity to make a mystery of their profession : they regret it, as much as we, that a contract is difficult to understand—and indeed impossible if it is heard instead of being studied visually. The sad fact is that regulations and deeds have to be drawn up with one's eye steadily on the potential cheat, not on the majority of us who merely want to know as simply as possible what our liabilities or rights are. To this extent, the style of legal English, too, then, is obligatory and not optional. As the late Lord Justice Birkett has said (*The Magic of Words*, English Association, 1953), 'the lawyer . . . must resolutely eschew the words that have colour, and content himself with the "hereinbefores" and "aforesaids" in order to achieve precision.' He does not actively wish to write obscurely, nor does he wish to omit the commas which would make his document so much easier to read. But a very 'light' punctuation is part of the tradition of statute composition, in deference to

167

such principles as 'Punctuation is no part of the English language' and 'Words should stand by their own strength'. There has thus been a feeling that if a statute requires punctuation to make it clear, then the wording must to that extent be deficient and perhaps dangerously ambiguous. On pp. 366ff of D. Mellinkoff's valuable study of legal language,[1] the reader will find a useful discussion of this point.

Here is an example of quite ordinary legal English:

3   Whereas the Insured described in the Schedule has by the proposal the date of which is specified in the Schedule which proposal and declaration the Insured has agreed shall be the basis of this Contract and be held as incorporated herein applied to The —— Assurance Company Limited (hereinafter called 'the Company') for insurance against the contingencies hereinafter specified Now this Policy witnesseth that in consideration of the Insured paying to the Company for this Insurance the First Premium specified in the Schedule the Company hereby agrees (subject to the conditions contained herein or endorsed or otherwise expressed hereon which conditions shall so far as the nature of them respectively will permit be deemed to be conditions precedent to the right of the Insured to recover hereunder) that in the event of any of the said contingencies happening. . . . (Preamble to a current Insurance Policy.)

The suffixed prepositions (as in *hereunder*) are well in evidence, and we see a good deal of the 'continuous chain' type of grammatical expression that has also been mentioned. Both are in fact long-standing characteristics of legal expression. In the eighteenth century, Shaftesbury writes of the suffixed preposition as being a feature of the 'complicated periods' which 'are so curiously strung, or hook'd on, one to another, after the long-spun manner of the bar'. What

[1] *The Language of the Law*, Boston 1963.

168

is called the 'hook'd on' manner can be seen in the compound reference expressions like 'which conditions' and 'the said contingencies', both making the reference back more precise and unambiguous (if clumsier) than an ordinary relative clause in the first case or an article without 'said' in the second. As a wit has said (*The Times*, 20 April 1963), a lawyer 'has a hereditament in his speech'.

The fact that we still have these characteristics 250 years later shows that legal language is very traditional. It is also, of course, formulaic. Thus *witnesseth* in this passage does not indicate a general use of *-eth* forms as in religious English (*agrees* also occurs in the passage); the archaic *witnesseth* stands in a set piece (additionally marked typographically in the original) dividing the preamble from the main undertaking. The way in which such a fixed formula can stand apart from ordinary linguistic structure reminds us of similar phenomena in (for example) proverbs.

The language of officialdom, which has some affinities with that of the Law, is worth a separate mention, though its features have been the object of much widely read criticism in the past thirty years, from the Fowlers to Sir Alan Herbert and Sir Ernest Gowers. One characteristic is the use of words and phrases that we condemn with the value-judgment 'pompous'. This generally means that words have been chosen which have as little popular echo as possible, since the composing official is afraid—and often with good reason—of being accused by superiors or the public of lacking a proper command of 'dignified', remote, impersonal English. The story is told of how Canning included the phrase 'He died poor' in the text of a monument to Pitt; an official was scandalised by this, feeling that it was grossly deficient in dignity, and he proposed instead of Canning's words, 'He expired in indigent circumstances.' Smile as we may, we must all have felt similar pressures and inhibitions at some time, even in drafting something simple to put up on a noticeboard. Official English has become a little less obtrusive in recent years, and here is a typical example of it:

4 The symbol † against a subscriber's entry in the Directory denotes that the telephone number is withheld from publication at the subscriber's request and the Post Office is not authorised to supply it to enquirers. The names and addresses of such subscribers are, however, shown in the Directory in cases where frequent enquiries are received by the Post Office for the exchange number, with a view to saving members of the public the trouble of fruitless enquiry. (*London Telephone Directory*, 1955.)

Even here, we may note the phrases 'in cases where' (reminding us of Quiller-Couch's devastating criticism)[1] and 'with a view to', not to mention the rather formidable 'authorised'. We notice also the impersonal style: the writer did not put 'We show the names and addresses', as he might have *said* if he had been explaining the system to an inquirer orally, but 'The names and addresses . . . are . . . shown'. Such a use of the passive (and it occurs a little earlier, too, in 'the . . . number is withheld') was attacked not long ago in a speech at Nottingham, which was reported in *The Guardian* beneath the headline, 'Too Much of the Passive Voice in Local Government' (4 September 1956). The speaker, Mr Derek Senior, had said: 'Half the dilatoriness, the passing of the bucks, the shirking of responsibility, the lazymindedness, and the want of initiative . . . could be eradicated overnight by the simple expedient of forbidding the use of the passive voice in any official document.' This is no doubt a little optimistic, but we can see what is in Mr Senior's mind.

There are similarities to both legal and official usage in the English of industry and commerce, but here we run

[1] In his fifth lecture *On the Art of Writing*, Cambridge 1916.

deeply into the much-discussed, much-misunderstood question of 'jargon'. Let us take the following passage:

5   The programme has included the replacement of existing coke ovens, a new material handling terminal, a sinter plant, the redesign and enlargement of the Company's eight fixed open hearth steel melting furnaces, the installation of two Bessemer converters and a mixer and blower to raise the potential of the melting shop, the installation of a combined slabbing, blooming and continuous billet mill and construction of a new basic refractory brick works at Jarrow.

    The five per cent. redeemable Debenture Stock 1975/85 was created by resolution of the Directors and will be constituted and secured by a trust deed charging the undertaking and all the property and assets of the Company present and future (including any uncalled capital) by way of a first floating charge. The stock will be redeemable by a cumulative sinking fund calculated to redeem by annual operation not less than half of the stock at par by 30th September, 1985. (Public Notice of the Consett Iron and Steel Company, December 1955.)

At 'melting shops' and 'floating charges' and 'sinking funds' many may throw up well-bred hands in horror, but though this be jargon, yet there is method in it. Indeed, since the word 'jargon' carries such overtones of disapproval, it would be best to reserve it for recurrent slipshod pomposities as distinct from technical expressions like 'sinter plant' which are admirably clear to those who understand these things, and which are therefore completely legitimate. One frequently hears writing like this condemned because it is incomprehensible, but criticism on this score is often grossly unjust: if we do not understand the *processes* of a given context of activity and situation, we cannot expect to understand the labels for those processes, however they are 'addressed', so to speak. Replacing the

171

terms *sinter plant* or *sinking fund* by something comprehensible to all would involve replacing them with manuals of instruction in metallurgy and finance respectively.

We find the same problem with modern scientific usage, which is particularly fertile in producing expressions totally obscure to the general public:

6 Neuraminic acid in the form of its alkali-stable methoxy derivative was first isolated by Klenk from gangliosides and more recently from bovine sub-maxillary gland mucin and from a urine muco-protein, its composition being $C_{11}H_{21}NO_9$ or perhaps $C_{10}H_{19}NO_8$. This substance has no reducing power, but is ninhydrin-positive. Sialic acid and the methoxy derivative of neuraminic acid are characterised by the purple colour they give on heating with Ehrlich's *p*-dimethylaminobenzaldehyde reagent even without alkali pretreatment (direct Ehrlich reaction), by the violet colour they produce on treatment with Bial's orcinel reagent and by the considerable humin formation on heating with dilute mineral acid . . . Neuraminic acid may be regarded as an aldol type of condensation product of 2-amino-2-deoxy-hexose with pyruvic acid, the aldol type of linkage rendering recovery of the amino sugar by acid treatment impossible. (Letter in *Nature*, November 1955.)

But quite apart from the *lexical* problems confronting us in these industrial and scientific passages, there is a prominent *grammatical* feature that has been subjected to a good deal of criticism. Thus, in place of what we find in passage 5, 'eight fixed open hearth steel melting furnaces', many critics of this style would prefer to see something like 'eight furnaces, of a fixed type with open hearth, for the melting of steel'. Similarly in place of 'bovine sub-maxillary gland mucin' in passage 6 they would prefer a rephrasing to 'mucin from the sub-maxillary gland of cattle'. In terms of the grammatical description explained in Chapter 11,

172

they would in other words prefer to see more 'postmodified nominal groups' and fewer of the heavily 'premodified' ones.

Premodification was roundly condemned by Dr John Baker, of Oxford (himself a scientist), in the number of *Nature* from which passage 6 was taken. As a matter of taste, of course, it must remain an open question, though obviously protagonists of the style will rightly advance its brevity on the credit side. But Dr Baker's objection seems to derive its vigour from his conviction that the habit of premodification is reaching Britain from the United States, where in turn it springs from the usage of the many German-born scientists now working in American laboratories. This seems rather dubious, since the premodification of nouns by nouns was a common feature of English before Germans studied science or America was discovered. Heavy modifications in this manner are very frequent in the most commonplace and least scientific English. We not only have 'refreshment room' and 'railway station' but also 'railway station refreshment room', which few would prefer to see broken down into 'room for refreshments at the station of that kind of way which consists of rails'.

Of course, we should always do well to remember that the excessive use of any stylistic device, be it never so genuinely native and natural, can become a serious source of irritation. Some of the varieties of English used in journalism bear this out only too well. In the last resort, the determiners of any linguistic form are mainly habit and fashion, however much we may like to believe there is some useful purpose justifying it. Probably, therefore, it is to these two that outstanding peculiarities in journalistic writing owe their persistence rather than to the demands of brevity and other factors sometimes offered as excuses. One such peculiarity is a piling up of adjectives and relative clauses, even though the information so conveyed is frequently not properly relevant to the rest of the sentence. Consider the following:

7 . . . this dark, slimly built young chemistry student from New South Wales is England-bound next April. A Sydney colleague tells me that the modest, 17-year-old Craig—who celebrated his recent double century against the South Africans by week-ending at his local Youth Club camp—is considered a certainty for the England tour. Craig, who has been handling a bat since he was eight, celebrated his entry into first-class cricket with a stream-lined 91 against South Australia at the belligerent age of 16. His tally to date is 654 runs in 13 first-class innings —twice not out. Complementary to his cricket, Craig was planning to have started a pharmacy course at Sydney University next March. (*Evening Standard*, January 1953.)

Apparently, the Sydney colleague did not say simply that 'Craig is considered a certainty for the England tour' but that '*the modest 17-year-old* Craig is considered a certainty for the England tour', which surely very few people would in fact be heard saying. And in the middle, the writer has interposed (presumably from other sources) the lengthy relative clause about 'week-ending' at the camp, which neither helps to identify Craig nor concerns the certainty of his 'England tour'. Craig's age, of course, is fair material here, but often age and other 'personal angles' dominate a journalistic sentence with less justification. Take the following, for example:

8 Mr John William Allaway, a 46-year-old plumber, his wife, Florence, aged 32, and their 15-year-old son, John, escaped unhurt in their nightclothes after fire broke out at their 200-year-old home, Rose Hill Cottage at Gallows Hill, Kings Langley, Herts. (*Ibid.*)

Notice first the special journalistic function of the indefinite

174

article—'a 46-year-old plumber': it conveys the information that Mr Allaway has not been in the news before (otherwise he would be 'the well-known 46-year-old plumber' or at any rate *the* something). It is the more noteworthy, therefore, that in this single sentence about a man we have not heard of, we are given not only *his* age but also that of his house and of its every occupant.

Now, this heavy modification of nouns leads to another fairly widespread feature in journalese. In the *Daily Mail*, July 1958, we find: 'Her 35-year-old Etonian husband, grandson of a millionaire steelmaster, said . . .' Here is a rhythm which is atypical in English structure, the heavy qualification of the subject (normally the first noun) of a sentence; in general, the English balance is found by making such heavy modifications to a noun after the main verb (normally the object or complement). And so there develops a tendency to inversion, illustrated in the same column, same 'story', in the *Daily Mail*; a paragraph begins: 'Said the new owner, 31-year-old Mrs Sheena Simmons, wife of a retired auctioneer from Bourne End . . .' We may compare the following piece from the *Daily Express*, August 1958: 'Presiding at the victims' funeral service will be rugged Army chaplain Captain Robin Roe, ex-Ireland international Rugby player, who was one of the first on the scene of the disaster.'

The stylistic traits shown here are widely current in an extreme form in some American journalistic writing, particularly that associated with *Time*. They were amusingly pilloried in 1937 by the late Wolcott Gibbs in *A Bed of Neuroses*; his by no means unfair parody includes the following:

Sad-eyed last month was nimble, middle-sized *Life*-President Clair Maxwell as he told newshawks of the sale of the 53-year-old gagmag to *Time*. . . . Behind this latest, most incomprehensible Timenterprise looms, as usual, ambitious, gimlet-eyed, Baby Tycoon Henry Robinson Luce. . . . Once to interviewer who said, 'I hope I'm not disturbing you,' snapped Luce, 'Well, you are.'

It would seem that writers in this style have reconciled a passion for piling adjectives on to the subject of a sentence with the English rhythmic pattern which requires heavily modified nouns to follow the verb; it has been done by reversing the normal English word-order with such results as 'Presiding . . . will be rugged Army chaplain Captain Robin Roe' and 'Sad-eyed last month was nimble, middle-sized *Life*-President Clair Maxwell'.

Not all writing in journalism is 'journalistic' in the sense that it necessarily embodies features found in the passages quoted here. That is to say, we define the features of this style only on positive grounds: they characterise journalistic writing in that they rarely occur outside it. A corresponding caveat is equally required when we come to consider 'literary' English; there are as many varieties of English in literature as there are outside it, to the extent that literature imitates life. When 'literary' is applied to style, therefore, the term is usually rather unfairly restricted to a *belles lettres* sense, referring to linguistic features which, although not having of necessity to be used in literary writing, are fairly rare in other kinds of usage. Let us consider the three following passages in this connexion:

9 It has given me pain to have to relate this incident. To suppress it indefinitely would be impossible. Besides, the Australian people have a right to know what happened and why. On the other hand, it must be remembered that, apart from the limitations of their rigid party system, the Australian Governments had little reason to feel confidence at this time in British direction of the war, and that the risks their troops had run when the Desert Flank

was broken, and also in the Greek campaign, weighed heavily upon them. (W. S. Churchill, *The Grand Alliance*, 1950.)

10 That a great many people in this country are but dimly aware of what the banishment of the artist has cost them is certainly true. The tidal wave of ugliness has swept away all but a few of the older, finer things which provided a salutary comparison.

Nor have many manufacturers perceived that the artist-craftsman of yesterday, who has been put out of business by their machines, might at least be replaced by the industrial designer of today, who could show them how to bring seemliness and beauty into the products of the machine. (Gordon Russell, in *The Observer*, February 1953.)

11 Although the power to communicate with others is no longer regarded as a characteristically human achievement, for which no other animal possesses the capacity, the habit of speaking in different languages is peculiar to Man. Thus there has arisen a situation which is biologically unique—the existence of a species in which some individuals are unable to understand the words and meanings of some other individuals. (T. Savory, *The Art of Translation*, 1957.)

If one had to say in three words how these passages differed from the varieties previously discussed, one might reasonably choose 'precision with elegance'. The writer seeks the *mot juste* from a fairly large vocabulary and embeds it in an elegant pattern of word-order and clause interrelationship. Thus in the second paragraph of the Russell passage, one recognises the precision of *perceived* (a word uncommon except in 'literary' usage) and the elegant network in which it appears; this opens with an inversion preceded by *nor* (again, a literary connective when used after posi-

177

tive statements) and proceeds to a pretty balance of 'yesterday' plus relative clause against 'today' plus relative clause.

Some other features in these passages which have a literary flavour may be mentioned briefly. As already stated, the typical and unremarkable English utterance has a light subject followed by the verb with the heavily modified parts then following; this pattern applies also to the disposition of subordinate clauses: they generally follow a part of the sentence which can be seen as in some way nuclear, thus conforming with the broad underlying pattern of having the main fabric of a structure take shape before the qualifications are added. The opening of the Savory passage illustrates how differently this matter can be treated in literary English: a concessive clause and a relative clause (one of an uncolloquial type) precede the nuclear part which even so begins with a 'heavy' subject. The second sentence of the Churchill passage and the first of the Russell one have as subjects a non-finite and a finite verb clause respectively; in spoken English, both would probably have had 'it' as the subject ('It would be impossible . . .' and 'It is certainly true . . .'). Churchill's last sentence has a noun clause interrupted by a lengthy parenthetic phrase, and a parallel noun clause whose subject is followed by a relative clause, a temporal clause and a parenthetic phrase before the verb, reserved in the majestic Ciceronian manner, makes its appearance.

Although in the criticism of a piece of literary English one may sometimes have occasion to draw attention to the flavours of religious, journalistic, scientific, or even legal style which the author has introduced, it is more usual to find oneself weighing the style against that of *colloquial* usage: 'literary' chiefly operates in contrast with 'colloquial'. Let us therefore turn to the features which characterise conversational usage, and consider first of all the following passage:

12   I often pop an odd paper in here. Do look at this! A
bell-ringer's outing to Skegness, before the war, in one
of those charabancs with a hood and, I should think by
the look of our hair, no mica side curtains that buttoned
and split half your nails! Would you remember those,
dear? This is the most likely spot in the house. I know I
put the recipe in just such a hidey-hole. The bicarb goes
with the warm milk. Take a look at that! Got up by a
crank uncle of mine. He had eccentric ideas on breathing. One long in, and two short out, I think he advocated,
or am I thinking of Morse? (*Punch*, February 1953.)

At once one notices words which would not appear in a
prayer or a law or in Mr Savory's book on translation:
'pop', 'hidey-hole', 'bicarb'. And there is colloquial syntax too: an expanded form of the imperative with *do* ('Do
look at this'), the indefinite *you* ('split half your nails'),
the special use of *would* ('Would you remember those,
dear?'). A noun clause introduced without *that* ('I know I
put') is also usually colloquial; compare Churchill's 'it
must be remembered *that*' and Russell's 'perceived *that*'.
Two verb expressions may also be mentioned as commoner
in colloquial than in other varieties of English. The first
is the 'phrasal verb' as it is usually called, illustrated in
'*Got up* by a crank uncle'; one may compare 'put up with'
meaning 'tolerate' and 'take in' meaning 'deceive'.
Secondly, there is the feature illustrated by 'Take a look at
that'—in other words, the use of a copula-type verb plus
noun in place of a fully 'lexical' verb; other common
examples are 'have a swim' for *swim*, 'have a smoke',
'have a try', 'take a bath'. It may be recalled that one of
the outstanding characteristics of C. K. Ogden's system of
Basic English is the replacement of practically all our verbs
by nouns preceded by one of a small number of 'operators':
instead of 'a war to end war', Basic has 'a war to put an
end to war'.

179

But the piece of spoken English quoted above was never spoken: it is a writer's imaginative attempt to capture the style of spoken English, and although it captures certain aspects of that style very well, one must not leave the impression that spoken English is typically and only this. The writer here is using literary conventions (punctuation marks, for instance) to convey one type of frivolous talk, and the conventions of writing cannot express such features as intonation, stress, tempo and rhythm which belong specifically to *speech*. Moreover, a great deal of spoken English is concerned with topics as serious as those which occupy the writers of 'literary' English. In the following passage, we have a transcript of a piece of serious conversation, recorded from life. The dashes indicate pauses; 'er' and 'um' give conventional expression to voiced pauses:

13 You see um the the um the chief lecturer there is is er um—he is the main lecturer though really he has one or two subordinates but he is the—he gives the lectures the main lectures—there are seminars as well and discussions following upon those but the main lectures are given by him—and he tries—to maintain—um a balance I mean he talks so far he's talked about I missed the last one um unfortunately but he's talked—er and given various sides he's given what he called the er the religious—um aspects of philosophy those who have— a religious point of view who believe in values you know er existing outside the human community—and then what he calls—the—the the secular point of view or the transsecular I think oh no secular point of view —opposed to the transsecular which embodies religious and er the other—er mystical er um approaches I suppose.
(Part of a conversation, transcribed from a recording.)

If we are struck by the clumsiness of expression and the inelegant hesitations, we must remember that the conventional orthography used for the transcription has no means of showing those features like intonation which were mentioned above, and which are described in Supplement I. Because of the features which belong *only* to speech, the conversation itself did not sound unduly clumsy. It was in fact fairly representative of the talk we hear around us every day. It serves to emphasise the art which the novelist has to cultivate in order to make his dialogue seem natural *and yet* readable.

There are numerous varieties of English that have not been illustrated in this chapter. It is important to realise, after all, that conversation itself can take place on many different subjects and that these subjects will influence the selection of linguistic forms in speech somewhat as we have seen them doing in the written language. And there are some spoken varieties, even among educated people, that we rarely find represented in writing. Mothers and fathers (or at any rate aunts and grannies) are still liable to address a baby with some such verbiage as:

> Will the baby-boodlum havums teeny-weeny drinkum-winkum now? Will he then! There now! Mummy wipum baby's mouffy.

Even this kind of 'specialised' language has its traditional characteristics. In his book on English grammar, the pioneer chemist, Joseph Priestley, noted in 1768 that in addressing very young children 'we sometimes use the third person singular instead of the second; as *will he* or *she* do it'.

It is hoped that enough of the varieties of English have been discussed to bring out the extent to which they have characteristic linguistic features. Whether or not we need to be proficient in *producing* all these varieties in our own usage, it is surely useful to be able to *recognise* them and to cultivate a sympathetic, urbane reaction to them. Each has a good deal of interest for the objective student of English and their degree of internal consistency should make us look with a critical eye on any handbook which would seem to suggest that there is a single set of Standard English forms which are 'right' for all occasions.

Exercises and Topics for Discussion

1   Reconstruct passage 4, imagining that your version is for *oral* delivery to an inquirer.
2   Passage 4 is dated 1955. Has the style of advice and instruction in telephone directories changed since that, and—if so—in what respects?

    Attempts are constantly being made to improve the language of what are called 'non-statutory documents'. Assume that you have been confronted with the task of improving the following note which appeared among the points of information circulated by the Income Tax authorities in 1961:

> **Unremittable Overseas Profits or Income.** Where overseas profit or income assessable on the amount arising is unremittable the person chargeable may give written notice before any assessment or assessments thereon have become final and conclusive that he desires to be assessed on the basis of no account being taken of such overseas income so long as it remains unremittable.

3   It was said of passages 5 and 6 that these kinds of language display 'similarities to both legal and official usage'. What similarities—and what differences—do you find?
4   Examine the report of Mr Senior's speech (quoted on p. 170). Why should he think abandoning the passive could have such results? Do you agree?

5 Select one of the passages 9-11 which you think could be written in a more natural and easy style: re-write it and comment on lexical and grammatical changes you make.

6 (a) Write a descriptive passage which could serve as an adequate introduction to what is spoken in passage 12, taking care that your introduction makes clear the situational context in which the speech could take place.

(b) Imagine you are going through last year's pocket diary with a friend. Attempt to write conversational reminiscences on the fragmentary entries.

7 (a) Re-write passage 13, giving it the form the speaker himself might have done if he had been *writing* an account of his tuition instead of *speaking* it. Explain why the spoken version is different from yours at several important points.

(b) If you have access to a tape-recorder, attempt a completely accurate transcription of a conversation with a friend. How might a novelist have written the same conversation?

8 Examine the following passage, listing and grouping the linguistic features which seem to be characteristic:

'. . . Next the jaws of the gaff were placed in position and parrels secured, then the peak halyards were rove. First the wire strops were passed through the bullseyes, wormed, parcelled and served, eyes spliced, put on gaff and seized. The masthead blocks were hooked aloft and moused, then the halyards rove to starboard and a purchase block spliced in lower end. When steam capstans came in, the purchase was often omitted as the fall was taken to the capstan. The main halyards rove through a treble block on a saddle at masthead and a double one on an iron tongue working in a slot at end of gaff near jaws. The hauling part went to port.

183

'Next a single block was spliced in one end of the topping lift and a thimble at the other to shackle on the boom end, the runner was spliced to a single block at masthead, rove through the first single block, back to the second and at the lower end was double block of luff tackle which was set up to starboard. The downhaul was fitted and the boom hung on its gooseneck.'

(J. March, *Sailing Trawlers*, 1953.)

9 Lord Chandos was reported as saying that 'scientists and engineers . . . have impoverished our vocabulary' (*The Times*, 25 April 1966). In what ways might this charge be (a) supported and (b) refuted?

11 : Grouping Words into Structures

IT must by now have become clear (particularly perhaps in the preceding chapter) that discussion of English usage and style is impossible without considerable reference to grammar, and indeed without a rather detailed knowledge of grammar and grammatical processes. For the most part in this book, grammatical distinctions have been made only as and when required, and the meaning of each necessary grammatical abstraction makes itself clear (it is hoped) in the course of actual usage: a principle in accord with the approach to vocabulary and meaning recommended here. It is time now to look again more closely at grammar itself, so that we may see the broad nature of grammatical structure and understand more clearly the nature of such individual units as 'clause' which hitherto we have been content to leave as self-explanatory.

Let us suppose that you look out of the window and see a little boy patting a dog. The impression constitutes a complex unity, all of which you are capable of contemplating simultaneously. Indeed, you would find it difficult to do otherwise—you could not readily assign an *order* to the boy, the patting, the dog, the boy's stoop, the dog's tail. On the other hand, as soon as you turn back into the room and try to report what you have seen, you find that you not only can but *must* assign an order to it and must break up your impression into pieces of your own choosing and present them, not simultaneously, but one by one: 'Some little boy is making friends with our dog' or 'John is patting a

185

flattered-looking mongrel' or 'The Wilsons' tyke is being fussed over by his usual admirer.'

This is not to deny that language has its own kind of superiority in simultaneous presentation—as is shown by a word like 'garden' as compared with the visual image which is a manifold of flowers, grass, shrubs, pathway, and greenhouse. But the fact remains that one of the striking characteristics of human language is its *serial* nature. Whether we are speaking or writing, we are obliged to produce linguistic signs in a linear string. A pianist playing a piece of polyphonic music (a fugue, for instance) is able to 'say' two or more things simultaneously: even when he strikes a single chord, one has an instance of the simultaneous transmission of a structure impossible for the human voice, which can produce only one note at a time. Mathematics too displays the advantageous power of simultaneous as opposed to serial presentation when we come upon such an expression as

$$\frac{\sqrt[3]{125}}{3}$$

and compare it with a 'linguistic' form which is as near as possible to it: 'the cube root of a hundred and twenty-five divided by three'.

Now, in this linguistic representation of the mathematical expression we at once notice a difficulty which did not occur with the expression in its mathematical form: how to punctuate it (in writing) or how to modify our voice (in speaking) in order to ensure that it will be interpreted as

$$\frac{\sqrt[3]{125}}{3} \quad \text{and not} \quad \sqrt[3]{\frac{125}{3}} \quad \text{or even} \quad \sqrt[3]{100} + \frac{25}{3}$$

186

For, of course, despite its necessarily linear presentation, a piece of language is a structure, or rather (as was pointed out in Chapter 7) is a structure of structures, not merely a long succession in which word is added to word like beads on a string. To maintain the comparison with mathematics, a linguistic expression is less like

$$(a) \quad 4+8+7+9+8+6+5+9+4$$

than like $\quad (b) \quad [(4+2)3] + [3(5+7)+6]$

This can be seen in the 'grammar of the word'. The word *denationalise* has four parts: the privative affix *de*, the base *nation*, the adjective-forming affix *al*, and the verb-forming affix *ise*. At first sight it might seem that the whole word is a simple sum of the four parts as in (a) above, but in fact it is more like the complicated expression (b): $\{de + [(nation+al)+ise]\}$. This way of putting it reflects a formation series as follows:

We are a *nation*
What we have in common is *national*
We add to that if we *nationalise*
We reduce it if we *denationalise*

At the same time, the formula acknowledges that *denation* and *denational* do not exist as words, since it shows that there is no direct link between the elements *de* and *nation* or even between *de* and the already complex *national*. We may therefore think of 'denationalise' as a *structure* which has two *substructures* within it; *national*, which as a structure combines with *ise*, and *nationalise*, which as a structure combines with *de*. Theoretically there is no upper limit to the complexity of a word; *antidisestablishmentarianism* is as possible as *rit*, and perhaps rather more probable.

In a similar way, however complex a structure a word

may have within itself, it operates as a whole—as one thing —when it is used in a stretch of language larger than the word. Let us examine from this point of view the slogan, 'Denationalise all road transport.' Just as there is no direct link between *nation* and *de*, as we have seen, there can be no direct link between *nation* and anything outside the word *denationalise*; nor does *de*, which has a direct link with *nationalise* as a whole, have a link beyond the limits of this word. In the same way, we find no link between the word *denationalise* and *all* or between *all* and *road* or between *all* and *transport*. Before we can find something with which *denationalise* has a link, we must discover another structuring of the elements *all* and *road* and *transport*, comparable with the structuring of elements within the word *denationalise*. That is to say, we must see *all road transport* as comprising a single structure, with a substructure *road transport* within it: [all + (road + transport)]. We now have a unit which can enter a direct relationship with *denationalise* to give us a still further unitary structure: [denationalise + (all road transport)].

We see, then, that despite the apparently simple linear progression language consists of layer upon layer of structure, each layer having its internal structure ignored and being treated as a single unit as it enters into the next layer of structural relationship. And we have chosen to distinguish and concentrate upon three particular layers which seem especially important stages in a hierarchy. In the *first stage*, we have seen infra-word structuring, yielding a unit which can operate in a different kind of structure; in the *second stage*, we have seen words themselves brought together to form one *group*, which can similarly then operate as a unit in a different kind of structure; and the *third stage* illustrates the way in which groups may operate as units to form a further unit which we may leave for the moment to be understood merely as a 'third stage' structure.

There are great differences, of course, between the three stages, but there are also great similarities. As between the word and the group we see a similarity in that both units characteristically have a recognisable *head*. Just as *denationalise* has been shown to result from a formation series beginning with *nation*, so with *all road transport* we have a series beginning with *transport*:

Trade depends on *transport*
Our vegetables come by *road transport*
The Highway Code applies to *all road transport*

And just as the complex word *denationalise* is treated exactly as the single word *run* in forming higher units, so a 'group' may consist of a single word *transport* as well as of several words, *all road transport*. Moreover, both in structures within the word and structures consisting of words, we may speak of lexical and grammatical elements: thus *denationalise* can be regarded as comprising the lexical element *nation* and the grammatical elements *de, al* and *ise*. Order is highly relevant in the three kinds of structure: indeed, in the word and to a large extent in the group, it is broadly speaking fixed. But of course a fixity in the succession of elements does not entail a fixity in the substructures which the elements may form. The elements in both *de-nation-al-ise* and *de-rail-ment* have an equally fixed order, but in the one our first breakdown is *de + nationalise* and in the other it is *derail + ment*; that is, *denationalise* does not comprise a substructure *denational*, and *derailment* does not comprise a substructure *railment*. Similarly, with group structures, we may compare the fixed linear order of

This ideal draught stabiliser

and

This Ideal Homes exhibition

with the important difference in substructuring between

This [ideal (draught stabiliser)]
and
This [(Ideal Homes) exhibition]

Nevertheless, despite this difference, these two nominal groups have one thing in common which they share also with the group *all road transport*, namely that the linear order of presentation leads up to the head as the final element. This characteristic (*premodification*) marks off one main type of nominal group, but it is by no means a characteristic of all nominal groups. In such units as *bravery of all kinds* or *bravery in the struggle against barbarism*, we meet the second main type, which involves *postmodification*. That the linear succession here does not present the head as the final element can be demonstrated by making the groups operate as an element in a 'third-stage' structure.

(*a*) All road transport is excellent
(*b*) Bravery of all kinds is excellent
(*c*) Bravery in the struggle against barbarism is excellent

Now, as we saw a moment ago, a premodification group like *all road transport* is an expansion of the final element in a formation series, so that instead of (*a*) we may have

Transport is excellent

Obviously, if *kinds* and *barbarism* were also premodified heads, we should have to admit extraordinary variants of (*b*) and (*c*):

Kinds is excellent
Barbarism is excellent

We can, of course, have mixtures of the two types of
190

modification within a single nominal group: *very great bravery of all kinds; the highest and most intrepid bravery in the struggle against barbarism*. As with the word, so with the group: there is theoretically no limit to its degree of complexity. We can have a group with postmodification where the postmodification is itself a substructure comprising a head with postmodification: 'bravery {in the [struggle (against barbarism)]}'. And we can have a group with premodification, where the premodification itself is a substructure consisting of a head with postmodification: 'The {[Port (of London)] Authority}', 'The head of the college's book of quotations', 'The Bishop of Durham's mitre of beautiful workmanship'.

The admissibility of this type, as against the commoner, 'simple' postmodification type whose head is the noun before the first *of*, provides the basis for the ambiguity in the old puzzle, 'The son of Pharaoh's daughter is the daughter of Pharaoh's son.' According to the structure and substructure we assign to the opening half, we may assign to the second half the structure and substructure

the daughter [of (Pharaoh's son)]

or

the [(daughter of Pharaoh)'s son]

This type has brought to our attention one important point of English grammar which must cause us to modify slightly what was said earlier to the effect that it is words as whole units (from 'stage one') which operate in groups (at 'stage two'). The last example quoted shows that the genitive ending can be used as what is appropriately called a 'group-genitive': *Pharaoh's* is not operating as a word-unit in the group structure—that is the whole point of the ambiguity; the genitive ending applies to the whole substructure 'daughter of Pharaoh'. It is preferable to admit this as an exception than to modify our definition of the

191

word in the light of it and either call such a substructure group as *daughter of Pharaoh* a 'word' or call the genitive ending itself a 'word'. There is something of an analogy to the extension of the genitive ending back over a group structure in the use of ordinal -*th* at the end of a numeral, as in 'the one hundred and twenty-fourth candidate'. We may compare also the extension forward of *the* over a group structure in what may be called the anticipatory function of *the*. If we contrast 'I admire bravery' and 'I admire the bravery of this man', we can perhaps see that the use of *the* in the second example is determined by (and might therefore be regarded as part of) the postmodification of the head, *bravery*.

A little earlier it was shown that, despite differences of substructuring, various nominal groups could be brought together by virtue of their premodification and seen in contrast with those groups whose heads are postmodified. We may now proceed to bring together all nominal groups, whether premodified or postmodified, by virtue of sharing a characteristic in contrast with the other main type of group structure, the verbal group. It can be said of all nominal group types that the head may be abstracted and used in a 'third-stage' structure exactly as the whole group may be used:

(a) All road transport is excellent

and

Transport is excellent

(b) Bravery in the face of barbarism is excellent

and

Bravery is excellent

In the verbal group, we may also speak of a 'head', but it is identified as being the last element in the structure, and we can rarely abstract from several words making up the group any single one which can operate without change as the whole group operates:

> It will be ruggling them

but not

> It will them

or

> It be them

or

> It ruggling them

Although it is usual to regard verbal groups that involve only one word as 'simple' (for example, *eat* in 'We eat'), all verbal groups equally—even if negatively—express all the relations that the English verb is capable of carrying. It is true, however, that we can more easily see the range of these relations by examining the complex verbal groups —that is to say, those more extensive than the unit 'word'. There are four main types, with terminations as follows:

(a) a present participle (-*ing*):
    '(he) × biting'
(b) a past participle (usually -*ed*, -*t*, or -*en*):
    '(he) × bitten'
(c) an infinitive (the basic form of the verb), not preceded by *to*:
    '(he) × bite'
(d) an infinitive preceded by *to*:
    '(he) × to bite'

When a group consists only of a single word, it overtly expresses (in modern English) little more than tense: *I bite* (present or 'simple present') ~ *I bit* (past or 'simple past').

We shall return to this presently and explain the limiting 'overtly'. In the verbal groups (a) to (d) something else is expressed too, and this 'something else' depends in part on the differing group structures (a) to (d). In part, however— and in most cases a very large part—it depends on what operates at the place in the groups marked x. This is usually a form from the 'closed set' of grammatical words.

The group (a) is especially associated with *aspect* (roughly 'the manner of the action') and expresses what is generally called the 'continuous' aspect. The x here is usually a form of the verb *to be*, 'he is (or was) biting', and since a tense distinction is made as well, the name 'continuous tenses' for expressions with this group structure is quite apt and useful. Some grammarians reckon as a group of the same structure one in which x is a lexical, 'open set' form, as in 'he keeps biting'.

In group (b), the place of x may be occupied by either a form of the verb *to have* or a form of the verb *to be*: *he has bitten* and *he is bitten*, and the group must obviously be subdivided accordingly. In the first type (bi) we have *perfective aspect* along with tense, making what is usually called the 'perfect tense' (*he has bitten*) and the 'pluperfect tense' (*he had bitten*), the one indicating the 'perfection' or completion of the action now, the other indicating the 'perfection' or completion of the action at some time in the past. In the second type (bii) we have an expression of the *marked* voice form, the passive, which is again accompanied by tense: 'he is (or was) bitten'. A few other verbs such as *get* and *become* may on occasion operate as x in this second type.

In group (c), the place of x is chiefly occupied by the closed set of verb-forms whose principal function is *modal*, indicating—that is to say—an attitude to the action (indicating that it is obligatory, permissive, and the like): *he may bite, he would bite, he should bite*, etc. They are often
194

referred to as the 'modal auxiliaries', but they include, of course, *will* and *shall*, whose function is primarily to supply the verb with a future tense (though it is also partly modal). The exception which justified 'chiefly' at the beginning of this paragraph is the verb *do*, which may occupy the place x to provide an interrogative, negative or emphatic *status* of the verb: *did he bite, he did not bite, he did bite.*

Group (*d*) is the most miscellaneous and the most extensible. There are a few 'closed set' forms operating at x, chiefly modal (*he ought to bite, he is to bite, he has to bite*), but there is one important and peculiar form which expresses a past tense habitual aspect (*he used to bite*). For the most part, however, the verb at x is from the 'open set' of lexical words in the language (*he wanted to bite, he started to bite*, and the like), and the limits of the 'verbal group' in this respect depend on how one wishes to account for the relations between different types of stage-three structures.

Long before we had finished discussing the nominal group it must have become clear that no fundamentally new types of structure were emerging, but only complexities in the arrangement of the two primary types, the premodification and the postmodification types, which we may represent in a simple form with *true bravery* and *bravery in battle*. Beside these, 'the Bishop of Durham's mitre of beautiful workmanship' and 'the rather agèd professor's book of quotations from Shakespeare' introduce only such complications as are referable to the two primary types. So too, these four types of verbal group, each comprising only two elements, are the basis of all the longer groups. Thus 'he ought to have been biting' should be seen as a structure with three substructures, each of which is referable to one of the four types: *ought to have* (*d*), *have been* (*b*), and *been biting* (*a*). We may see the layers

195

of the structure more clearly with the following
examples:

ought to	bite	d
	has bitten	bi
	was biting	a
ought to have been	biting	$d + bi + a$
may have been	being bitten	$c + bi + a + bii$
	was bitten	bii

It should be noticed, however, that some longer groups
are only *apparently* compounds of two or more types. On
the one hand we have 'I am trying to climb' which is
composed of type (*a*) and type (*d*), as we can see by the
fact that it is possible with only a change of tense and
aspect to reduce the group to 'I tried to climb' (type *d*
alone). On the other hand, we have 'I am going to climb'
or 'I am willing to climb' which are type (*d*) only, despite
the superficial similarity to 'I am trying to climb': this can
be seen from the fact that a corresponding change in tense
and aspect does not produce 'I went to climb' or 'I willed
to climb'. Clusters like 'be going to' (one of the chief ways
of expressing future tense in English) and 'be willing to'
may therefore be regarded as simple elements in type (*d*)
structure, showing only the same range of inflexion as *be*
to (as in 'I am to climb') and showing an expansion of *be to*
similar to that in 'be about to' and 'be eager to':

I am/was going to climb	(*d*)
I am/was able to climb	(*d*)
I am/was about to climb	(*d*)

but

I am/was trying to climb	(*a* + *d*)

196

It is not the case, however, that an expression like 'I am going to climb' is always a verbal group of type *d*? If it is possible to make such an expansion as 'I am going (over there) (in order) to climb', we should not regard this as a single group at all. In the first part (*I am going*) there is a type *a* group (which can be replaced by *I went*), and in the second part an additional element not of group structure but of 'stage three' structure, and to this we shall return later in the chapter.

We may conclude this discussion of the verb by returning to re-consider the 'simple' forms, 'I bite' and 'I bit'. These, it was said (p. 193), overtly express little more than tense, but it must now be emphasised that they *covertly* express the 'unmarked' term in each of the relationships in which the marked term is expressed by the various types of complex group; for example

> I bit ~ I was biting
> I bit ~ I have bitten
> I bit ~ I was bitten
> I bit ~ I *did* bite
> I bit ~ I had to bite

For some of these 'unmarked' expressions, we have quite familiar names such as 'active' for *I bit* in contrast with *I was bitten*. Moreover, the unmarked present is so often used with a particular aspectual sense that it is commonly referred to as the 'habitual' present. On the other hand, some grammarians prefer not to call it a 'present' at all, but the 'non-past', because it is often used without reference to time, as in 'Penguins live in the Antarctic'. One further point: an actual modal contrast—the 'subjunctive' is still possible (though rather rare) with several of the simple forms of the verb *to be* and with the third person singular present of other verbs:

If I *were* you; if he *bite*; I suggest that he *go* now.

Traces also survive, of course, of the use of the subjunctive in expressions like 'God save the Queen'. This is somewhat akin to a much wider use of the simple form of the verb in that modal function which we call 'imperative' (*bite him!*), while for first and third person use, a roughly equivalent function is performed with a verbal group which has affinities with type (*c*): 'let's bite', 'let *s* be the distance travelled'.

Now that we have explored some of the characteristics of the two chief types of group which operate as 'second-stage' units, we may look at the types of 'third-stage' units. If we slightly complicate our original example without altering its third-stage structure, it will be easier to bring out some necessary points here. Let us say, then, that our model is 'Don't denationalise all road transport', a structure comprising two elements. What are these elements in terms of the third stage? It will be recalled that a complexity of elements at one stage becomes a single element at the next. Thus the complex arrangements of parts which made up *denationalise* are ignored at stage one, where this is recognised as a word no more nor less than *car* or *try*. Just as the parts have no relevance at the stage of the word, so the words have no relevance at the stage of the group: *denationalise* is now part of a recognisable verbal group structure with *don't* (marked negative status, modally imperative), and the words *all*, *road* and *transport* constitute a single unit, a premodified nominal group. So now at the third stage, the groups themselves are no longer relevant as such. *Don't denationalise* operates not as a verbal group but as a Verb (V) which enters into construction not with a nominal group but with a *Complement* (C). At this degree of abstraction, therefore, 'Don't denationalise all road transport' is structurally identical with 'Eat fruit' and 'Keep

198

fit'. Such a structure does not of course exemplify the full list of elements possible at stage three. In particular, it is usual to find a Subject, as in *She sang* (with a structure SV); and there is commonly at least one Adjunct, as in *She sang afterwards* (with a structure SVA). All four elements appear in

She sang it afterwards

which thus has the structure SVCA.

A word here on terminology. From what has been said, it will be agreed that it would be appropriate for terms at stage three to be independent of terms at stages one and two. One would obviously find it quite inadequate to describe the structure of 'She sang it afterwards' as consisting of four 'words'; equally, terms like 'noun' and 'pronoun' have no direct relevance at this stage—after all, both *she* and *it* are pronouns. For this reason, *predicator*, abbreviated as P, is in many ways preferable to V in referring to an element at stage three: it is not adopted here because V is well enough established for this purpose and because P might be confused with *predicate*, an abstraction comprising V, C, and even A, in some alternative modes of analysis to that proposed here. Most important, perhaps: the symbol V reminds us of the significant fact that the verbal group can enter a stage-three structure only as V and that, conversely, alone of the four elements in a stage-three structure, V can be realised by only one type of structure, the verbal group.

On the other hand, it has seemed best to use *complement* in a rather different way from that observed in many handbooks, since it can be useful to recognise a level of abstraction at which all elements that are necessary to the completion of the basic structure are 'the same': elements which are final in the following examples—

199

He saw *a dog*
He taught *a dog*
The puppy became *a dog*
It was *a dog*
He kept *a dog*
He kept *fit*
He was *fit*

Only after recognising this degree of identity is it advisable to sub-classify these into 'direct object', 'indirect object', 'predicatives', 'complements' with a small *c*, to whatever degree of refinement or with whatever labels may seem useful.

Obviously, then, with our four distinctions S, V, C and A we are capable of a very high degree of abstraction or generality in describing our language. It is a degree of generality which exactly equates the structure of

1 She sang it afterwards

with the structure of

2 The distinguished soprano who had been waiting on the stage was going to sing what the audience most wanted when her accompanist eventually arrived.

Refinement in the description is a matter of successively analysing the exponents of the elements in both, labelled S, V, C, A. The exponent of S in the latter case, for instance, is the nominal group 'The distinguished soprano who had been waiting on the stage': it might have been another nominal group such as 'The State Opera Company of Vienna's most distinguished singer', and the difference between these groups would appear when we moved 'down', so to speak, from stage three to stage two in the analysis, stating the exponents of the elements in the pre- or post-modification structures of the groups. With a progressively

200

increasing degree of specific detail (and hence with a decreasing degree of abstraction), we can carry the analysis of the 'structures-within-structures' as far as we wish.

Just as the S in (1), *She*, corresponds to something much more complex in (2), *The distinguished soprano who had been waiting on the stage*, so too the A and C are much more complex in (2). Instead of the simple adverbial *afterwards* as A, we have a cluster of words which is itself a stage-three structure, *when her accompanist eventually arrived* (ASAV). Similarly, instead of the simple *it* as C in (1), we have *what the audience most wanted*, again a stage-three structure, this time one with the four elements CSAV. This is why the structures at stage-three were left so vaguely labelled at the point when they were introduced in this Chapter. Since any SVCA structure may have an SVCA structure 'embedded' in it as exponent of its S, C, or A, we need two separate labels such as 'sentence' and 'clause' to distinguish structures which otherwise can have identical elements. From this point of view, we may define *clause* as an SV(CA) structure which is exponent of an element in another SV(CA) structure, or of an element in a structure which is itself an element in another SV(CA) structure.

By contrast, we may say that a *sentence* derives its 'completeness' from the fact that, whatever its internal constitution, it is *not* the exponent of an element in another structure. This means that quite short pieces like 'Fire!' or 'Some water, please' may be regarded as sentences while far longer and more complex stretches like 'When the dreary game which had exhausted most of the players despite their previous claim that they would not weaken' may not.

One important characteristic of a clause will by now have been noticed: the first word is usually one of those grammatical words which we may bring together in this sketch as 'subordinating conjunctions'. For example, '*when*

201

her accompanist eventually arrived'. A conjunction in a clause may correspond to an adjunct in a sentence, as we may see by comparing '*when* he arrived' with '*then* he arrived', or '*where* he went' with 'he went *there*'. Often, the subordinators function as S or C in the clause-structure or the corresponding sentence-structure, and we may sub-classify these as 'conjunctive pronouns'; we may compare '*who* had been waiting' with '*she* had been waiting', or '*what* they wanted' with 'they wanted *that*'. Sometimes they are simply subordinating signs, not corresponding to an element in sentence structure, as we may see in comparing '(the claim) *that* they would not weaken' with the sentence-form of this clause, 'they would not weaken'.

Just as there are sentences (such as 'Fire!') which lack the range of sentence elements such as S and V, so too there are clause types without V ('*His voice angry*, he shouted to them'), without S ('*Feeling angry*, he . . .'), or without either ('*Angry and full of disgust*, he . . .'). In particular, the clause whose exponent of V is a non-finite verbal group is of great importance in English structure: 'He came *wanting the car*'; 'He came *to get the car*'; 'He came *followed by his dog*'. With the recognition of the non-finite verb clause, we can describe the difference noted on pp. 196f between 'I am going to climb' (past: *was* . . .) and 'I am going to climb' (past: *went*). The first has the structure SV, where the exponent of V is the verbal group *am going to climb*; the second has the structure SVA, where the exponent of A is the non-finite verb clause *to climb*.

There is a further structure that we have not yet mentioned. This too can operate as an element in any other structure, but we may look upon it as intermediate between the group and the clause: it is the *phrase*. It will be remembered that the characteristic of a group is to have a head: *great bravery of many kinds* has *bravery* as its head, and

202

bravery can work as well in another structure as *great bravery of many kinds* can. In a somewhat analogous way *came* can work as well in another structure as can *ought to have come*. Groups are for this reason sometimes called *endocentric*. By contrast, phrases cannot be reduced to a single head. If we take the prepositional phrase, 'completely within large square boxes', we may see that this structure is still maintained in the simpler form, 'in boxes', so that both phrases could expound A in the sentence 'We keep the clothes (A)'; but no simpler form is possible. Like clauses and sentences, therefore, phrases are characteristically what some linguists call *exocentric*.

Finally, although it is right and natural to see the structures *sentence, clause, phrase, group* as forming a hierarchy (from 'high' to 'low'), it is important to remember that any of the last three may be exponent of an element in the structure of the sentence or of each other. This may be illustrated as follows:

Group, phrase and clause in Sentence structure:

> I saw him *a few times*
> I saw him *during the holidays*
> I saw him *when I was home*

Group, phrase and clause in Phrase structure:

> From *the dark corner*, crept a . . .
> From *under the chair*, crept a . . .
> From *where he sat*, crept a . . .

Group, phrase and clause in Group structure:

> *The surface* of the dusty road seemed . . .
> The man *beside the dusty road* seemed . . .
> The man *that he saw on the dusty road* seemed . . .

Even so brief a sketch of grammatical analysis must not end without some reference to one further—and very well-known—type of grammatical relationship. In addition to the hierarchical structure already explained and illustrated, there is a *co-ordinate* structure which brings together items of equal rank in the sense that they operate as though they were a single element from the viewpoint of hierarchical structure. Consider, for example:

(1) The *men and women* of London (were pleased).
(2) Liking *neither the dull street nor the look of this particular house*, (he turned away).
(3) *When I knew him and while he worked in this office*, (he seemed happy enough).

In (1) we have co-ordinate words in group structure. That is to say, the exponent of S in the sentence is the nominal group, *the men and women of London*; the group structure is 'head plus postmodification', and the exponent of the head is the structure of co-ordination, *men and women*. In (2), on the other hand, we have co-ordinate nominal groups which operate (despite their own differences—the one premodified, the other postmodified) as a single element in clause structure. In (3) we have co-ordinate clauses which are bracketed together as exponent of A in sentence-structure: and again we note that the 'equality' of the co-ordinate parts does not lie in their internal structure.

Exercises and Topics for Discussion

1 Re-form the following nominal groups so as to intro-
    duce postmodification:

    (a) the coke oven replacement programme

(b) the five per cent redeemable Debenture Stock

(c) the dark, slimly built cricket-playing chemistry student.

What advantages and disadvantages do you see as between premodification and postmodification in those instances?

2 'At no stage of the war was the area bombing offensive wanton' (*The Observer*, 1 October 1961). Analyse the sentence structure and explain why one might have momentary difficulty in reading it.

3 Carefully explain the difference in grammar between

(a) What did you bring the parcel in? *and* Why did you bring the parcel in?

and between

(b) Are you going to be doing it? *and* Are you going to be long doing it?

4 Explain (a) why each of the following sentences is unsatisfactory, and (b) why, at the same time, the writer in each case has apparently thought he was using common and acceptable grammar:

(i) Agile as his mind is, he has produced a book which has not and does not attempt the clarity and conciseness of De Bello Gallico (*Daily Telegraph*, 5 September 1957).

(ii) He said he had promised that the weekly staff would be paid this week, but he did not know if, when or how much the monthly staff would receive.

5 The prosecuting counsel in a murder case was reported as having asked the following question: 'Did you used

to visit her at that flat?' (*Daily Telegraph*, 4 July 1955).

Comment fully, explaining the analogy illustrated here. List the verbs with which *do* does not usually operate in indicating 'status'. What variation is there in Standard English (and between educated and substandard usage) in this respect?

6 State the component types in the following verbal groups, indicating the respective functions, in terms of tense, aspect, etc.:

(a) he did not have to be beaten
(b) he ought to have been trying
(c) she may be going to have (measles)
(d) they used to keep shouting
(e) didn't he get beaten?

7 Turn back to passage 11 in Chapter 10, and analyse the structure of the first sentence in terms of S, V, A, C; proceed then to analyse the exponents of these elements, until you arrive at the point when the group structures have been analysed. Now attempt a similar procedure with the first sentence of passage 6 in Chapter 10. At what points in the structure of the two sentences does the greatest complexity lie? In what ways do the sentences differ in complexity?

8 (a) In what ways do the *clause* types and structures differ as between passages 5, 6, 7, 10, and 11 in Chapter 10?

(b) In what ways do the nominal group structures differ in these same passages?

(c) List the structures of the verbal groups in these passages, and note whether there is a preponderance of certain types in certain passages.

(d) On the basis of what you have found in (a), (b),

and (*c*), try to characterise the language of the five passages.

9 The following is the exact text of the endorsement to an insurance policy. Present a full analysis of it in terms of clause, phrase, and group structures:

The Insured having removed to the private dwelling brick stone or concrete built and roofed with slates tiles concrete asphalt metal or sheets composed entirely of incombustible mineral ingredients situated and known as described below the property insured by the within policy is declared to be insured at that address in lieu of the address stated in the policy.

10 The following sentence was heard on the BBC News, and it happened to be read in a way that made two interpretations possible:

'Nigerians say Whitbreads are happy people who enjoy drinking beer.'

Present analyses showing the two interpretations, and (after studying Supplement I) explain how the utterance would be said so as to allow both interpretations and how it might be said to give each interpretation in turn unambiguously.

12: Processes of Construction

I<small>T</small> has been argued (pp. 44f) that a language is equipped
to say anything its users want to say. What is true for
vocabulary is in this instance true also for grammar, and it
means that we are able to devise sentences that have never
been heard before and relate sentences to one another in
such ways that we communicate ideas and experiences
never previously communicated. Conversely (as is rather
more relevant to most of us perhaps), we have decoding
devices in our linguistic faculty that enable us to understand 'new' sentences and new interrelations of sentences
and their parts. We are so apt to take these skills for
granted that it is difficult for us to realise how much we
depend on them or even to realise what an extraordinarily
powerful, efficient and complicated mechanism it must be
that operates them. Certainly, the mechanism is so complicated that we still have no certain idea (and only the most
rudimentary hypotheses) about how it works. We can do
little more than roughly sketch some of the processes that
seem to be involved in its operation.

Among these processes it may not be too hazardous to
suggest that *abstraction, abbreviation,* and *assumption* are
of basic importance and that every discourse cumulatively
involves them. Consider for example:

> When I asked if John would play a tune for me, he did.

In the last two words, the pronoun *he* replaces *John* while
did is an abbreviation not of a clause that has already
occurred but of the one we can assume at this point:

'played a tune for me'. And the relevance of 'cumulatively' becomes clear when we reflect that the two words in question are both abbreviative and sequential in the discourse; we cannot re-order the sentence so as to begin, 'He did, when I asked . . .'

We can understand 'abstraction' very generally in this context, even to the extent of including the very use of names. Just as currency enables us to dispense with the direct barter of 'real' object for 'real' object (a farmer handing his newsagent a turnip in order to buy his daily paper), so language enables us to handle the 'not here' and 'not now' by a symbolic abstraction from the 'promiscuous bundle' in which objects in their 'concrete state' have been 'tied together by the hand of Nature'.[1] The name 'Rover' enables me to refer to my dog without needing to have him there to point to, though even with the object present, naming serves to 'abstract' it or 'chop it out of the flux', as we put it on p. 60. Moreover, with a very big jump in abstraction, calling 'Rover' a 'dog' enables us (as was pointed out on p. 164) to relate him to an indefinite number of other 'animals' (a word which in turn carries the abstraction process a great deal further), of very different size and appearance, without having to gather specimens round us and point to that one and that one. The power to abstract can thus be seen as that propensity to generality and imprecision which we have noted (pp. 65f) to be an indispensable feature of language.

The abstraction process takes on another dimension when we move from 'I saw a dog' to 'I saw a fight', since fight involves not only abstracting a common core from an indefinite range of hostile activity, but also our being able to treat this abstraction from activities as though it were a nameable 'thing', like a three-dimensional object. The

[1] J. Bentham, Works, vol. 8, p. 26.

abstraction process is thus fundamentally concerned with metaphor, requiring an imaginative leap towards seeing resemblances across ontological frontiers; this occurs with other parts of speech beside nouns, of course: one can be *in* a fight as well as *in* a room, *see* an idea as well as a fight. But because *fight* refers to activity, we may also regard this as an example of the *abbreviative* process in language. The expression 'a fight' has to be understood as a summary of a sentence '. . . was fighting with . . .' in which we can ask for the blanks to be filled. If now we change the example from 'I saw a fight' to 'I saw the fight', we illustrate the *assumptive* process in language, since the use of *the* indicates the speaker's assumption that his hearer knows the fight to which he is referring.

No one has yet mapped out for any language the enormously intricate and elaborate rules that govern the operation of these conventions for abstraction, abbreviation and assumption, and it is the modest purpose of this chapter only to look a little more closely (and this time from a 'process' point of view) at the units such as clause and group that were discussed in Chapter 11 from a chiefly analytic point of view. It will be recalled that reference was made there to carrying 'the analysis of the "structure-within-structures" as far as we wish' with 'a progressively increasing degree of specific detail (and hence with a decreasing degree of abstraction)' (pp. 200f). Instead of unfolding the structural units that have been compressed and packed away and explaining their relation to the structures in which they have been packed, let us now consider some of the packaging procedures and the kinds of linguistic entity that have been subjected to them.

We are a long way from reaching agreement—for any language—on the types of pattern that might be regarded as truly primitive, and we are equally far from agreement on the types of fundamental 'selection rules' which, as we shall see, control the formation of acceptable linguistic sequences. Nevertheless, generations of linguists have tried to see the endless complexity of language in terms of a small number of simple patterns, and there is no reason to under-estimate the insight that such attempts can give us as we try to frame hypotheses about the nature of linguistic processes. Thus, it seems plausible to explain the similarity that we recognise between

1 The wise man knew the way.
2 The man, who was wise, knew the way.
3 Being wise, the man knew the way.

by postulating a sentence 'The man was wise' which in some sense is an underlying part of all three. Indeed, such a postulation may seem not merely plausible but obvious and inevitable, and to this extent an 'analysis' which seems to dwell on the differences between the sentences (a premodi-fied nominal group in one, a non-restrictive relative clause in another, a non-finite adverbial clause in the third) can seem perverse and irrelevant. We have of course insisted in this book (cf. pp. 115ff) that labelling is only of value to the extent that it gives us an insight into the working of our language. In recent years, linguists have increasingly argued that, since we all know immediately on reading any of these three sentences that 'The man was wise', this justifies a wholehearted attempt to devise rules, however complicated they may become, that will relate such a sentence to any sentence it appears to underlie. Rules attempting to do this will postulate 'embedding' (p. 201), as though one were to envisage a sequence like

The man + *The man was wise* + knew the way.

with 'pronominalisation' of the repeated item (*the man*) together with a grammatical selection rule which would allow the pronoun *who* but disallow *which*. Sentence (1) might involve a rule putting the relative clause of (2) in front of *man* and abbreviating it by 'deleting' the *who was* part, or a rule permitting the original underlying sentence to be embedded in front of the subject of the embedding (or 'matrix') sentence, again with appropriate deletions. Sentence (3) will clearly require deletion of *The man* of the embedded sentence, 'The man was wise', but it will also require 'non-finitisation' of its verb from *was* to *being*. It is essential, moreover, to provide for rules to be 'recursive' (that is, re-applicable indefinitely), so as to account for the nesting effect of 'structures within structures' that we noticed in Chapter 11. Recursiveness thus accounts for our awareness that such a sentence as

The shrewd young man won his case

results from a formation series (cf. p. 187) like this

The man was young
The young man was shrewd
The shrewd young man . . .

rather than from an additive process co-ordinating

The man was young + The man was shrewd → . . .

This also accounts for what we take to be the difference between the following pair

Her lovely dark eyes . . .
Her dark, lovely eyes . . .

where the latter may indeed be referred to a co-ordination process.

Needless to say, descriptive rules of this kind to account

212

less form, English grammar will no longer permit it to be the subject of a passive verb, and even the anticipatory *it* process is impossible (*It was thought the girl pretty*). Instead, a curious re-analysis of the structure takes place such that the subject of the embedded and transformed sentence can be made the subjective in a passive construction:

> The girl was thought pretty (by the man).
> The girl was expected (by the man) to swim gracefully.

Some insight into the nature of this re-analysis may be gained by considering for a moment the non-finitisation of an adjunct clause whose relationship is basically very different. If in the type C.1 sentence

> The man saw the girl.

we introduce as adjunct the type B sentence

> The girl was swimming then.

we form the composite sentence

> The man saw the girl when she was swimming.

Adjunct clauses can readily be made non-finite with deletion of the subject, provided the subject can be inferred or 're-covered' through a neighbouring nominal group. Thus the difference between the pair

> The man saw the girl swimming
> Swimming, the man saw the girl

is that in the former we are obliged by English grammar to infer that the girl was swimming whereas in the latter the man was swimming. Now, just as the composite fully finite

221

sentence can be made passive like any other C.1 sentence (*The girl was seen by the man when she was swimming*), so can the sentence when the embedded clause is made non-finite:

The girl was seen (by the man) swimming.

and we note that the original relationships can be preserved in that it is possible to infer that it is the girl that is swimming and not (despite propinquity) the man. Thus, however different the relations in their embedded clauses, the two sentences

The man saw the girl swimming.
The man expected the girl to swim.

are treated as partially alike in their grammar, so far as passive transformation is concerned. In part, the reason doubtless lies in the fact that verbs such as *see* can appear in both C.1 and C.3 patterns; for example,

He saw the girl when she was swimming.
He saw that the girl was swimming.

In making the embedded clauses non-finite, we neutralise the contrast between them or rather conflate the two relationships so that either may be assumed according to the context: in *He saw the girl swimming* we are saying both that he saw her and that she was swimming. It is in this way, by the overlapping of certain properties, that grammar provides for one series of structures to shade over into another; such 'serial relationship' in grammar is no more than a special application of the metaphor principle that we have discussed earlier.

In now seeing that, although C.3 begins by having a single complement element, it develops into having a segmentation of this complement ('*The girl* was seen *to*

222

arrive', '*The boy* was thought *a genius*'), we can now turn to the last sub-class of type C:

C.4 The man sent the girl a book.

Here the two-part complement is basic and in fact it is a feature of C.4 that each of the complements can become a passive subject:

The girl was sent a book (by the man).
A book was sent (to) the girl (by the man).

For some people (and for some verbs that appear in C.4 sentences), the preposition parenthesised in the latter example is obligatory to make this passive form acceptable. But whether obligatory or not, it is a useful hint as to the similarity between the 'indirect object' and an adjunct in sentence structure. We may see this example as a metaphorical extension of the purely locative adjunct in

A book was sent *to the cottage* (by the man).

which cannot have a prepositionless active form (*The man sent the cottage a book), nor—without losing the locative function and without, as it were, being personified—can the cottage be made a passive subject as the girl could: *The cottage was sent a book.* Thus, just as the non-finite clause in C.3 was shown to have affinities with a complement-plus-adjunct sequence, so the two complements of C.4 are seen to be related to such a sequence. Moreover, the fact that in C.4 the indirect object comes before the direct object (and possibly even the fact that it is typically 'personal') reminds us of the similarity between the indirect object and the subject of the embedded clause in a type C.3 sentence—as though C.4 were to be understood as The man sent (that) the girl (got or had) a book.

223

In a short treatment concerned only with some basic principles in grammatical processes, it is natural not only that there can be no detailed exposition but that many important constructions are left out of account entirely. This must be so of the comparison structures, despite the amount (and fascinatingly different kind) of abbreviation and assumption involved in two sentences like

His car travels faster than 90 m.p.h.
His car travels faster than mine.[1]

It will be recalled (p. 31) that Etiemble was struck by the deletions in English expressions like 'It washes without boiling', and it is no bad thing for the reader to be left pondering for himself the unmentioned problems, not least the variants of the three main types of sentence discussed in this chapter. He will find that there are non-finite verb clauses which, although having to be understood in terms of fully finite embedded sentences, have no finite verb versions; for example, *He enabled John to go* (as compared with *He expected John to go* which has a more explicit finite version *He expected that John would go*). He will find that with some such sequences there can be no passive (for example, *He liked John to go* beside which there is no *John was liked to go* analogous to *John was enabled/expected to go*) or even no active (thus *John was said to go* has no corresponding *N said John to go*).

But although much has been left untackled and obscure, there will have been a certain amount of progress. In the previous chapter it was shown that a linguistic sequence was not like a string of numbers in a simple addition sum but rather more like a bracketed string involving other mathematical operations besides addition. Now, rather than

[1] R. Huddleston's article in the *Journal of Linguistics* 3, 1967, p. 91ff, which also refers to other recent studies of this subject.

either of the formulations (*a*) or (*b*) given on p. 187, we can see that a linguistic expression is more like

(*c*) $3x + 3y + 6$

where it has been independently established that $x = 4 + 2$ and $y = 5 + 7$. This surely corresponds more closely to the way we understand *John's . . . hat* ('John has a hat'), *The . . . dark-haired boy* ('The boy has dark hair'), and the like. In other words, if the reader has been helped to grasp the kind of processes and the kind of continuous inter-relationships operating in English grammar, this itself is a worthwhile achievement.

Indeed, it is important for him to realise that even a study several volumes in extent could not fully explicate these processes and interrelationships in our present state of knowledge. What is left out here is in no sense just a matter of detail, and it may be salutary to end the chapter with an attempt to illustrate the depth of our ignorance. Let us consider the following two sets of sentences:

1 (*a*) The man was nasty enough to splash bitumen on my friend.
   (*b*) A crony of mine had pitch splattered over him by this spiteful wretch.
   (*c*) My friend was spotted with tar by that nasty man.
   (*d*) This beast of a fellow dirtied my buddy with pitch.
   (*e*) That nasty man spotted my friend with tar.
2 (*a*) When he was with Mum, my pal was noticed by this unpleasant fellow.
   (*b*) It was by that frightful chap that Mother and my buddy were seen.
   (*c*) My friend was spotted with Ma by that nasty man.
   (*d*) This beastly wretch observed my friend in Mum's company.
   (*e*) That nasty man spotted my friend with Ma.

It does not need to be argued that all of the sentences within each set have more in common with the other members of the set than any does with any of the members of the other set. Within each set we can sometimes describe the formal grammatical process by which one sentence is related to another (1c and 1e, for example). Sometimes we can label certain aspects of the relationship in terms of 'lexical synonymy' (*friend* and *crony* in 1a and 1b, or *noticed* and *spotted* in 2a and 2c, for example), though this of course is far from explaining what is involved. Sometimes we have a mixture of grammatical and lexical relationships that we cannot even label. In two instances (1c and 2c, 1e and 2e), we find that the two sets themselves appear to be related and that they are distinguished only by a small graphic or phonic contrast; in British 'RP', indeed, the distinction in the spoken form appears to rest on the contrast between a single pair of phonemes, /m/ and /t/. Yet just how trivial this type of contrast is becomes clear when we reflect on the deeper distinction that goes with it: a sharply different meaning of *spotted* and a sharply different relationship between *with* + N and the rest of the sentence. How is it that, despite the minimal contrast, 1e seems less like 2e than like 1a? It is a sobering thought that truths obvious to any child should continue to elude explication.

Exercises and Topics for Discussion

1   (a) In terms of the three basic pattern types, set out the elementary sentences that have been brought together to form the following:

   (i) While the tutors and specialist lecturers are at meetings, the authorities expect students to be taught their subjects and to work just as carefully as they normally do.

(ii) It is usual to find it forbidden to swim near waterfalls.

(b) 'What did you bring this book to be read to out of up for?' Improbable as this question may be, it is grammatically possible. Set out the perfectly normal and common structures that underlie it and explain the grammar of each.

2 In Chapter 11 it was pointed out that a closer analysis of 'C' (complement) in sentence and clause structure would reveal several sub-categories. Some of these are illustrated in *bons mots* like 'He can neither teach chemistry nor students' or 'You water a horse but you don't milk a cat'. Others are illustrated in the story of the guests leaving a Buckingham Palace reception: a rather pompous man approached the waiting figure of J. H. Choate, the American Ambassador, and said imperiously, 'Call me a cab!' At this, it is said that Mr Choate looked him up and down mildly, shrugged, and said, 'Okay, you are a cab.' Attempt a classification of complements which will accommodate these and other types.

3 In view of what was said (p. 217) about concord and selection restrictions on subject and complement in sentences of type A.2, how would you account for the following: 'Ruritanians are a funny people'; 'John is a failure'; 'I am glad we invited Jill but Mary was a mistake'; 'Two's company but three's a crowd'?

4 Compile sets of sentences corresponding to the pattern types B and C. Are there other sub-types besides those distinguished in this chapter? Describe the properties of any additional patterns you decide to establish. Do

the verbs used in your sets of sentences fall into classes with describable properties?

5 Consider the type and sub-type to which the following sentences show most affinity: 'The weather turned cold'; 'The man became a teacher'; 'John seemed lazy'. (Account should be taken of such additional sentences as 'John seemed to be lazy' and 'It seemed that John was lazy'.)

6 In describing the pattern types, emphasis was placed on the features distinguishing one type from another, but reference was also made to inter-relationships. What similarities do you see between the various patterns and what additional interrelationships do these seem to make possible?

7 How would you explain the difference between

I stayed at home because it was impossible to go out.
I stayed at home because it was impossible for John to go out.

and in what underlying sentences would the difference be explicit?

8 Return to the sets of sentences compiled for Exercise 4 above. Try introducing plausible -ly adverbs in each example and observe (a) the restrictions upon introducing certain adverbs into certain sentences, and (b) the different types of adverb that appear to exist.

9 (a) Write out ten sentences each containing *utterly* but otherwise as different as possible from each other. What common features do you discern in the finished sentences that may help you describe the usage of *utterly*?

(b) Repeat (a) with *really* instead of *utterly*. How many different uses of *really* are involved in the finished sentences and how would you characterise them?

10 What would selection rules have to specify in order to show that *The dog scattered tidily tomorrow is an impossible sentence?

ALL of us at some time have marvelled at the miraculous feat of complex co-ordination that we perform every time we walk. We are not in the least surprised that the poor centipede whose attention had been drawn to this skill was never able to walk properly again, because he was now too preoccupied with how he did it.

Every time we use language to explain something to a friend, we are performing a far greater feat of co-ordination, and the story of the centipede's fate might be urged upon us in this connexion, with the warning that if we become too self-conscious about *how* we use language we shall never do it properly again. Up to a point this would be a fair warning. If we are self-conscious about it, we shall certainly not be at our best in using language, and that is why in this book it is being repeatedly stressed that the shibboleths of traditional 'correctness' handicap us rather than help us to move about confidently and pleasingly in our language.

But the analogy of the centipede must not be pressed too far. There are many differences between walking and talking, and an important one for our present purpose is that when we walk no one else need be involved. From this point of view, walking is a *private* activity : so long as our method of locomotion gets us from A to B, we may be content; we do not depend on other people's approval, co-operation, or indeed presence. But talking—the use of language—is *social*; it depends for its success on doing something not merely as we ourselves like to do it, but in such a way as

230

will fit in with what other people like (or expect or understand).

If we use language solely for self-expression, the centipede parable might be more relevant, but this would involve us in only one part of the complex act of co-ordination. Self-expression is a valuable aspect of the use of language but there can be few who would regard it as the most valuable to cultivate. We need language for *communication*, and this complicates enormously the degree and kind of necessary co-ordination.

Moreover, while we do not want to use our language *self*-consciously, there is no reason why we should try to avoid using it *consciously*: every reason, in fact, why we should strive to express ourselves in full consciousness, not only of what we are saying, but how we are saying it, and what effect it is having. We spend our lives adding to our knowledge of vocabulary and practising our skill in the easy, ready manipulation of whatever complex grammatical patterns are necessary. This always remains in part a fully conscious process, and even the most skilled practitioners in what seems a 'natural', 'easy', or at any rate 'inevitable' form of expression have often torn up several early versions of what you may be judging in these terms. Even after 'twenty years . . . Trying to learn to use words', T. S. Eliot confessed that every attempt was 'a wholly new start', leaving him 'still with the intolerable wrestle with words and meanings'. And Mr Robert Graves has recently insisted that 'every English poet should . . . master the rules of grammar before he attempts to bend or break them' (*The Times*, 21 October 1961).

Those who favour relying on a haphazard self-expression in the use of English will find little support from practised writers. The fact that we ourselves know perfectly well what we mean is simply not enough. Indeed, it is not enough even if we are in communication with ourselves, as for in-

231

stance in making notes for future reference. The 'self' who has to read and understand these notes a year or so hence may find them baffling, even though the 'self' who wrote them felt they were a perfectly adequate expression. Reflections on one's own diary were amusingly handled in a Fourth Leader in *The Times*:

> What *can* the phrase 'Loaded be blowed', which appears underlined three times in the space devoted to Thursday, April 27, ever have meant? (30 December 1961.)

We should therefore be all the more careful when what we say or write is addressed not to ourselves but to other people.

Every time we express ourselves we have to co-ordinate not merely muscular movements in the speech organs or in the hand which is grasping the pen. We have to relate the *simultaneously* apprehended topic of discourse to the necessarily linear linguistic signals which must communicate it: moreover, we must do so in such a way that we can be sure our companion or our reader is able to apprehend the topic in the way we ourselves do—which means selecting linguistic expression which will not merely suit the topic but which will suit our audience.

Now, in the 'primary' use of language we are able to manage this highly complex task fairly well for the most part. This is largely because speaking comes more easily to us than writing (we are more used to it) and because the normal speech situation—face to face—provides liberal opportunity for what communication engineers call 'feedback'; we watch our companion's eyes and note his expressions of comprehension or doubt, and adjust our delivery accordingly. There is also the fact that in the ordinary speech situation we usually know our companion and have in consequence some experience of what he is able to understand. With strangers we may have difficulty even in speech.

232

A man may find it hard to understand a motor mechanic who tries to explain what is wrong with his car, and will turn to a friend to explain it: the same topic, but the friend is in a better position to know how the explanation should be put—and at what point it needs to start.

The speech situation is perhaps at its most difficult when one is addressing a mixed audience, some of whom will understand one kind of expression and others a different kind. The radio talk sees this situation in its acutest form, since the speaker cannot even see whether most of his audience is nodding approval or wearing a puzzled frown. There was an amusing instance of this problem in a television programme in the autumn of 1959. The Prime Minister was entertaining President Eisenhower at 10 Downing Street and discussing political problems with him while at the same time indirectly addressing the public. One remark by Mr Macmillan baffled most of us, though no doubt each in his own way made some kind of sense out of it. *The Times* reported him next day as having said 'We know the job backwards' and several other papers had several other versions; in *The Listener*, for instance, the report read 'We've never jogged backwards'. In *The Times* on 4 September 1959 it was stated that from a replay of the recording the Prime Minister's words had been transcribed as 'We never jog backwards', and the following day the mystery was finally cleared up in a letter from Mr C. G. Bernstein, Director of Granada Television, who wrote:

we listened many times to the recording of the Macmillan-Eisenhower broadcast. It was not quite clear whether Mr Macmillan said 'job' or 'jobbed' and, as practically every newspaper reported his using a different word, we telephoned 10 Downing Street. We were eventually advised that the word the Prime Minister used was 'jobbed'. He said 'We never jobbed backwards'. (*The Times*, 5 September 1959.)

233

The solution indicates that Mr Macmillan had used a vivid technical term, meaning roughly 'We haven't spent our time resentfully thinking of what *might* have been'. It is an expression well known in financial circles and readily understood by statesmen, but it turned out to be beyond the linguistic experience of most of us.

The only things that all the versions had in common were the first and last words, *we* and *backwards*, together with a word beginning with /n/ somewhere between them. In making sense of the puzzle, it can be seen that reporters were very much influenced by normal collocations of the word *backwards*. The one who decided on 'We know the job backwards' was influenced by a specific stock phrase. If we found the words '. . . job backwards' on a torn scrap of paper, we would immediately assume that they had been preceded by a part of the verb *know*: and we should probably supply 'the job' just as readily if we found the words 'we know' and 'backwards', with something illegible in the middle. The version in *The Listener* ('jogged backwards') is influenced by the directional sense of *backwards* in expressions like 'moved backwards', 'swung backwards', 'jerked backwards'. It is significant that all the reporters managed to produce quite sensible versions by putting into grammatical framework words that customarily belong together. They failed to make an accurate report not because Mr Macmillan's grammar was unusual (a simple SAVA structure as in 'We always work quietly'), but because he was putting words together in what is for most people an unfamiliar collocation.

Effective communication of the simplest utterance depends on the extent to which its fits in with the listener's expectations, and these expectations are largely derived from his previous experience in the language. We cannot therefore over-emphasise the importance of taking care in both grammatical arrangement and lexical selection. This

234

can be tested out in a simple experiment. See how quickly the following sentences can be read with understanding:

1 The table was of polished mahogany and it gleamed in the bright light.
2 The car was of corrugated plastic and it swayed in the ploughed sand.

Or try dictating them at the same speed to a friend. Grammatically the two are identical, and one cannot object that the second is 'nonsense' or 'not English'. Experimental cars have been made of odder materials than corrugated plastic, and what more reasonable than to test the springing by ploughing a stretch of beach for it to be driven over? Nevertheless, sentence (1) can probably be assimilated faster and with less error than (2) and this is because 'table' collocates with 'polished mahogany' (and 'mahogany' with 'polished') more often than 'car' with 'corrugated plastic' (or 'plastic' with 'corrugated'); polished mahogany is often said to gleam and lights are often described as bright.

So we see that, when grammar is a constant, ready comprehensibility may still vary sharply, according to expectedness or unexpectedness in the selection or collocation of words. Similarly, when vocabulary is a constant, a variation in grammar may bring about sharp differences in the ease of comprehension. In *The Ring and the Book*, there is a passage where Browning is talking about the contrast between what a child and what a scientist may see in the same ordinary events. The child, for instance, may regard a rough sea as being 'angry', whereas the scientist will ponder upon the physical laws operating in the turbulence of the waves; and Browning writes:

3   To both, remains one and the same effect
      . . . change cause
      Never so thoroughly   (Book X)

Compare the degree of concentration necessary to absorb this with what is necessary for the following 'paraphrase' in which the same lexical words are used but in which the grammar has been changed:

4   However thoroughly the cause may change, the effect remains the same for both.

We scarcely need to be reminded that where both grammar and vocabulary are rare, our concentration has to be doubly great. We may see this in the following poem by Roy Campbell, which by no means reaches extremes in 'difficulty':

5   In bare country shorn of leaf,
    By no remote sierra screened,
    Where pauses in the wind are brief
    As the remorses of a fiend
    The stark Laocoon this tree
    Forms of its knotted arm and thigh
    In snaky tussle with a sky
    Whose hatred is eternity,
    Through his white fronds that whirl and seethe
    And in the groaning root he screws,
    Makes heard the cry of all who breathe,
    Repulsing and accusing still
    The Enemy who shaped his thews
    And is inherent to his will.

It should be clear, after reading this poem, that there can be no question of recommending a mode of expression which has as its sole criterion the ease with which it may be understood. There are plenty of occasions when ease of comprehension must take its place in the queue with other priorities. But it should never be wilfully or carelessly neglected: as we address our friends, write letters or memoranda, even attempt a poem, linguistic tact demands that we should *care* for the ease and comfort of the 'receiver'. Indeed, self-interest enjoins it: we cannot expect to be accorded the concentration we are willing to give Browning or Roy Campbell, and unless we do not mind being half or totally misunderstood, we must make a conscious effort to communicate fully and speedily. Deliberate obscurity is a ridiculous vanity and obscurity through carelessness is a form of insolence.

When we were considering the 'jobbed backwards' crux, it was pointed out that *job backwards* on a scrap of paper would lead us to suppose that this had been preceded by the verb *know*, because *know* and *job* and *backwards* are habitually collocated. In other words they constitute a cliché, and because (whether we like it or not) most of the ordinary use of English is thoroughly saturated with clichés, most of us come to expect that there is a good deal of redundancy in what we are hearing or reading. Indeed, redundancy is a natural and necessary factor in all use of language: without it, any momentary inattention or mispronunciation or misprint or the intrusion of 'noise' of any kind would make comprehension impossible; and even without such intrusions, the degree of concentration necessary to understand anything would exhaust most of us.

The question of redundancy can perhaps be most readily grasped with reference to the *transmission* side of language (and it is discussed by Professor Gimson below), but it concerns grammar and vocabulary no less. We intuitively recognise its importance when we ask a policeman the way to a particular street (which we probably enunciate very distinctly, because we know he cannot be expecting us to name a particular street) and when, on the other hand, we finally thank him with 'I'm very grateful for your help' (which we may say very indistinctly, because the words in this utterance so very much 'belong together' that any single one is highly redundant). We also intuitively acknowledge the existence of redundancy in the irritating habit we sometimes have of not completing an utterance. A man waits at Oxford Circus and at last his friend turns up; their conversation may begin somewhat as follows:

6 I'm sorry if I'm er—— Shall we go and have a bite to——? Or have you had your—— Oh, by the way, we can't go for a drive in my—you see, I've failed my—— Ugh, the examiner was an absolute——

This is not the kind of acknowledgment of redundancy that is to be commended. Rather, what we should conclude is that since linguistic usage does in fact condition an expectancy of the redundant and of the habitual collocation, we must take special care to anticipate and forestall this expectancy when what we are saying involves fairly rare relationships and collocations, with a fairly low degree of redundancy. Consider the following opening paragraph of a news-item in *The Times* on 21 June 1958:

7 There was a massive vote—345 to 12—in the House of Representatives last night for amendments to the McMahon Act which will enable the United States to provide Britain and, to some extent, other allies with far less restricted information about its most recent advances in the development of atomic weapons.

It is quite likely that many readers at that point concluded that American security measures were being tightened and that Britain in future would be left still more in the dark about trans-Atlantic atomic research. Yet the converse proved to be the case and the writer no doubt felt perfectly sure that it was the converse he was conveying, since the grammar of the crucial part is not in itself ambiguous, as one can see by looking at the following unequivocal instance:

8 She gave him a far less expensive gift.

238

The writer should have noticed that while 'gave him a far less expensive gift' would be unambiguous to everyone, the same grammar in 'gave him far less restricted information' could not be unambiguous; that whereas in the first the nominal group structure would be recognised as basically 'a (far less expensive) gift', it might be taken in the second as '(far less) restricted information'. In other words the writer should have been conscious of an existing collocation in the language ('restricted information') which would interfere with reception of his intended (and in itself perfectly acceptable) grammar. Being clear oneself as to what is meant is not enough: one must be conscious of the receiving end and satisfied that things will be equally clear there.

Similarly, let us take the following sentence:

9 A policeman and an old woman, who was dressed in a dirty shawl, stood talking in the lane.

The relative clause here creates no difficulty, because the singular *was* and the lexical congruence of *shawl* with *old woman* makes its relationship perfectly clear. But the same grammatical arrangement in the following sentence from a newspaper is by no means so fortunate:

10 A British destroyer and a cargo steamer, which had been making for Algiers, spent hours searching the area.

Again the writer should have had sufficient regard for his readers to be aware that the grammar here, which was clear to him and which would be equally clear to anyone else in (9), might now be misunderstood.

In that example, difficulty could have been avoided by an elementary precaution in punctuation and it must be emphasised that, when we write and so are obliged to manage without features of language like intonation, we must be careful to give the reader all the help that is possible

239

from the resources of punctuation. Again, we readily agree, it will not matter in some instances. 'After all I'm a man now' and 'After all this time I've forgotten' are both straightforward enough without internal punctuation, but a sentence like the following is susceptible of several interpretations:

11 After all this life in the rough country towns would seem ghastly.

Even here, the context might be sufficiently explicit as to make it possible to argue that no pointing is necessary, though in general one might say that any sentence which is liable to hold up a reader—even momentarily—should be improved if possible. Thus for instance the following excerpt from a newspaper does not actually need punctuation (in fact comma-punctuation would be improper here), but it is certainly difficult to read and the writer's best course would have been to re-cast it entirely:

12 June output of tin concentrates for a number of companies under the management of British interests showed declines over the May period.

Again, when we write 'stainless steel sink plugs' we know exactly what we mean, and we know also that we are using a nominal group of a perfectly normal and acceptable type. But we must *also* anticipate the reader's difficulty and realise that *in this case* it would be better to use a structural type that can be more discriminating: 'plugs for stainless steel sinks' or 'sink plugs of stainless steel'. We must always bear in mind the potential problems of both grammar and vocabulary.

But, as we saw in connexion with example (12), care with grammar and vocabulary is not solely directed to avoiding ambiguity: we must seek to avoid any momentary interference with communication. Such momentary interference can arise through clumsiness or obscurity, but equally it may arise through the reader's attention being deflected from what is being said to how it is being said. This often takes place when we thoughtlessly utter *double entendres* ('There's a bloody patch on the floor') or use collocations which evoke the discomfort or facetiousness of mixed *metaphor* rather than pass unheeded as clichés. A question like 'How is your mind working?' involves a common and unremarkable collocation. Similarly, when we say 'Try to put the whole thing in a nutshell', no fear of a liberal-minded reaction need trouble us. But when an unfortunate BBC interviewer said to one of Her Majesty's Ministers, 'In a nutshell, how is your mind working?' there was material for a derisive letter in the *Radio Times*. Compare the following report of a speech by a prominent actress:

13   Some people are saying that the theatre is dying. They have been saying so since the days of Greece, but it is impossible to kill something which has roots and blood. (*Daily Telegraph*, 23 July 1956.)

The speakers unnecessarily spoil their effect in these cases not by causing ambiguity but by deflecting the hearer's attention in some trivial way. It is in this respect that the common grammatical shibboleths retain some importance: they are liable to be obtrusive to the hearer or reader and so take his attention from the communication itself. While there remain people who are moved by these things, linguistic tact (not to mention self-interest) requires that we avoid them at points where they are apt to interfere with our communication. Thus we may sympathise with the *Sunday Pictorial* sub-editor who wrote 'This is him' beneath a photograph of Mr Arthur Miller; he may well have felt

241

that 'This is he' would be even more obtrusive and open to the possibly more serious criticism of being 'unnatural'. But if he had thought of putting 'This is the man', he could have evaded the difficulty and avoided the exaggerated rebuke of Peter Simple:

14   But where is her? And whom is what?
           And when did him meet she?
           Her must be it if him is not.
           Thou doesn't know. Does me?

                            (*Daily Telegraph*, 26 July 1956.)

The fact that English lacks an 'epicene' pronoun in the singular (with the convenience of the plural *they*) often causes difficulties of this kind. 'Everyone can do it if they try,' we say, and in speech this seems to be universally accepted. Similarly an invariable *who* (especially interrogative *who*) is often acceptable colloquially. Not long ago, a woman prominent in social and public life used the following expressions in a broadcast interview: 'Everybody has private sorrows, don't they?' and 'History is written about who?' But when such expressions appear on paper (especially in print), many people who not only tolerate but actually *use* them in speech will find them obtrusive and objectionable: will find that they have an effect on the smooth in-take of the text comparable to the effect that an obscurity or ambiguity would have. And although some 'dangling participles' are universally acceptable (as for instance in 'Roughly speaking they are the same length') and others can pass muster in speech, they may be considered slovenly when they appear in writing; for example:

15   Not being an engineer this suggestion may be something of a pipe dream. (From a letter in *The Times*, 27 October 1961.)

Very often, of course, when we put pen to paper we are

quite aware that the tolerances and constraints of written English are different from those of the spoken language, but we may still spoil our communication if we leave the reader able to see all too clearly that we have simply twisted an idiomatic spoken form in the hope that it might 'look better'. 'How stupid can the English become' (the opening letter in *The Times*, 27 April 1961) is paralleled to some extent in the report that executives were 'requesting for English secretaries' (*The Times*, 21 March 1960), where it would seem that *requesting* has been hastily substituted for *asking* because it had a more rotund tone. Some years ago, a serious article in *The Guardian* mentioned 'the girl from a progressive school who had not a lipstick' (21 March 1955): the writer has apparently hoped that this would be read as 'hadn't', which he was reluctant to see in print, but in fact it was liable to be read as the first part of a correlation ('who had not a lipstick but a—'). A full awareness of the reader's position would have led him to substitute a different negative expression ('who had no lipstick') which would occasion no pause or stumble.

This is by no means a full account of what is involved in the subtle co-ordination necessary for effective communication: the discussion must be continued in the next chapter. But it is hoped that enough has been said to make it abundantly clear that language must be used not merely to 'get out' what we have in our minds but also to 'get it across' as completely and effectively as possible to someone else. For this latter part of the process we must bear *his* needs and problems consciously and sympathetically in mind.

Exercises and Topics for Discussion

1   Write two sets of instructions for replacing the rear

243

tyre of a bicycle. In the first, assume that your readers are experienced cyclists who understand the names of tools and parts of the cycle. In the second, assume no such experience: your readers are young people owning their first cycle and doing their first repair.

2 Tabulate linguistic features of grammar and vocabulary (including collocation) in the poem by Campbell (example 5) which seem to you relatively uncommon.

3 Explain in detail why example 10 is misleading while 9 is not.

4 What are the 'several interpretations' that could be given to example 11? Attempt to write a set of introductions that would give sufficient context to lead us to each interpretation in turn, even without punctuating the example.

5 Write a comment on the theatre which achieves the force of example 13, without allowing the effect to be spoilt by loose expression or by unfortunate collocations. Comment on the ways in which your version differs. To what extent would you defend the example as it stands?

6 Re-write the following comment on the Common Market problem, making it rather easier to grasp the argument:

> If industrialists are so keen for Britain to join why does not the Government make it possible for those who want to get into Europe, without the sacrifice to British sovereignty, not to mention agriculture and horticulture, which must be the inevitable result of our joining if we are to rely on M. Debré's words recently that the Common Market is unworkable without the Treaty of Rome. (From a letter in *The Times*, 18 July 1961.)

7 Explain why the burlesqued features in example 14 are 'more ungrammatical' than the caption it criticises.

244

8　Many would find obstructions to easy and acceptable communication in the following quotations; explain why, and comment on the probable objections that a reader might raise:

(a) Boards of directors should not wait for strikes but should voluntarily offer themselves the higher pay they admit their workers should have.

(b) He now learns for the first time that she is now under contract, and he would at no time be a willing party to any artist breaking their contract with another management.

(c) Guy Fawkes was put on the rack but he would not split.

(d) The Exmouth scheme involves work being carried out to the Withycombe Brook, which overflowed into the town twice last winter and was sent to the Ministry by the Devon River Board in August.

(e) He told her he had reason to believe that she had a man there who he knew as Fred Harmsworth and who he wished to interview.

(f) It is said that everything comes to he who waits.

(g) Let us go then, you and I.

14: Style and Purpose

PART of the intricacy of co-ordination in using language lies, as we saw in the previous chapter, in the different constraints operating in speech and writing. But, as we know well, the constraints do not fall neatly into a twofold division, 'speaking' versus 'writing'. The stylistic range of English is wide and ultimately the gradations are infinite. When we are putting words together, we have to see that they are congruous with the expectations at some point on this scale and that they are arranged according to the conventions of collocation and grammar—with reference to the same point on the scale.

It may seem paradoxical to lay such stress on being conventional in the use of English when we may well feel that the big prizes go to people who are original and *un*conventional in their English. It is by no means certain that the big prizes *are* so awarded, but whatever our opinion of this, there seems to be a general agreement that cries of 'Look, Mother: no hands!' are especially unimpressive when we have still not properly mastered the art of cycling in the conventional manner. Before trying to write like Gertrude Stein, we have to school ourselves to observe and to use English within the strictest conventions—and we have support in this from the words of Mr Robert Graves quoted in the last chapter.

Without a norm, it is difficult to recognise or practise originality. You may have sampled a variety of ice-cream which has little bits of crystallised ginger in it, and you may have come across it being marketed with the rather

246

fetching gimmick, 'freezing hot ice-cream'. Here is a case where a departure from conventional collocation is very effective. The title of Noel Coward's play, *Bitter Sweet*, is a better known example, and most of us have at some time been amused by hoary witticisms like 'The hand that rocked the cradle has kicked the bucket'. In all these examples, we are departing from conventional arrangements—but we are not ignoring them. It is *because* we recognise that 'bitter' and 'sweet' are mutually exclusive and not normally collocable that the junction of them can be effective. The effectiveness of 'freezing hot ice-cream' depends on the tension that is set up between this and the normal collocations of 'freezing' and 'hot' (such as 'freezing cold' and 'boiling hot').

The order of events in our strategy, then, must be first to observe the conventional arrangements and the points to which they belong in the stylistic range: again, it is necessary to insist on the central importance of keeping in line with *actual usage*. We observe that if people we respect begin a letter 'Dear Mr Jones', they will close it with 'Yours sincerely', but that if they begin with 'Dear Sir', they will end with 'Yours faithfully'. Experienced and well-educated people will not mix these formulas—and they tend to think poorly of those who do. And, of course, it is not merely the beginnings and endings that are not mixed: the type of grammatical construction and the selection of the words—the whole style—will tend to be different (and consistently so) in the two types of letter.

It is true that many enlightened business firms have now given up the sillier, stiffer formalities that used to spoil commercial letters (expressions like 'Further to yours of the 23rd ult.'): but a shapely sense of formality remains. The letter to or from a business firm or government department will now say (after the 'Dear Sir') something like 'In reply to your letter of 23rd June . . .' It will *not* begin with the

247

informal and imprecise words, 'Thank you for your recent letter', which are more suitable for one beginning 'Dear Mr Jones'. Needless to say, there are other expressions that are appropriate to other types of letters on the scale which runs from distant formality (especially in dealings with an *organisation*, when personalities are kept in the background) to the completely familiar and intimate (where personalities matter as much as anything): 'My dear Frank, It was awfully nice to get your note the other day.' In each case, the experienced letter-writer adopts a style fitted to the degree of formality that his letter requires and maintains that style consistently throughout. He will not say, 'My regards to your wife' in a *Dear Sir* letter, and he will not end with 'Cheerio for now' in a *Dear Mr Jones* letter.

Letters are convenient for illustrating stylistic range, but of course a scale of styles exists in all our use of English. Each of us works not just with one English but with many Englishes, and the wider the range of our life and the more various the contacts we have, the wider and suppler must be our command over a range of English styles, each of which we know how to use consistently. A haphazard knowledge of several styles may be worse than useless if we do not know the type of occasion on which each is appropriate, or if we do not know when we are sliding from one to another. We do not say, 'It was extremely gracious of you to invite me, Lady Jones, and I've had bags of fun', because 'bags of fun' does not mix with 'extremely gracious', and because to use an expression like 'bags of fun', we should need to know Lady Jones well enough to be addressing her by her first name.

It is not—we must never tire of insisting—that *bags of fun* can be labelled 'bad' or 'slovenly' English, 'a lazy substitute for thought'. 'Bags of fun' is no more a lazy substitute for thought in its appropriate setting than is 'extremely gracious' in the setting that is appropriate for *this* expression. As we have seen repeatedly (and especially in Chapter 10), it is the height of naïvety to go round with a single yardstick, measuring English as 'good' or 'bad'. Take the opening suggested earlier for an informal letter: 'My dear Frank, It was awfully nice to get your note the other day.' Here are words that would greatly please the receiver with their warmth and friendliness, yet they include *awfully*, *get*, and *nice*, three words which have been condemned so often that many people cannot write them without having a slight feeling of guilt. They have been called 'slovenly' and even 'meaningless'. Such an attitude is plainly ridiculous and can do nothing but harm to the good use of English.

But it would be equally ridiculous to *reverse* the judgment just as flatly. It is the type of judgment that is wrong: it is not merely that the judgment is faulty in this particular instance. If we were studying a review and found the comment 'This is an awfully nice book', our reaction to the words in this situation might well be to call them 'slovenly', 'meaningless'. We do not want merely polite noises in a review: we want some precise observations about the book's content and quality. Equally, however, we should disapprove of the English used if we were greeted by a friend at a party with the words, 'I apprehend an atmosphere of spontaneous delight with your arrival', whereas 'Awfully nice to see you here' would strike us as just right.

This must take us back to what was said in the previous chapter about expected collocations. Frequent and thoroughly expected collocations (like 'freezing cold') are most apt to strike us as clichés when they are used on occasions which lead us to expect relatively high precision and relatively low redundancy. As so often in matters of language, it is not usually a question of whether a given expression *out of context* is or is not a cliché. If we are strolling during an interval at the theatre and our companion says, 'I admired Pinter's incredible insight in that act', we may not feel any of that distaste that constitutes reaction to a cliché. Indeed, we can imagine many informal contexts of situation in which 'incredible insight', so far from being a cliché, might sound rather high-flown and technical: everything depends on what is expected at particular points in the stylistic range. But if 'incredible insight' is acceptable when used in criticism that is *spoken* on an informal occasion, it does not mean that these words are equally acceptable in *written* criticism of a formal kind.

All too frequently we tend to pick up the collocations of the most commonly heard criticism and then to use them indiscriminately, without realising how empty they seem in a setting where precision is expected. In a set of essays written by an undergraduate class recently, it appeared that the following are among the commonest collocations which must be branded as clichés in serious commentary on literature:

> lofty flights of imagination; inimitable narrative technique; organic unity; consummate skill; consummate art; heights of majesty; heights of tragedy; inherent atmosphere; essential atmosphere; inherent appeal; essential appeal; essential characteristics.

And this is to ignore expressions which descend from the hackneyed to the tautologous, like 'basic fundamentals'! We must develop the critical awareness to recognise that such expressions, which may impress the inexperienced, are largely automatic, neither reflecting any precision in our judgment as we write them nor conveying any precise information to the reader. The reader may in fact conclude that the writer is incapable of judgment and is trying to deceive with a show of verbiage: a conclusion which may well be completely just in many cases. The use of clichés in essay-writing is often accompanied by a woolliness of expression which confirms the impression that no hard thinking has been taking place: 'his verse is packed with special meaning'; 'his poems have a character all their own'; 'he paints the very body and soul of English industrial life'; 'his decorative imagery always follows a structural line'. Do these reflect laziness or the will to deceive?

Again, we must emphasise that absolute judgments are inappropriate. Most of our vagueness in expression comes from a lazy inconsiderateness towards our hearer or reader. An example may be given from a recent BBC news bulletin which fell below the usual high standards of competent clarity: 'Mr Dean Rusk said there ought to be a temporary appointment pending agreement. He suggested an outstanding world figure.' This was the end of the news-item, and listeners were left wondering whether or not Mr Rusk had actually named someone.

In all probability, this example resulted from a sub-editor's oversight, but there are occasions when a vague way of putting things can achieve more than an attempt at precision: many of the best novels and poems demonstrate the importance of the studiously equivocal. Even in ordinary day-to-day discourse, we may wish to veil what we are saying and we know that this can be as difficult as achieving clarity. Let us assume that we have to persuade a relative, suspected of having a serious complaint, to see a doctor: she is terrified, perhaps because she too suspects the seriousness of her complaint. After the visit, one may say comfortingly, 'Well, the doctor was quite reassuring after all, wasn't he? Let's hope you won't ever again be worried by having to visit him.' Such a form of words may be taken as meaning 'Let's hope you won't have to see the doctor again' or 'Let's hope you'll never find a visit to the doctor worrying': and as in all useful equivocations, its value lies not in the 'either—or' but in implanting both suggestions without commitment.

But it will be noticed that this was called being 'studiously equivocal': the vagueness is conscious and deliberate. Moreover, the motive in this instance would be widely approved. Often there are less commendable motives. A cigarette advertisement some time ago bore a picture of Gigli with the caption '"Smooth" is the key word says Gigli', in large type above the picture, and the words 'Smooth to the lips . . . to the taste . . . to the throat' in similar type beneath the picture and beside the brand-name. The implication here is that Gigli is testifying to the 'smoothness' of this particular cigarette, but in fact a closer reading (if our eyes are good enough to manage the small type) reveals that Gigli's word 'smooth' is quoted from one of his comments on voice-control and has no reference to cigarettes of any brand—or even to smoking.

When we are reading, we have to study carefully the unintentional ambiguities that may—as we saw in the previous chapter—make us run away with the impression that America is going isolationist or that British destroyers are threatening Algiers. We need to exercise equal care in order to respond to the deliberate ambiguities and subtleties in a novel or a poem—and in order to protect ourselves against the deliberate ambiguities of the advertiser and propagandist.

'Scientific experiments have proved that our product makes your clothes whiter.' This is intended to give the impression that 'our product' is the most efficient on the market, and that in fact 'science' has proved it so. But of course this is not actually claimed in the text, and when we study advertisements of this kind carefully we see that very little indeed is ever 'actually claimed'. The words 'scientific experiments have proved' certainly seem a strong opening, but a moment's reflection is enough to give us doubts. Are they not rather vague? What were the experiments? Who performed them? Under what conditions? Even in a world where 'science' is a magic word, the layman must still venture to ask questions like these. But what in any case are the experiments said to have proved? That 'our product' makes clothes 'whiter'. Makes them whiter than *what*, we must ask. Whiter than when they are washed under absolutely identical conditions using every other relevant product on the market? Or merely whiter than when they are washed in cold water without soap? Or perhaps, indeed, just whiter than they were before they were washed! The advertiser is wisely content to avoid such details, and we too may be content enough, provided that we realise that this is the deliberately vague language of persuasion and that we need not be awed by the gesture of science.

Let us remember, however, that there is no hard and fast line to be drawn between the 'language of persuasion' and the 'language of fact'. It is very difficult to say or write anything without adopting some 'angle' and without betraying some point of view, even if we *want* to be objective: and for the most part we do not very energetically seek to be so. In fact, it is easy to persuade ourselves that our angle on the world is the objective one and that it is the 'facts' that we are seeing. As we noted in Chapter 4, the 'real facts' are in any case very much determined by the use of language itself, and so cultivating objectivity is often not so much a matter of seeing reality clearly as seeing other people's vision of reality sympathetically. The lesson from this for the present purpose, however, is that we must scrutinise other people's language, as we read or listen, not merely for 'facts' but for a *viewpoint* on 'facts', and that we must not expect these always to be distinguishable.

The best way to appreciate this point fully is no doubt to read a full account of a lawsuit and to notice how the arguments on both sides make the same 'facts' seem very different. It would require too much space to examine one here, and we must content ourselves with some newspaper comment on a minor court-case. Not long ago, a man was sentenced to six weeks' imprisonment for hurting a dog in a London park. This is probably as objective a summary as it is possible to write—yet even this, with the expression 'hurting a dog', seems to make the man's offence culpably cruel. How much more can viewpoint enter when the actual attempt is being made to express one! In one account of the case, written by someone who obviously thought the sentence harsh, the man was described as 'an elderly gentleman' who was 'reading his Sunday newspaper in the park' when 'a dog jumped upon him and upset him'. In the shock and confusion, the elderly gentleman 'kicked at the animal'. Here we have a selection of words which reveal the writer's sympathies and which—unless we are careful to note that this *is* what they are doing—are liable to condition ours. An elderly gentleman cannot easily be thought of as nasty, but the words 'old man' are quite often preceded by 'nasty'. But we may readily grant that there are no 'lies' here: most men in advancing years can be described as 'elderly gentlemen', and the writer might well protest that it was a 'fact'—he *was* an elderly gentleman; and he *was* reading his Sunday newspaper; this, too, is a 'fact', though of course it is a fact that is more likely to be noticed if one wants to emphasise the inoffensive, peaceful behaviour of the defendant. A dog disrupts the serenity by jumping upon him and upsetting him, and all he does it not to *kick it* but to *kick at it*: another illustration of the dependence of fact upon viewpoint. From one point of view an idly swinging foot may *kick* something; from another, it may simply *knock* it. From one point of view, if you kick at something you are making a kicking motion without commitment to the intention of

254

actually kicking; from another, if something is struck by the foot, it is kicked whatever the intention.

In another account of the same episode, things are put very differently. The dog has become a 'lively puppy', and the elderly gentleman is coolly referred to as 'a man', because it now appears that he did not merely kick at the lively puppy: he 'stamped on it' and showed no 'feeling for our dumb friends'. Language can scarcely be more slanted than that! Having made it virtually certain that animal-lovers (or at any rate those animal-lovers who do not read very critically) are already won over to his view, the writer now daringly seeks to widen his appeal with a peroration in which he says how serious a crime is cruelty of any kind, but especially 'cruelty to animals *or children*'.

A critical, mature reading of accounts like these helps us to judge the 'facts' for ourselves but, just as importantly, it also helps us to a sympathetic understanding of differing viewpoints sincerely held. Often, however, the latter aspect is by no means so important (the expressed viewpoint may not be sincerely held at all), and our principal concern is self-protection. History—and not least the history of our own times—presents all too many examples of people and even whole nations being duped by high-sounding but meretricious political rhetoric and slogans, and our law-courts all too often deal with sad cases of people losing their money because of golden-tongued racketeers.

One such case was described by C. K. Ogden[1] as 'an example of the power of symbols without parallel in any age'. Horatio Bottomley was so golden-tongued that he managed to raise from a gullible public no less than £20,000,000: this, according to his secretary, was 'the outstanding fact in his remarkable career'. He was sentenced to seven years' imprisonment in 1922 after a trial which revealed the appalling, unscrupulous power of the

[1] See *Psyche*, vol. 18 (1952), pp. 8off.

man. Perhaps more revolting than any other aspect of the case was the way in which he exploited the piety and patriotism of simple people during the war of 1914-18. While his chairman would be giving him a glowing introduction, his cynical eye was estimating the size of his audience and hence his box office receipts for the occasion ('He was never more than a few pounds out'), deciding in consequence which of his graded perorations he would give the audience in return. It is said that if he expected at least £75 he would conclude like this:

When this great nation emerges from its period of trial—as please God it will—we shall stand erect shoulder to shoulder before the world and declare with one voice that Britain is the Land of Hope and Glory, Mother of the Free . . . God who made us mighty shall make us mightier yet.

For a return of between £75 and £100, his audience would hear:

When this tragedy is over, we shall be able to look the whole world in the face and say that this country, this England, has come out of this ghastly conflict with its name unsullied, its escutcheon clean. . . .

If he was assured that he would receive more than a hundred pounds, his reaction was, 'Right! I will trot out the Prince tonight.' And this, as Ogden demurely tells us, 'was a reference to the fact that the peroration concluded with an allusion to the Prince of Peace.'

He used to be paid £250 a week by a popular Sunday paper for a column claiming to be a 'soul-stirring message, perhaps the most inspired words ever penned by a layman'. As an example of these 'most inspired words' we may quote the following:

Therefore, dear mothers, sisters, wives and sweethearts,

whose men and lads have fallen or shall fall upon the field, or on the sea, have no misgiving. They are not dead. You have lent them to God.

The Editor of *Truth* (31 May 1922) reported that, among his intimates, Bottomley 'did not trouble to conceal his contempt and derision. "That's the stuff to give 'em," he would say, sometimes adding blasphemies which I should not care to print. But the public guilelessly swallowed the stuff.'

Perhaps, we may say to comfort ourselves, the public today would not guilelessly swallow such stuff. Perhaps, indeed, our public today has been so exposed to sentimental, high-sounding, highly-charged language that it has grown some kind of protective skin. The story is told of a couple outside a cinema looking at a garish sign which read 'Colossal! Stupendous! The Great Cinematic Attraction of All Time.' And the woman turned to her husband and said reflectively, 'I wonder if it's any good, dear.'

If such scepticism were widespread, it could hardly represent any gain so far as our language and its use are concerned. A totally apathetic cynicism in the face of a communication would be no more an advantage to the effective use of English than a totally naïve gullibility, since it would indicate a devaluation of our linguistic currency to near worthlessness. It is likely, however, that scepticism is not in fact widespread enough, and that increased and constant scrutiny of language must be encouraged not only to protect ourselves from being duped but so that we may understand more fully the society in which we live.

We may end this chapter by quoting from an account of a prominent Kentucky politician's campaign for the state governorship in 1963. Mr A. B. (Happy) Chandler

evokes cheers and tears from his audience with equal ease, and does not hesitate to shout and weep with them. He quotes

257

(or misquotes) the Bible, Shakespeare or his Uncle Ben with equal facility, calls on the Lord frequently and with easy familiarity . . . If the day is warm, he throws aside his jacket and loosens his tie before addressing the faithful . . . On the platform beneath the trees of the courthouse lawn, he manages to hug each local dignitary, all the while calling and waving to the audience, 'Hello, there, John', 'Howdy, Bob', 'Hello, there, Preacher'.

There may not be a John, Bob, Tom or Preacher in the audience, but if there is, he will be sure that Happy's greeting is for him alone. Happy knows this . . . After a prayer and eulogies by local supporters, he gets down to business. If he feels he has his opponents on the run, he launches into a burst of scorn and ridicule; but if he is himself under fire he likes to divert his listeners by an appeal to emotion. Once . . . he interrupted his explanation because, he said, he had just spotted a 'dear little, grey-haired lady' in the audience, whose face had taken him back to the days of the war. He described how he went to North Africa 'to see how they were treating our boys'. There he made his way to the front line.

'And suddenly,' he recounted, 'I saw this fine young boy, lying wounded there on the ground, and he looked up at me and said: "Why, it's Happy Chandler!"

'"Yes, son," I said, and he reached out his hand and he said, "I'm from Kentucky, Happy." And I knelt down there on the sand beside him, and I could see the hand was on him, and he was about to cross over, and he reached out and said, "Take my hand, Happy, 'cause I'm about to go."

'I'm not ashamed to say there were tears on my face as I held the hand of that brave boy, dying there so far from the old Kentucky home he loved, and he said to me, he said, "Happy, I want you to promise me you'll take a word back for me, 'cause there's a sweet little old lady waiting for me, and I'm not coming home. Tell her I died facing the enemy, Happy, but thinking of home." And I said, "I'll do it, son."'

The story continued with his return to Kentucky and a visit to the 'sweet little Kentucky mother'. Then he stepped down and led to the platform a small greying woman, weeping copiously, and with his arm round her shoulders he faced the audience. By this time there was hardly a dry eye in the crowd.

(*The Times*, 5 March 1963)

Let him who knows he would have been without tears cast the first stone.

Exercises and Topics for Discussion

1   Write a letter to a local government official (whom you do not know personally) outlining a limited parking scheme for a street in the shopping centre, and asking him to have it considered by the council. Write also letters to a close friend and to your doctor, outlining the scheme, telling them what you have done, and asking for their support.

2   Write an account and an evaluation of a play or film that you have seen recently, taking particular care to convey your own reaction and to avoid critical clichés. Alternatively (since we see clichés less easily in our own writing than in other people's), watch a play or film with a friend, and when you have both written reviews of about 500 words, exchange them and act the role of a brutal sub-editor.

3   Here is a modern English rendering of a verse in Ecclesiastes (IX. 11):

I saw that under the sun the race is not to the swift, nor the battle to the strong, nor bread to the wise, nor riches to the intelligent, nor favour to the men of skill; but time and chance happen to them all. (Revised Standard Version, 1952.)

This is not the only kind of modern English that can replace the language of the Authorised Version. In what he calls 'a parody, but not a very gross one', George Orwell offers the following in his essay, 'Politics and the English Language' (1946):

> Objective consideration of contemporary phenomena compels the conclusion that success or failure in competitive activities exhibits no tendency to be commensurate with innate capacity, but that a considerable element of the unpredictable must invariably be taken into account.

What is Orwell parodying? Examine these two pieces of English and explain in detail how they differ. Compare your analysis with Orwell's own commentary on his version, and follow up his argument by close study of his essay as a whole. (It appears in the Collected Essays, London 1961, pp. 337-51.) Do you always agree with him?

4 Examine what has been called 'studiously equivocal' language in a poem of your own choice, explaining the point of the equivocations and the means by which they are achieved.

5 Write a frankly partisan argument for or against public schools or the game of Rugby or a change in the licensing laws. Then, in a contrite tailpiece, confess the ways in which your argument has been unfair to 'the other side'.

6 Collect from a paper or periodical

  (a) instances of language used with careless woolliness; re-write them in what seems to you an improved way;
  (b) instances (especially in advertisements) of language deliberately vague or misleading; write an exposure of them.

7 Miss Marghanita Laski once wrote an article (New

Statesman, 13 November 1948) with the title 'Cheap Clothes for Fat Old Women'. From an examination of advertisements in the newspaper you read, write on the words which seem to be avoided and the words that seem to be preferred.

8   Write a critical commentary on Bottomley's use of English as exemplified in this chapter, and discuss the sources and kinds of similar emotional and meretricious argument today.

9   The British press magnate, Mr Cecil King, was reported as telling the American Society of Newspaper Editors in April 1967 that 'interpretation is fact and fact without interpretation is not fact at all'. Explain this view, and give arguments both for and against it.

15 : *The Intolerable Wrestle with Words*

A S we strive, in our ordinary day-to-day use of English,
to put into words what we want to say in the best
possible way for our hearers and readers on a specific
occasion, it is perhaps some comfort to remember that those
who use English best of all—our poets and novelists, for
example—experience the same difficulty. As we saw in
Chapter 13, poets regard the use of language in literature as
a wrestle with the fundamentals of grammar and vocabulary. One thinks of Dylan Thomas, struggling

> to twist the shapes of thoughts
> Into the stony idiom of the brain,
> To shade and knit anew the patch of words
> Left by the dead who, in their moonless acre,
> Need no words' warmth.
>
> ('From love's first fever'.)

Elsewhere, too, he writes of the yearning to articulate, the
long bitter discipline to give his passion its full expression:

> Were that enough, enough to ease the pain,
> Feeling regret when this is wasted
> That made me happy in the sun,
> How much was happy while it lasted,
> Were vaguenesses enough and the sweet lies plenty,
> The hollow words could bear all suffering
> And cure me of ills.
>
> ('Out of the sighs'.)

Talk of vaguenesses, sweet lies, hollow words, with the

implicit assertion that they are *not* enough, reminds us sharply of the *Four Quartets* and of Eliot's austere arraignment of degenerate expression in 'East Coker':

So here I am, in the middle way, having had twenty
    years . . .
Trying to learn to use words, and every attempt
Is a wholly new start, and a different kind of failure
Because one has only learnt to get the better of words
For the thing one no longer has to say, or the way in
    which
One is no longer disposed to say it. And so each venture
Is a new beginning, a raid on the inarticulate
With shabby equipment always deteriorating
In the general mess of imprecision of feeling,
Undisciplined squads of emotion.

It is earlier in the same poem that he has shown his dissatisfaction with 'periphrastic study in a worn-out poetical fashion', which leaves him 'still with the intolerable wrestle with words and meanings'.

With this intolerable wrestle, I take it, we have the area in which the interests of the writer, the critic, the linguist, the grammarian converge. And it is an area of special interest in an age like ours which rejects 'poetic diction' and accepts the view that the spring supplying literary language must be 'ordinary language'.

In his essay 'The Music of Poetry', Eliot reminds us that 'Every revolution in poetry is apt to be, and sometimes to announce itself to be a return to common speech. That is the revolution which Wordsworth announced in his prefaces and he was right; but the same revolution had been carried out a century before by Oldham, Waller, Denham and Dryden, and the same revolution was due again something over a century later', because, as he goes on to say, poetic idiom tends regularly to become traditional while language itself, equally regularly, tends to change.

It is noteworthy that in succeeding generations the urge has been felt to make a search in this direction, to find the received language of literature inadequate for the expression of the keenest sensibilities, and to feel that only a re-engagement with something rather gropingly called 'ordinary language' can equip the literary artist for what he wants to express. To Dryden and Wordsworth we may add, for instance, Shelley, who in his Preface to *The Cenci* agrees that 'in order to move men to true sympathy we must use the familiar language of men'. One might also add Gerard Manley Hopkins, whose concern was for poetry to base itself upon 'current language' (*Letters to Robert Bridges*, p. 89), and W. B. Yeats, who singled out 'the lack of natural momentum in the syntax' as the mark of inferior and 'pretty' poetry: and by this—as Professor Donald Davie supposes—he must refer to the necessity for contact with living speech (*Articulate Energy*, p. 95).

The urge itself to turn from traditional language is surely a sound reflection of general linguistic experience. It is not only poets who find that 'one has only learnt to get the better of words, For the thing one no longer has to say'. In Dryden's time, in another field, it was this problem that exercised Thomas Sprat in the interests of achieving a written prose style which should break with a tradition of rhetorical tropes and figures and be an adequate vehicle for experimental science. For both Dryden and Sprat, as for Eliot and Einstein, outworn modes of expression have to be replaced for the sake of contemporary needs, and the primary source to turn to is the unwritten language of daily discourse which —whether it is adequately expressing them or not—is certainly in full engagement with these contemporary needs. From this viewpoint one may say, as Eliot in fact does, that 'the task is to catch up with the changes in colloquial speech, which are fundamentally changes in thought and sensibility' ('The Music of Poetry').

The extent to which spoken language is, from an expressive viewpoint, so to speak 'ahead' of the corresponding sphere of written language, and the means by which it achieves a lead, are matters still in need of thorough investigation, but what little experimental evidence we already have would seem to confirm the impression that such a lead exists. But this is not by any means to say that spoken language, merely as such, is wholly effectual: still less that it is to be bodily transferred on to paper to constitute an ideal literary medium, whether for scientific or poetic purposes. Coleridge, Shelley and Sir Walter Raleigh are among those who have uttered warnings about carrying the 'ordinary language' approach too far. While conceding that people must be addressed 'in their accustomed tongue', Raleigh goes on:

> The public, like the delicate Greek Narcissus, is sleepily enamoured of itself; and the name of its only other perfect lover is Echo. (*Style*, pp. 66f.)

In consequence

> He who has a message to deliver must wrestle with his fellows before he shall be permitted to ply them with uncomfortable or unfamiliar truths. (*Ibid.*, p. 80.)

The advent of a mass audience, coupled with the advent of a naturalistic style, may dangerously invite a reduction of language to a prime factor of banality:

> We talk to our fellows in the phrases we learn from them, which come to mean less and less as they grow worn with use. Then we exaggerate and distort, heaping epithet upon epithet in the endeavour to get a little warmth out of the smouldering pile. (*Ibid.*, p. 87.)

We have seen something of the truth of Raleigh's remarks

265

in Chapter 14, and it must be obvious that it is not in Eliot's mind to imitate such features when he speaks (in his essay on 'The Social Function of Poetry') of regaining contact with the 'language as it is actually spoken around him'. Sweeney's language is not the ideal:

> That's all the facts when you come to brass tacks:
> Birth, and copulation, and death.
> I've been born, and once is enough.
> You don't remember, but I remember.
> Once is enough . . .
> I tell you again it don't apply
> Death or life or life or death
> Death is life and life is death
> I gotta use words when I talk to you
> But if you understand or if you don't
> That's nothing to me and nothing to you
> We all gotta do what we gotta do
> We're gona sit here and drink this booze . . .

One might, however, just add in parenthesis that the poet finds it no less a wrestle to compose language like this: it is no easy task to create on paper an image of even the most 'ordinary' of 'actual language'. A threefold distinction has to be made between kinds of 'usage': *actual usage*, *believed usage*, and *preceptive usage*. The forms that a person in fact uses are often different from what he believes he uses, and these in turn may be different from what he thinks he *should* use. It is 'believed usage' that a writer usually puts on paper to represent natural English. Or else he abstracts from speech, or from *some* speech, features which seem particularly striking and which he takes to be the essence of speech. Perhaps it may be disjointed fragmentary syntax like Mr Jingle's; or the recurrent modifiers like 'well' that Swift satirises; the exaggerated and overworked epithets in Thackeray's *Book of Snobs*; or—used

266

more seriously—the hypocritical repetitious syntax of Mr Casby in *Little Dorrit*; or the clipped, staccato, tongue-tied language of the narrator in *The Catcher in the Rye*, a work as remote from *traditional* accounts of boyhood as Thomas's 'Fern Hill', and indeed explicitly distinguished in the first paragraph from 'all that David Copperfield kind of crap'. In short, whether for satirical or for serious purposes, the imaging of actual speech on paper *is* imaging and not a transcript of the real thing. It involves the working out of conventions, a deliberate weighing of words, at least as much as any other kind of writing, and the relationships of such conventions to those of ordinary speech are, incidentally, much in need of serious study.

Sweeney's language, then, is not what Eliot is referring to when he speaks of the poet's catching up 'with the changes in colloquial speech, which are fundamentally changes in thought and sensibility'. Rather, it is the converse: it is a dramatisation of the 'shabby equipment' with which the inarticulate pathetically make do. This is what justifies the raid. And the 'intolerable wrestle' is poignantly made Sweeney's own problem: 'I gotta use words when I talk to you'—the more poignant because so banal, so inadequate for expressing 'thought and sensibility'. The wrestle is something which confronts not merely the poet, the thinker, the scientist.

Eliot's interests in the functioning of language and in the problems of communication are in fact far more deliberately therapeutic than Wordsworth's. He is far more concerned than most of us about the defects in ordinary speech, what he calls (in his essay 'Poetry and Drama') 'its fumbling for words, its constant recourse to approximation, its disorder, and its unfinished sentences', and he explicitly draws attention to these features as sharply distinguishing speech from either prose or poetry. 'No poetry', he in fact says in 'The Music of Poetry', 'is ever exactly the same

267

speech that the poet talks and hears', but poetry has to have a direct linguistic relationship to ordinary speech, the poet 'must, like the sculptor, be faithful to the material in which he works'. Let us look at what he means by being 'faithful'.

In 'East Coker' he speaks of conquering 'By strength and submission' and later on, with a different metaphor, 'We must be still and still moving Into another intensity For a further union, a deeper communion'. In 'Little Gidding' he is again concerned with speech, and these concerns impel him 'To purify the dialect of the tribe And urge the mind to aftersight and foresight'. These themes recur again and again in his essays. In the 'Social Function of Poetry', for example, he says that a poet's foremost 'duty is to his *language*, first to preserve, and second to extend and improve'. Elsewhere (in 'The Music of Poetry'), he writes: 'I believe that any language . . . imposes its laws and restrictions and permits its own licence, dictates its own speech rhythms and sound patterns. And a language is always changing; its development in vocabulary, in syntax, pronunciation and intonation—even in the long run, its deterioration—must be accepted by the poet and made the best of.' Here we see the 'submission' and the being 'still' of 'East Coker'; but he goes on: '[The poet] in turn has the privilege of contributing to the development and maintaining the quality, the capacity of the language to express a wide range, and subtle gradation of feeling and emotion; his task is both to respond to change and make it conscious and to battle against degradation below the standards which he has learned from the past.'

The poet's position is thus closely analogous to that of the scientist. 'Last year's words belong to last year's language', but, in rejecting the outworn periphrasis of an earlier age, the poet can afford no more than the scientist to fall back on the 'habitual phrases' of a contemporary sleepy Echo. As Joshua Whatmough says in his somewhat eccentric book on *Poetic, Scientific and Other Forms of Discourse* (1956), the poet and the scientist are equally creative in their use of language, prompted by analogous urges. Both kinds of language 'are precise, each in its own way, the one in its probabilities of choices (*le mot juste*), the other in logical and mathematical forms'. 'The creative imagination of a Shakespeare or a Milton, of an Einstein or a Newton; both demand the total resources of form and meaning of a language.' 'In both kinds of discourse, scientific and poetic, there is a goodness of "fit".'

To relate Eliot's purification image to Whatmough's engineering metaphor, 'goodness of "fit"', and to bring both into the terms of linguistics, we need only say that both poet and scientist must undergo the discipline of basing their expression on the vocabulary, grammar and transmission system used naturally in speech and *as* used naturally in speech, if they are to perform the social function of communication. Moreover, in proceeding from this point to ply us, as Raleigh says, 'with uncomfortable and unpalatable truths', such new expressions as are necessary must conform to the graphic, phonemic, grammatical and lexical conventions obtaining in the language. Poetic—like scientific—language must be creative, but creative in terms of the language's own 'laws and restrictions', as Eliot says.

Thus our language permits many consonant clusters, as in *triumphs, squibs,* or *judged,* but there are restrictions which make it very unlikely that our scientists will call their next synthetic product *zdabf* or *ftrime-goshk*. Eliot's *aftersight* is not, according to most dictionaries, from our actual word-hoard, but it accords with his theory of submission to the restrictions of ordinary language, as one can see from its parallelism to the collocated *foresight* ('urge the mind to aftersight and foresight'), and also in fact from our being unsure whether or not it is already part of our vocabulary until we have looked for it in the dictionaries.

269

The word conforms with the conventions of the everyday English around us in a way that a projected synonym such as *sightafter* or *vision-post* would not.

What is true of word-formation in this example, or of the slightly more linguistically complex 'at smokefall' in 'Burnt Norton' or Thomas's 'windfall light', is true also of syntactical structures, where the poet can exploit the language's own licence but again with adherence to its own restrictions. We have seen earlier in this book that words are related in sentences both by grammar and collocation, that both grammatical analogy and semantic analogy operate when we use language. To take a simple example, in the utterance 'He's an odd sort of man', there is decidedly more restriction upon occupation of the place filled by *sort* than there is upon the place of *odd*, and more upon the place of *odd* than there is upon the place filled by *man*. Moreover, both semantic and grammatical analogy must control the replacement of *odd* and *sort*: the replacements will not merely have to be adjective and noun respectively but will tend to be like *odd* and *sort* semantically as well: *queer* and *type*, for instance.

Now, when in his poem 'Fern Hill' Dylan Thomas uses an expression like *all the sun long*, he is tampering with the paradigmatic system of a phrase which might be set out for ordinary usage as comprising the following terms: 'all the day long', 'all the night long', 'all the week long', and perhaps a few others. The commutation *day/night/week* involves both grammar (a noun) and meaning (a unit of time). By partial compliance with this paradigmatic structure, replacing *day, night, week* by a form which is *grammatically* commutable (another noun, *sun*), Thomas obliges us to consider it as semantically commutable as well, making a new member of the paradigm with *sun* functioning as a unit of time (the notion that is being explored in the poem), *as well as* continuing to carry the semantic value
270

that it has independently of this context: a new member which is a sub-class of one of the existing terms, 'all the day long', because not all days are sunny, and it is the sunniness of his memories of the days that Thomas wishes to convey. Later in the poem, by a further extension of the paradigm, we have 'all the moon long', which is in a similar sub-class relationship to the 'all the night long' of everyday language.

There are many instances of this device in Thomas's poems, some of them with ironic effect, some poignant, some amusing. They admirably illustrate Thomas's striving to infuse with new life the 'vaguenesses' and the 'hollow words' that he refers to in 'Out of the sighs', and they illustrate also the 'submission' to ordinary speech which accompanies and conditions—as Eliot sees it—the paradoxical struggle to move beyond ordinary language.

But how far, we may wonder by this time, does poetry move from 'ordinary language'? For Eliot, after all, poetry 'is essentially a disturbance of the conventional language' and disturbs the conventional consciousness 'by its syntax more than by its sentiments' (F. O. Matthiessen, *The Achievement of T. S. Eliot*, p. 86). And the Hopkins letter already quoted says that the ideal poetic language is 'current language heightened, to any degree heightened and unlike itself, but not an obsolete one'. It would thus appear that if poetry can depart from ordinary language in the direction of creativeness based on the structure of ordinary language it cannot depart from it in the direction of the past.

Yet one may have doubts here too. Whence comes, for instance, the widespread popular belief that the proper language of poetry has an archaic flavour? How does it happen that Hopkins's assertion seems so flatly to contradict Gray's, that 'The language of the age is never the language of poetry'? By what odd chance is it that this seems to be so thoroughly accepted by a general public to whom its author's *Elegy* remains the only poem they know well and a poem which epitomises for them poetic expression at its best? Surely it is the mating of current speech and the poetic tradition from generation to generation that provides poetry with a good deal of that range of licence that Eliot talks of. And does not this range result from the co-existence with the *actually* current of a *potentially* current wealth of linguistic patterns and forms, readily associable in the receiving mind with the discourse of sensibility? It is this potential currency which enables even Eliot to express himself through *a carvèd dolphin* in 'A Game of Chess', though it is doubtful if a dissyllabic *carvèd* is current outside what one might provisionally call the language of the poet; which enables him in 'The Fire Sermon' to postpose an adjective as in 'the young man carbuncular', to use a highly restricted word-order like 'him shall heavenly arms enfold' in 'The Hippopotamus' or 'Issues from the hand of time the simple soul' in 'Animula'. And if it is objected that Eliot expects his reader to react to the echo from else-where—another age, another poem—is not this only an-other way of saying that the poet takes his language not only from that around him, together with what he can add to it by his own creativeness, but also—delicately and selectively—from the accumulated Golden Treasury of the past? Michael Hamburger's lines 'Creation's monster, meta-physical man Across the garden moves his soft machine'; C. Day Lewis's 'Yet fools are the old who won't be taught'; and Edmund Blunden's 'Sweet this morning incense, kind This flood of sun': all these embody linguistic, syntactic arrangements which are not current in everyday speech but which are manifestly current in the language of poetry.

We may accept Hopkins's assertion that poetic language must not be obsolete, if we bear in mind that this can only refer to the use of forms and arrangements which are no longer susceptible of being *received* as poetic. And we may accept Gray's assertion, too, if it can bear the interpretation that the language of poetry tends to be not *merely* the language of the age: it extends from a given age in two directions, so to speak. But it would seem that the extension in one of these directions—the past—is more liable to be suspect, more liable to seem out-worn and to ring false and hollow, than the more difficult and creative extension in the other direction.

And it is especially in this other direction that we find the most striking and interesting, if not the most typical, poetic uses of English: poetry, for example, in which the special use of language *is* the poem. Take the following lines from W. H. Auden's 'It was Easter as I walked':

> Is first baby, warm in mother,
> Before born and is still mother,
> Time passes and now is other,
> Is knowledge in him now of other,
> Cries in cold air, himself no friend.
> In grown man also, may see in face
> In his day-thinking and in his night-thinking
> Is wareness and is fear of other,
> Alone in flesh, himself no friend.

Here we have something of a *tour de force* in which we may well speak (with Eliot) of being disturbed more 'by its syntax than by its sentiments'. The sentiments are fairly straightforward, but Auden may well claim that by his suppression of subject pronouns and articles he has been able to suggest more powerfully the anonymity of the un-born child and relate it to the bitter loneliness of the individual in the larger, less protective matrix of the world.

As so frequently in discussions of this kind, one finds oneself talking of the literary artist in terms of the type *par excellence* of the literary artist, the poet. It is impor-

273

tant to remember that 'current language heightened' can be found in prose also. Few writers, surely, can have indulged more in mimetic syntax than the voluble (if now rarely heard) Carlyle: 'So wags and wavers this unrestful world, day after day, month after month. The streets of Paris, and all cities, roll daily their oscillatory flood' (*The French Revolution*, V. ix). He makes the syntax oscillate with the flood. Not surprisingly, perhaps, *flood* is an important word for Carlyle; notice it in this passage where he is writing of Coleridge:

To sit as a passive bucket and be pumped into, whether you consent or not, can in the long-run be exhilarating to no creature; how eloquent soever the flood of utterance that is descending. But if it be withal a confused unintelligible flood of utterance, threatening to submerge all known landmarks of thought and drown the world and you!—I have heard Coleridge talk, with eager musical energy, two stricken hours, his face radiant and moist, and communicate no meaning whatsoever to any individual of his hearers,—certain of whom, I for one, still kept eagerly listening in hope; the most had long before given up, and formed (if the room were large enough) secondary humming groups of their own. (*John Sterling*, viii.)

It requires no pedestrian *explication de texte* to see here the tie between 'a passive bucket' and the grammatical passive 'be pumped into', but there are other features to note. For example, the sentence which describes the unintelligible flood becomes itself a flood in which the writer is so to speak drowned, and he does not finish it.

More interesting than Carlyle, however, in his syntactic experiments to make language work impressionistically, is Charles Dickens—especially in his maturer writings. While Flora Casby in *Little Dorrit* is his best known comic attempt at a technique analogous to the more recent 'stream of consciousness', the device is rather more ambitious and less of a caricature in a later and minor work, *Mrs Lirriper's Lodgings*:

> I am an old woman now and my good looks are gone but that's me my dear over the plate-warmer and considered like in the times when you used to pay two guineas on ivory and took your chance pretty much how you came out, which made you very careful how you left it about afterwards because people were turned so red and uncomfortable by mostly guessing it was somebody else quite different, and there was once a certain person that put his money in a hop business that came in one morning to pay his rent and respects being the second floor that would have taken it down from its hook and put it in his breast-pocket—you understand my dear—for the L, he says of the original—only there was no mellowness in *his* voice and I wouldn't let him, but his opinion of it you may gather from his saying to it 'Speak to me Emma!' which was far from a rational observation no doubt but still a tribute to its being a likeness, and I think myself it *was* like me when I was young and wore that sort of stays.

Another experimental device which had attractions for Dickens, and which played a more elaborate structural role in some of his later writings, has been called his *surrealist* technique. There is, for instance, the wildly daring interpenetration of sensation and language in the chapter describing a journey 'From Dover to Calais' in *The Uncommercial Traveller*. All one needs to appreciate the linguistic effects is a genuine aptitude for seasickness, and a knowledge of the words of a Victorian ballad by Thomas Moore, the author of 'The Minstrel Boy' and a score of other well-known pieces. The author represents himself as sheltering on deck as best he can, looking at the derisive lights of Dover, the terrifying sea, a lighthouse, and trying *not* to look at a fellow-passenger being audibly sick beneath an umbrella. He tries to keep his mind on happier things than the convulsions of the ship by means of this ballad. As already said, one needs to know the words in advance because Dickens assumes a knowledge of them and does not present them without considerable linguistic interference:

> Rich and rare were the gems she wore,
> And a bright gold ring on her wand she bore;
> But oh her beauty was far beyond
> Her sparkling gems or snow white wand.
>
> Lady! dost thou not fear to stray
> So lone and lovely through this bleak way?
> Are Erin's sons so good or so cold
> As not to be tempted by woman or gold?
>
> Sir Knight, I fear not the least alarm,
> No son of Erin will offer me harm;
> For though they love woman and golden store,
> Sir Knight, they love Honour and Virtue more.
>
> (from *Irish Melodies*, by Thomas Moore.)

There is space here only for some extracts which will illustrate the purposive linguistic fantasy sufficiently, perhaps, to make you want to read or re-read the whole:

> The wind blows stiffly from the Nor-East, the sea runs high, we ship a deal of water . . . I am under a curious compulsion to occupy myself with the Irish melodies . . . 'Rich and rare were the ge-ems she-e-e-e wore, And a bright gold ring on her wa-and she bo-ore, But O her beauty was fa-a-a-a-r beyond'—I am particularly proud of my execution here, when I become aware of another awkward shock from the sea . . . 'Her sparkling gems, or snow-white wand, But O her beauty was fa-a-a-a-a-r beyond'—another awkward one here . . . 'Her spa-a-rkling ge-ems or her Port! port! steady! steady! snow-white fellow-creature at the paddle-box very selfishly audible, bump roar wash white wand.'

As my execution of the Irish melodies partakes of my imperfect perceptions of what is going on around me, so what is going on around me becomes something else than what it is . . . Still, through all this, I must ask her (who was she I wonder!) for the fiftieth time and without ever stopping, Does she not fear to stray, So lone and lovely through this bleak way, And are Erin's sons so good or so cold, As not to be tempted by more fellow-creatures at the paddle-box or gold? Sir Knight I feel not the least alarm, No son of Erin will offer me harm, For though they love fellow-creature with umbrella down again and golden store, Sir Knight they what a tremendous one love honour and virtue more: For though they love Stewards with a bull's-eye bright, they'll trouble you for your ticket, sir—rough passage to-night! (*The Uncommercial Traveller*, ch. 18.)

Still more important is another impressionistic technique which makes an appearance in this passage. From the time when Charles Bally in a classic article examined ' le style indirect libre ' as it had been exploited by Flaubert, many writers have extolled the value of this device in the French novel, but even today it has too often been disregarded as a feature in the English novel both contemporary with and anterior to Flaubert: *Madame Bovary*, it should be remembered, was published in 1857. Its first extensive and serious use in English seems to be by Jane Austen, who achieves with it that sense of realism which is curiously greater when this device rather than direct speech is used to focus our attention on a character's linguistic peculiarities and through them on the character's individual facets of personality. The selfish, hypocritical clucking of Mrs Norris, for example, is often given expression by this means:

Mrs Norris was sorry to say, that the little girl's staying with them, at least as things then were, was quite out of the question. Poor Mr Norris's indifferent state of health made it an impossibility: he could no more bear the noise of a

277

child than he could fly; if indeed he should ever get well of his gouty complaints, it would be a different matter: she should then be glad to take her turn, and think nothing of the inconvenience; but just now, poor Mr Norris took up every moment of her time, and the very mention of such a thing she was sure would distract him. (*Mansfield Park*, ch. 1.)

The value of the technique lies not only in the subtlety with which fast flowing narrative can be coloured by the characteristic idiom of a particular speaker, but also in the ability to convey the unspoken reflection of the speaker in the suggested language of his reflection—and even the suggested impact of one speaker upon another—without the clumsiness of explanation which would coarsen and over-sharpen the impression, and fatally simplify what the author would prefer to leave equivocal. Consider this further example from *Mansfield Park* (ch. 33): 'Mr Crawford was no longer the Mr Crawford who, as the clandestine, insidious, treacherous admirer of Maria Bertram, had been [Fanny's] abhorrence. . . . He was now the Mr Crawford who was addressing herself with ardent, disinterested, love.' This has the grammatical structure of reported interior monologue without the operative verb that would declare it so; in consequence, the reader cannot tell exactly how much of this is indeed Fanny's reflection and how much is endorsed by the author as narrator: in particular, is an omniscient author telling us that Crawford's ardent love *is* disinterested or have we only Fanny's fallible opinion? 'Free Indirect Speech' enables the author to leave the reader wondering.

Dickens was keenly alive to the potentialities of this device and we find it put to subtle and effective use throughout his writings. To illustrate his skill, we may cite a simple instance for which we happen to have his source. In January 1850, *The Household Narrative* printed the report of a boy giving evidence in an assault case. The report uses the direct speech of undistinguished journalism:

Alderman Humphrey: Well, do you know what you are about? Do you know what an oath is? Boy: No. Alderman: Can you read? Boy: No. Alderman: Do you ever say your prayers? Boy: No, never. Alderman: Do you know what prayers are? Boy: No. Alderman: Do you know what God is? Boy: No. Alderman: Do you know what the devil is? Boy: I've heard of the devil, but I don't know him. Alderman: What do you know? Boy: I knows how to sweep the crossings.

Now, let us see what Dickens makes of this in the eleventh chapter of Bleak House, when the Coroner interrogates Jo, the crossing-sweeper boy:

Here he is, very muddy, very hoarse, very ragged. Now, boy!—But stop a minute. Caution. This boy must be put through a few preliminary paces.

Name, Jo. Nothing else that he knows on. Don't know that everybody has two names. Never heerd of sich a think. Don't know that Jo is short for a longer name. Thinks it long enough for *him*. *He* don't find no fault with it. Spell it? No. *He* can't spell it. No father, no mother, no friends. Never been to school. What's home? Knows a broom's a broom, and knows it's wicked to tell a lie. Don't recollect who told him about the broom, or about the lie, but knows both. Can't exactly say what'll be done to him arter he's dead if he tells a lie to the gentlemen here, but believes it'll be something wery bad to punish him, and serve him right —and so he'll tell the truth.

In this passage, free indirect speech has enabled Dickens to give us simultaneously the narrative of the interrogation, the sequence of question, answer, and record, the boy's reaction, the boy's impact on the coroner and perhaps also on the clerk whose muttered, truncated note-taking is also suggested.

Important mimetic and impressionistic devices have been evolved, then, for prose as well as for verse. But poetry offers one outstanding possibility for the disturbance of ordinary syntax that prose does not, through the fact that metre provides units—the stanza, the couplet, the line—which have a 'syntax' of their own. And this 'syntax' may (as usually, perhaps) either have a precise correspondence with ordinary syntax and so endorse it; or it may be significantly in contrast with it.

For example, it is normal for Eliot's metrical unit (the line) to be at the same time a grammatical unit, as in

> Tell her I bring the horoscope myself:
> One must be so careful these days.

By contrast, let us re-read the opening lines of this section of 'The Waste Land':

> April is the cruellest month, breeding
> Lilacs out of the dead land, mixing
> Memory and desire, stirring
> Dull roots with spring rain.

Here the 'ordinary syntax' (marked by punctuation) is supplemented by a 'poetic syntax' (whose units are marked by the lines), suggesting a connexion between breeding and the cruelness of April, pointing the paradox of lilacs and dead land, and commenting upon the stirring of memory and desire.

It should now be apparent that there is a close similarity between what has here been called 'poetic syntax' and the contextual relationship of words through *collocation*, which was discussed earlier in this book (for example, Chapters 8, 13, 14). What Eliot calls, in a rather special sense, the *music* of a word is

at a point of intersection: it arises from its relation first to the words immediately preceding and following it, and indefinitely to the rest of the context; and from another

280

relation, that of its immediate meaning in that context to all other meanings which it has had in other contexts, to its greater or less wealth of associations. . . . This is an 'allusiveness' which is not the fashion or eccentricity of a peculiar type of poetry; but an allusiveness which is in the nature of words, and which is equally the concern of every kind of poet. ('The Music of Poetry'.)

Nor of course is this solely a property of words in poetry. In the writing of another Eliot (*Adam Bede*, Ch. 6), we are made to hear that 'the calves are bleating from the home croft', and it is worth pondering on why this unusual collocation has been chosen. Hugh Kenner, in *The Poetry of Ezra Pound* (p. 256), goes so far as to define 'le mot juste' in terms of the reciprocal tension which is operating between words independently of their grammatical relationship; he points the distinction in suggesting that whereas this grammatical relationship can survive even a poor translation, the former tends to be lost even in a careful, sensitive one.

We may perhaps clinch the point by looking at two very different translations which confirm the importance of observing both grammatical and lexical relationships. The text translated is from Horace's *Odes* (I. xxxvi):

> Omnes in Damalin putres
> deponent oculos nec Damalis nouo
> diuelletur adultero
> lasciuis hederis ambitiosior.

The first translation was done by Conington in the nineteenth century:

> Every melting eye will rest
> On Damalis' lovely face: but none may part
> Damalis from our new-found guest;
> She clings, and clings, like ivy, round his heart.

The second is the more recent translation by C. K. Ogden:

> Though all on beauteous Damalis
> Repose their putrid optics twain,
> Never will that ambitchious miss
> Unclasp her last adulterous swain;
> Like ivy clinging to the oak
> Lasciviously, she's nailed her bloke.

It is impossible in a sketch of this kind to bring out the full richness and complexity of language in literature. We have, however, attempted in this chapter to draw together some of the threads of thought and argument that have been spun earlier, by showing that the use of English in literature involves an 'intolerable wrestle' similar in kind if not in degree to the one we face in our own day to day use of English. Our concern in this book is how words are used and how they make their impact, whether spoken on the top of a bus or printed on handlaid paper in a slim, expensive volume. And it has seemed fitting to conclude by reflecting that English at its best—when poets have wrestled with it—has a value not only in what they make it say, but also in showing us how subtly, richly, powerfully our language can be used.

Exercises and Topics for Discussion

1   Analyse what can be achieved by the following phrases, and explain their connexion with everyday English: 'once below a time', 'once upon a dream', 'dressed to die', 'a grief ago'.
2   Examine in some detail the way in which the words of 'Rich and rare' become fused with the objective and subjective events which take place in the passage from *The Uncommercial Traveller*.

3 Explain fully and precisely the value of 'free indirect speech' in the passage quoted from *Bleak House*, and examine the use of this device in a novel of your own choice by a present-day writer.

4 Analyse the relationships of the italicised words in the following, and find further instances of this richness in other poems.

    (*a*) Tell me, moon, thou pale and gray
        Pilgrim of heaven's homeless way . . . (Shelley.)
    (*b*) Full many a glorious morning have I seen
        Flatter the mountain-tops with sovereign eye . . .
                                  (Shakespeare.)
    (*c*) Lay your sleeping head, my love,
        Human on my faithless arm . . . (Auden.)
    (*d*) Let the winds of dawn that blow
        Softly round your dreaming head . . . (Auden.)

5 Compare the two translations of Horace, noting the contrast in tone and the means by which the tone is established in each.

6 With the material of this chapter and earlier chapters in mind, study and discuss the following:

    (*a*) The winged bull trundles to the wired perimeter.
        Cumbrously turns. Shivers, brakes clamped,
        Bellowing four times, each engine tested
        With routine ritual. Advances to the runway.
        Halts again as if gathering heart
        Or warily snuffing for picador cross-winds.
        Then, then, a roar open-throated
        Affronts the arena. Then fast, faster
        Drawn by the magnet of his *idée fixe*,
        Head down, tail up, he's charging the horizon.
           And the grass of the airfield grows smooth as a
            fur.
        The runway's elastic and we the projectile;

Installations control-tower mechanics parked aero-
planes—
Units all woven to a ribbon unreeling,
Concrete melts and condenses to an abstract
Blur, and our blood thickens to think of
Rending, burning, as suburban terraces
Make for us, wave after wave.
                                        The moment
Of Truth is here. We can only trust,
Being as wholly committed to other hands
As a babe at birth, Europa to the bull god.
                        (from 'Flight to Italy', by C. Day Lewis.)

(b) GEORGE: . . . Shall I tell you a story? Yes, do tell
        me a story. Well, it happened to me when I was
        in the R.A.F. during the war.

    RUTH: I didn't know you were. You've never men-
        tioned it.

    GEORGE: The one thing I never shoot lines about
        is the R.A.F. Just a gap in my life. That's all. Well,
        it happened like this: It was one night in particu-
        lar, when it wasn't my turn to go on ops. Instead,
        we got a basinful of what we gave the Jerries,
        smack bang in the middle of the camp. I remem-
        ber flinging myself down, not so much on to the
        earth as into it. A wing commander type pitched
        himself next to me, and, together, we shared his
        tin-helmet. Fear ran through the whole of my
        body, the strange fear that my right leg would be
        blown off, and how terrible it would be. Suddenly
        the wingco shouted at me above the din: 'What's
        your profession?' 'Actor,' I said. The moment I
        uttered that word, machine-gun fire and bombs
        all around us, the name of my calling, my whole
        reason for existence—it sounded so hideously
        trivial and unimportant, so divorced from living,
        and the real world, that my fear vanished. All I
        could feel was shame. (*Epitaph for George Dillon*,
        by John Osborne and Anthony Creighton.)

(c) The human brain functions by making comparisons. Every individual, faced with a particular situation, deals with it by comparison with other situations through which he has passed, which have left their imprint on the memory system of the brain. Each new situation is matched by this memory system, until an adequate response is produced. Obviously there is no brief way of describing the method by which this matching and selection are achieved; indeed we do not know how it is done. When we make a real effort to find out we shall have made a tremendous step forward.

Yet, we can see already that there is something cognate between the aspects of any situation that we select for attention and observation, and the motor response by which we deal with it. The brain reacts to those features of environmental change that have produced effective motor responses in the past. In particular, it selects features that it can call to the attention of others by a name. This is the activity that gives language its central importance in determining both the observations a doctor makes and the actions he takes on behalf of his patient; and that is why it is impossible for science or medicine to proceed with the motto *nullius in verba*. To a large extent words determine observations. We see what we can name and speak about, neglecting the rest.

Anyone who studies the fashions and conventions of a science at any epoch must be struck by this fact. For example, at present many physiologists make observations on nerve impulses and the excitation of one nerve-cell by another. Few try to study the processes by which organisms discriminate visual forms. Most physiologists would probably say that the time is not ripe for this, and that we have no language adequate to deal with such complex processes. But how are we to make the time ripe? Does language develop automatically? The matter has been so little investigated that it is difficult to be sure, but it seems that a science goes on finding out more and more detail within one language system until new comparisons are introduced —usually as a result of the discovery of a new technique or invention in a different field. (J. Z. Young in *Studies in Communication*, 1955.)

SUPPLEMENT I

The Transmission of English

BY

A. C. GIMSON

Professor of Phonetics in the University of London

The Transmission of English

1 SPEECH AND WRITING

WE use language primarily as a means of communication with other human beings. Each of us shares with the community in which we live a store of words and meanings as well as agreed conventions as to the way in which these words should be arranged to convey a particular message; the English speaker has at his disposal a vocabulary and a set of grammatical rules which enable him to communicate his thoughts and feelings, in a variety of styles, to other English speakers. His vocabulary, in particular, both that which he uses actively and that which he recognises, increases in size as he grows older, as a result of education and experience. But, whether the language store is relatively small or large, the system remains no more than a psychological reality for the individual, unless he has a means of expressing it in terms able to be perceived by another member of his linguistic community; he has to give the system a concrete, transmission, form. We take for granted the two most common forms of transmission—by means of sounds produced by our vocal organs (speech) or by visual signs (writing). Yet these are among the most striking of human achievements.

Speech, as was seen in Chapter 3, must be considered the primary means of using language both for the individual and for the community. We normally speak, using words and a restricted grammar, several years before we acquire the more sophisticated medium of writing. In the history of language, too, alphabetic writing develops from speech, in the sense that, originally, such writing sets out to mirror the sounds of speech. Moreover, in our everyday lives, we make use of speech as a vehicle for language, either in speaking or in listening, far more frequently than visual signs, either in reading or in writing. It is, therefore, reasonable to consider the spoken form of language to be its primary and most important manifestation and to base our first analysis of linguistic usage on speech.

2   THE MECHANISM OF SPEECH

The infant is able to produce sounds and tunes from its mouth long before it is able to organise these sounds within any linguistic framework: it is, moreover, capable of hearing and reacting to sounds, and, at an early age, shows considerable powers of mimicry. But it must be remembered that man, in speaking, has imposed habits on certain organs of the body which have quite other primary biological functions; our use of the respiratory tract (lungs, larynx, pharynx, mouth and nasal cavity) for speech must be regarded as a secondary activity of these organs.

Any effective act of speech, learnt by a human being over years of trial and error, is an exceedingly complex operation. The transmission in sound of the simplest concept in the mind involves the setting in motion of a complicated chain of events. The psychological stimulus, conveyed to the organs of speech by the nervous system, activates the lungs, the larynx and the cavities above in such a way that they perform a series of movements which, as we have learned by experience, will have the effect of producing a particular pattern of sound (the *articulation* stage of speech). These movements of the organs of speech create in the air variations of pressure which will be received by a listener's hearing apparatus. This information is transmitted through the nervous system to the brain, where the linguistic interpretation of the message takes place (the *reception* stage of communication by speech). The hearing apparatus of the speaker also functions as a mechanism controlling his own speech.

Though the listener's reaction as well as the speaker's activity must be taken into account when considering what is linguistically relevant in the sound signals transmitted in speech, the analysis of the sound material of speech will obviously be concerned mainly with the articulatory stage. We must, therefore, examine the role in speech of the organs mentioned above.

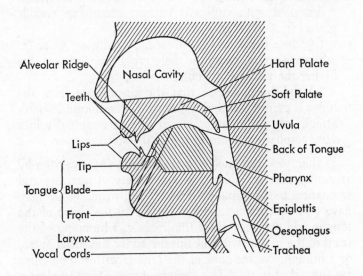

1 *Lungs.* The lungs supply our most usual source of energy in speech, the air-stream being directed outwards through the mouth or nose, or both. Sometimes, we make noises which do not require lung air, e.g. the *tut-tut* of irritation, but such sounds must be considered extra to the normal sound-inventory used in English.

2 *Vocal cords.* These are contained in the larynx (a

hard casing which may be felt—the 'Adam's apple') and consist of two folds of ligament and elastic tissue which may be brought together or parted; the opening between the cords is called the *glottis*. Biologically, the cords act as a valve to prevent the entry into the trachea and lungs of any foreign body, or, when closed, assist in any muscular effort of the arms or abdomen. In speech, they may assume a variety of positions:

(*a*) Wide open, allowing the air to escape freely as in breathing (as when we say an *s*), or, when the air-stream is expelled with sufficient energy, producing audible glottal friction (as in a strong *h* sound);

(*b*) close together and vibrating, producing *voice* (as when we say *ah* or *z*), the more rapid the vibration, the higher the pitch of the note;

(*c*) tightly closed, so that the air-pressure from the lungs is pent up behind the closure—the so-called 'hard-attack' or 'glottal stop' which may occur initially in a very emphatic pronunciation of the word *anyone*.

3   *Pharynx and mouth cavities.* These upper cavities by assuming different shapes, give a variety of qualities and resonances to the sound produced. Thus, vowel sounds may have their quality determined largely by the shape of the tongue and the position of the lips, e.g. a humping of the front of the tongue with the lips spread for the vowel in *tea*, or a humping of the back of the tongue with rounded lips for the vowel in *two*. This change of shape may be clearly felt if the vowels *ee* and *oo* are said one after the other. Alternatively, there may be a complete closure made by the lips or by the tongue with some part of the roof of the mouth, e.g. the lips in *p*, *b*, or the tongue and the upper gums (alveolar ridge) in *t*, *d*; or there may be a narrowing which causes friction, e.g. between the lower lip and the upper teeth in *f*, *v*, between the tongue and the teeth in *th*

sounds, or between the tongue and the alveolar ridge in
s, z; or again, there may be a contact simply of the tongue
tip, e.g. on the upper alveolar ridge in the case of l.

4 *Nasal cavity*. In normal breathing, the soft palate is
in its lowered position, allowing the air to escape through
the nose. In English speech, we usually have this type of
air escape only in conjunction with a complete closure
in the mouth, e.g. in the sounds of m, n, ng; all other
English sounds are said with the soft palate in its raised
position, the nasal cavity being shut off. If the nasal passage
is blocked, as when we have a cold, our m, n, ng sounds may
cease to be nasal and become b, d, g (*bordig* for *morning*).

In general terms, the English vowel sounds may be said
to be characterised by voice, given various resonances
(qualities) by the position of the tongue and lips; the consonant sounds may be voiced or voiceless, with a closure
or narrowing in the upper cavities, and, in the case of
m, n, ng, with the addition of the nasal cavity.

3   THE SIGNIFICANT ENGLISH SOUNDS (PHONEMES)

It is possible to describe the articulation of any sound
produced by the organs of speech but, when we speak,
there is a continuously changing pattern of movement and
sound which it is not always easy to reduce to small seg-
ments. Articulations merge into one another, or, alternatively, more than one articulation may count as a single
sound in the language. It is important, therefore, to determine which sound distinctions are significant in English.
If we compare monosyllabic words, we may find that a
change of meaning is related to a variation of one part of
the syllable, at the centre or the margins. In this way, we
can establish that there are a certain number of *oppositions*
possible in various positions in the syllable; we can then
give a general articulatory label or identification to each
of the terms or classes in this series of oppositions. Such

distinctive terms or classes are known as *phonemes*; the oppositions between them are said to be phonemic.

1 *Central in the syllable—vowels*. If we compare the pronunciation of the following monosyllables, in one widespread type of British English, we find that they differ in their central element, to which a labelling symbol is here assigned in / /[1]:

heed/i/; hid/ɪ/; head/e/; had/æ/; hard/ɑ/; hod/ɒ/; hoard/ɔ/; hood/ʊ/; heard/ɜ/; hide /aɪ/,

giving a series of 10 oppositional central elements. But the /i/ of *heed* also occurs in *feel*, which may be opposed to:

fool/u/; foal/əʊ/; fowl/ɑʊ/; fail/eɪ/; foil/ɔɪ/,

giving an additional 5 oppositions. Again, the /i/ of *feel* occurs in *bead*, which may be opposed to:

bud/ʌ/; beard/ɪə/; bared/eə/,

adding 3 more; and the /i/ of *bead* occurs in *pea*, which is opposed to *poor*/ʊə/. We thus have a total of 19 oppositions or phonemes in this vowel position in the syllable. Some speakers may add another by opposing *saw*/ɔ/ to *sore*/ɔə/.

If we take into account the unaccented parts of polysyllables, we find, in addition to the above oppositions, one other illustrated by the pair *city, sitter*, /ɪ/ to /ə/. Our total inventory of central syllabic oppositions consists, therefore, of 20 (or 21) phonemes for this type of English.

But if we examine the precise quality of these vowel

[1] It is customary in linguistic description to enclose a transcription denoting phonemic categories in / / and one which shows precise phonetic values in [ ]. The symbols used here are those of the alphabet of the International Phonetic Association, the use of which is described in a pamphlet obtainable from the Secretary of the Association, at University College, London, W.C.1.

phonemes, as they occur when the words are uttered, we may distinguish three types:

(a) short—7
     hid, head, had, bud, hod, hood, sitter
     /ɪ   e   æ   ʌ   ɒ   ʊ   ə/

(b) long pure (non-gliding)—5
      heed, fool, hard, hoard, heard
      /iː uː ɑː ɔː ɜː/
(where the additional symbol [ː] after the vowel sign indicates length)

(c) long gliding (diphthongal, composite)—8
fail, foal, hide, fowl, foil, beard, bared, poor
/eɪ əʊ aɪ   aʊ   ɔɪ   ɪə   eə   ʊə/
i.e. 3 glides to [ɪ], 2 to [ʊ], and 3 to [ə] (with the possible additional glide /ɔə/ to [ə]).

If we compare the tongue-raising of the first two types, in terms of the region of the mouth in which it takes place (front, centre or back) and the degree of raising (close, i.e. high in the mouth, or open, i.e. low in the mouth), we can establish a table of rough articulatory relationships:

	Front	Centre	Back
Close	iː		uː
	ɪ		ʊ
	e	ɜː	
		ə	ɔː
	æ		
		ʌ	
Open		ɑː	ɒ

(The English back vowels usually have some degree of lip-rounding associated with them.)

In the same way, the glides may be represented thus:

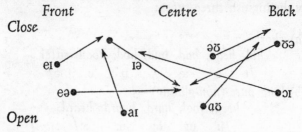

Front   Centre   Back

Notes:

(i) The so-called 'long pure' vowels are often pronounced with a slight glide; they are 'pure' in a relative sense, compared with the considerable glide of the diphthongs.

(ii) /ə/ differs from other vowel phonemes in that it occurs only in syllables which are unaccented.

(iii) Some vowel phonemes occur more frequently in connected speech than others, /ə/ and /ɪ/ being the most common and /ɔɪ/ and /ʊə/ the rarest.

(iv) The long vowels and diphthongs are considerably shorter when a voiceless consonant (e.g. *p, t, s*) follows in the same syllable; cf. /iː/ in *bead* and *beat,* /eɪ/ in *plays* and *place.* Thus, the opposition between *bead*/iː/ and *bid*/ɪ/ is achieved by a complex of quality and length, whereas that between *beat*/iː/ (= [i]) and *bit*/ɪ/ is primarily one of quality.

(v) The English diphthongal phonemes have all the prominence associated with the first element, e.g. the [e] element of /eɪ/ is long compared with [ɪ], which is only lightly and briefly touched upon.

(vi) Some linguists (especially in America) analyse the long vowels and diphthongs as complex syllabic units made up of combinations of the short vowels with /ə/ (or /h/), /j/ and /w/ (see following section for these

296

consonantal phonemes), e.g. /iː/ = /ɪj/ or /ij/, /ɑː/ = /aə/ or /ah/, /eɪ/ = /ej/, /əʊ/ = /əw/, etc. If this is done, the basic vowel phonemes are the 7 short syllabics.

2 *Marginal in the syllable—consonants.* If we examine in the same way those sounds which occur at syllable boundaries, we can establish a list of consonantal phonemes. Thus, by comparing the following initial oppositions in monosyllables, we arrive at twelve phonemes:

pin/p/, *bin*/b/, *tin*/t/, *din*/d/, *kin*/k/, *chin*/tʃ/, *gin*/dʒ/, *fin*/f/, *thin*/θ/, *sin*/s/, *shin*/ʃ/, *win*/w/.

Four more phonemes are added by the oppositions:

tame, dame, game/g/, *lame*/l/, *maim*/m/, *name*/n/;

three more by:

pot, tot, yacht/j/, *hot*/h/, *rot*/r/;

two more by:

pie, tie, thigh, thy/ð/, *vie*/v/;

and one more by:

two, do, zoo/z/,

giving a total of 22 consonantal oppositions in syllable initial positions.

Most of these phonemes are also distinctive in final positions, but, in the present analysis, /w, j, h, r/ do not occur finally. On the other hand, the final /ŋ/ of *sung* (opposed to *some, sun*) occurs only after a vowel, and the medial /ʒ/ of *leisure* (opposed to *letter, leather*) occurs only between vocalic sounds, or, occasionally, finally in such a word as *rouge*. Thus, in positions following the vowel, there are 21 possible consonantal oppositions, though for any term in the series the occurrence may be restricted, e.g. /ŋ/ occurs normally only after /i, æ, ʌ, ɒ/.

In all positions, we have the possibility of 24 consonantal phonemes, of which 6 (/w, j, h, r, ŋ, ʒ/) have restricted occurrence.

These consonantal phonemes may be labelled and classified according to their general articulatory characteristics, i.e. taking into consideration the place and organs of articulation, the type of obstruction to the air-stream, and the presence of vibration of the vocal cords (voice):

(i) *Place of articulation*

Bilabial—articulation by the two lips—/p, b, m, w/

Labio-dental—articulation by the lower lip and upper teeth—/f, v/

Dental—articulation by the tongue and upper teeth —/θ, ð/

Alveolar—articulation by the tongue and upper teeth ridge—/t, d, n, s, z, l/

Post-alveolar—articulation by the tongue and the back part of the teeth ridge—/r/

Palato-alveolar—articulation by the tongue and both teeth ridge and hard palate—/tʃ, dʒ, ʃ, ʒ/

Palatal—articulation by the tongue and hard palate —/j/

V*elar*—articulation by the tongue and soft palate— /k, g, ŋ/

Glottal—articulation largely in the glottis—/h/

(ii) *Type of articulation*

Stop—involving a total interruption of the air-stream

Plosive—a total closure with possible rapid explosive release—/p, b, t, d, k, g/

Affricate—a total closure with slow, fricative release—/tʃ, dʒ/

Continuant—the air-stream escaping with different
degrees of freedom

Nasal—a total closure in the mouth, but, the soft
palate being lowered, a free escape of air through
the nose—/m, n, ŋ/

Non-fricative (lateral)—a point closure made between the tongue and the teeth ridge, with free
escape of air at the sides—/l/

Non-fricative (vowel-like)—a relatively free escape
of air, with no great constriction or closure—
/w, j, r/

Fricative—a constriction sufficiently close to produce friction—/f, v, θ, ð, s, z, ʃ, ʒ, h/

(iii) Voicing. Certain consonants are typically said with
relatively great energy (*fortis*) and are never voiced—
/p, t, k, tʃ, f, θ, s, ʃ, h/; others are more weakly arti-
culated (*lenis*) and may be voiced—/b, d, g, dʒ, m, n,
ŋ, l, w, j, r, v, ð, z, ʒ/.

The following table classifies these consonantal articulations, the voiceless (*fortis*) articulation, in the case of pairs,
being placed on the left:

	Bilabial	Labio-dental	Dental	Alveolar
Stop—Plosive	p, b			t, d
Affricate				
Continuant—Nasal	m			n
Non-fricative (lateral)				l
Non-fricative (vowel-like)	w			
Fricative		f, v	θ, ð	s, z

299

	Post-Alveolar	Palato-Alveolar	Palatal	Velar	Glottal
Stop—Plosive				k, g	(ʔ)
Affricate		tʃ, dʒ			
Continuant—Nasal				ŋ	
Non-fricative (lateral)					
Non-fricative (vowel-like)	r		j		
Fricative		ʃ, ʒ			h

Notes:

(*i*) The alveolar consonants /t, d, n, l, s/, followed by /ð/, have the highest frequency of occurrence in connected speech, while /θ, ʒ/ occur the least frequently. The high place of /ð/, despite a restricted list of words containing this phoneme, may be accounted for by the existence of such common words as *the*, *that*, etc., with /ð/.

(*ii*) *Vowel-like consonants.* Certain of the consonants included in the table above share phonetic or distributional characteristics with vowels. /j/ and /w/, being equivalent to short [i] and [u] and often called semi-vowels, are most frequently entirely vowel-like in their articulation, i.e. they do not involve a complete closure of the organs of speech nor a stricture producing friction; but they behave like consonants in that they do not occur centrally in the syllable. Moreover, in certain situations, e.g. in *tune* /tjuːn/ and *quite* /kwait/, they tend to be both voiceless and fricative, i.e. phonetically consonantal. /r/, too, frequently has an articulation similar to that of a vowel (and, in some kinds of English, functions as a syllabic centre, e.g. *water* ['wɔːtr̩][1]), but again this phoneme is generally marginal in the syllable, and sometimes

---

[1] ' indicates that the following syllable carries a stress accent; , below or above a symbol indicates that the consonant is syllabic.

is voiceless and fricative, e.g. in *try* /traɪ/ and *cry* /kraɪ/.

/m, n, l/, on the other hand, have the total or partial closure typical of consonant articulations, yet, being voiced, non-fricative continuants, frequently have the central syllabic function of vowels, e.g. in the polysyllables *rhythm* ['rɪðm̩], *sudden* ['sʌdn̩], *middle* ['mɪdl̩]. Thus, in the following two lines from 'Come live with me and be my love' by C. Day Lewis, the words *handle* and *maiden*, normally pronounced ['hændl̩, 'meɪdn̩], must for metrical reasons be taken as consisting of two syllables, the second being furnished by /l/ and /n/ without a vowel:

'I'll handle dainties on the docks. . . .'
'Care on thy maiden brow shall put. . . .'

/m, n, l/, therefore, and sometimes /ŋ/ (e.g. in *bacon*, if pronounced ['beɪkŋ̩]), function both as consonants and as vowels.

(*iii*) *Voice as a distinctive feature*. The pairs of consonants /p, b; t, d; k, g; tʃ, dʒ; f, v; θ, ð; s, z; ʃ, ʒ/ are shown in the table above as being distinguished by the presence of voice. This opposition, however, operates only in medial positions, e.g. *caper—caber, writer—rider, catches—cadges, racer—razor*, etc. In initial, accented positions, the plosives are distinguished rather by the puff of air (aspiration) accompanying the stronger series /p, t, k/, cf. *pie—buy, two—do, curl—girl*, whereas, in the case of the so-called voice (lenis) members of the other pairs, partial voicing and weak articulation are distinctive.

When these consonants follow a vowel or voiced continuant consonant, the opposition relies less on the presence or absence of voice than on the reduction of the length of the preceding vowel or continuant consonant before /p, t, k, tʃ, f, θ, s/, cf. *rope—robe, write—ride*,

back—bag, lunch—lunge, leaf—leave, loath—loathe,
pence—pens, etc. (Initial and final oppositions between
/ʃ/ and /ʒ/ do not arise, since /ʒ/ does not occur initially
and only exceptionally in final positions.)

(iv) /tʃ, dʒ/ *as simple or complex phonemes.* Native
speakers usually feel that the words, *chin, gin* consist
of three distinctive elements in the same way as *tin, kin,*
din, etc. Nevertheless, it is possible to make a more economical statement of the consonantal phonemes if /tʃ, dʒ/
are treated as /t/ + /ʃ/ and /d/ + /ʒ/. A difficulty arises
when /t/ and /ʃ/ come together at the boundaries of
adjacent morphemes (this being no problem in the case
of /dʒ/ since /ʒ/ does not occur initially). Thus, the /t/
and /ʃ/ of *hat-shop* are not as close-knit, nor is the /ʃ/
as short, as in the case of /tʃ/ in *ketchup*. The difficulty
is overcome if the sequence of /t/ + /ʃ/ is distinguished
from the close-knit form /tʃ/ by means of a space or
special sign, e.g. /ˈhæt ʃɒp. ˈhæt + ʃɒp/.

(v) *Glottal stop.* A consonantal articulation which
occurs frequently in many kinds of English but which
often has no distinctive function of its own is the glottal
stop [ʔ], where the total closure is made by the vocal
cords. This articulation is used:

(a) generally, for emphasis on an initial, accented
vowel, e.g. *anyhow* [ˈʔenɪhaʊ], or as a syllable-marker at
a vowel hiatus, e.g. *geometry* [dʒɪˈʔɒmətrɪ];

(b) as a reinforcement of final /p, t, k, tʃ/, either before
the consonant, or at the same time as it, or as a replacement for /p, t, k/, e.g. in *sharp, luck, much* [ʃɑːʔp, lʌʔk,
mʌʔtʃ];

(c) in various dialects, to replace medial /t/, e.g.
daughter [ˈdɔːʔə], *mutton* [ˈmʌʔn̩], and, less frequently
/p/, e.g. *supper* [ˈsʌʔə], and /k/, e.g. *lucky* [ˈlʌʔɪ].

(vi) /w/—/ʍ/. In several kinds of English, *witch,*

302

wine, weather, etc., are distinguished from *which, whine, whether*, etc., by the use of a voiceless fricative [ʍ] initially in the second group or by a complex /hw/.

3   *Phoneme Clusters.* Only a restricted number of all the possible combinations of the English phonemes occur. We have already seen, for instance, that long vowels and diphthongs do not normally precede /ŋ/; or again, /e, æ, ʌ, ɒ, ʊ/ do not occur finally. Consonant clusters, initially and finally in the syllable, are also limited in their types.

Initially, for example, /tʃ, dʒ, ð, z/ do not combine with other consonants; /v, h/ combine only with /j/ (*view, hue*); /b, d, g, θ, s, ʃ/ occur only as the first members of clusters (*brown, dune, grow, through, spot, shrink*); /r, j, w/ occur only as non-initial members (*pray, pew, dwarf*); initial clusters of three consonants must consist of /s/ + /p, t, k/ + /l, r, j, w/ (*splint, spray, spew, stray, stew, scream, skewer, square, sclerosis*). Certain initial sequences such as /ðr/, /zw/, /fs/, /mh/, /nd/, /rw/, /tl/, /dl/, /stl/, /spw/ are un-English. Others, such as /fθ/ in *phthisis* or /zl/ in *zloty*, occur only in rare learned or foreign words.

Finally, even if cases of syllabic /m, n, l/ are excluded, more numerous combinations of consonants occur because of the addition of such morphemic, inflexional elements as /s, z, t, d, θ/, e.g. /lp, lps, lpt/ (*help, helps, helped*), /ks, kst, ksts, ksθ, ksθs/ (*fix, fixed, texts, sixth, sixths*), /lm, lmz, lmd/ (*film, films, filmed*), /ps, pt, mps, mpst/ (*drops, dropped, glimpse, glimpsed*), etc. Nevertheless, many possibilities are excluded, e.g. /h, r/ (and /j, w/ in the present analysis) do not occur finally alone or in clusters; only /l/ may occur before non-syllabic /m, n/, but non-syllabic /l/ does not precede final /g, ð, ŋ/; only /t, s/ normally constitute the last member of a cluster of four consonants. Thus, such final combinations as /hf/, /nm/, /lð/, /ʃp/, /mpsp/

303

are un-English, and, in the type of English being considered, such clusters as /rt, rst/ are unknown.

This restriction of sequential possibilities means that the succession of phonemes in a word is to some extent pre-determined by what precedes, e.g. word initial /ð/ must be followed by a vowel; a consonant must follow /e, æ, ʌ, ɒ, ʊ/; word initial /st/ must be followed by a vowel or by /r, j/, etc.

4 THE FUNCTION AND IDENTITY OF PHONEMES

We have referred to phonemes as significant elements of speech, i.e. the use of one or other phoneme may change the meaning of a word. In this sense, phonemes are meaningful, but on a lower level than the morpheme or word of which usually they are a constituent part. It is rare for an English phoneme to constitute a word. In the present phonetic analysis of English, examples of words consisting of a single phoneme would be: /ɑː/ (are), /ɔː/ (awe, or), /aɪ/ (I, eye), /ɪə/ (ear), /eə/ (air). Single phonemes are sometimes meaningful outside the usual linguistic system: thus, /əʊ/ (Oh!), /ɜː/, /m/ (hesitation noises), /ɔɪ/ (summoning attention), /ʃ/ (calling for silence). More frequently, a single phoneme may constitute a morphemic element of a word, e.g. /s/ in (laɪts/ (lights, light's) means plural, possessive, light + the unaccented form of is, has, or the third person singular of the verb to light, as does /z/ in /rɪŋz/ (rings, ring's); or /ə/ in /ˈbɪɡə, ˈraɪtə/ (bigger, writer) means the comparative form of an adjective or the 'actor' form of a noun. The examples of /s, z/ given above illustrate the fact that a phonetic entity may have several morphemic functions or that a single morpheme, e.g. plurality in a noun, may be realised by more than one phoneme. To this extent, single phonemes are meaningful at the word or morpheme level. But, generally, they function as constituent parts of a word or morpheme composed of several phonemes; in such cases, their

304

meaning is oppositional rather than intrinsic. For instance, the meaning of /p/ in *pin* is not so much that it is /p/, but rather that, together with the subsequent phoneme sequence /-ɪn/, it is not *bin* or *tin* or *din* or any other words with a different first phoneme, or, as in the case of *in*, with no phoneme in this place—zero phoneme.

A phoneme, in our analysis, may correspond to what we perceive, or may learn to perceive, as more than one sound segment. Although every sound we utter contains variations of quality which are revealed by instrumental techniques of analysis, we tend to hear the /ɪ/ of *bit* or the /s/ of *sit*, for instance, as consisting of an unvarying stretch of quality. But we have seen that we may treat a gliding sound such as English /aɪ/ as a complex but single phonemic unit, occurring centrally in a syllable. Similarly, but less obviously to the English ear, the initial /p/ of *pin* consists of more than one sound segment. The bilabial plosive [p] is followed by aspiration [h], i.e. a puff of air before the vowel. But, in English, there is only a two-term opposition of bilabial plosives (*pin—bin*), in which the aspiration feature is present mainly in initial, accented positions, but is less relevant in, for instance, medial unaccented positions (*rapid—rabid*). It is simpler, therefore, to treat [h] as a constituent element of /p/ in initial, accented positions. In the same way, the /t/ of *tin* often has an [s] quality following the release of the plosive; again, since [tˢ] is here a variant of, and not in opposition to, [tʰ], we consider the complex as a single phonemic entity.

Allophonic variants. The phonemes which we have established for English are based on oppositions; they are, although we have given them for convenience general articulatory labels, negative and abstract concepts. In concrete terms, as far as the pronunciation of English is concerned, they have an infinite number of different realisations. In the first place, if we say the word *cat* (the same sequence of

305

phonemes) several times, there are likely to be measurable differences in the sounds which we utter; yet these utterances count as the *same* as far as our linguistic signal is concerned, and we may need very keen hearing to appreciate the minute differences there are. We may, however, be able to detect more easily variations in the realisations of phonemes which are due to the influence exerted on them by their environment or which are related to a particular situation of the phoneme. Thus, we may perceive the nasalisation of /æ/ in *man*, due to the nasal environment, which is not present in the /æ/ of *cat*; or we may feel that the /k/ of *key* is made at a point further forward on the roof of the mouth than the /k/ of *car*, due to the influence of the front vowel in *key* and the back vowel in *car*. Alternatively, we may notice that the /p/ in *pin* is followed by a puff of air (aspiration) whereas the /p/ in *supper* has much less aspiration and the /p/ in *heap* may not be exploded at all: these are the different ways in which we habitually pronounce a /p/ in these situations in the word. Or again, it is evident that the qualities of the two realisations of /l/ in *little* are different: we habitually use one type of /l/ before vowels and another kind before consonants or silence. These different articulations are not distinctive in the sense that they may serve to change the meaning of a word: they are *allophonic* variants, or *allophones*, of the phonemes, and, each occurring in a predictable and exclusive situation, are said to be in *complementary distribution*.

It sometimes happens that the same sound may be treated as an allophone of two phonemes. The nasal consonant preceding the /f/ in both *infant* and *comfort* tends to be neither an alveolar nor a bilabial consonant, but rather a labiodental sound [ɱ] anticipating the labio-dental /f/. If we assign the sound in *infant* to the /n/ phoneme and that in *comfort* to the /m/ phoneme, this is an arbitrary decision largely dictated by the spelling or by a slow, unnatural division of the words into two syllables; it may equally well be treated as an allophone of /n/ or /m/. Again, though we distinguish the phonemes /p/ and /b/ in *pin*, *bin*, there is no such opposition after /s/. Since the plosive in *spin* has neither the aspiration associated with accented, initial /p/ nor the slight voicing often accompanying /b/, the sound may be classed with either /p/ or /b/. The spelling influences our usual phonemic transcription /spɪn/, though the form /sbɪn/ would be equally unambiguous. These examples illustrate the fact that, where oppositions do not occur, phonemes may coalesce in their realisations and be neutralised.

5   STANDARDS OF PRONUNCIATION

Although we agree by and large about a standard English usage in matters of vocabulary and grammar, in both the written and the spoken forms of the language, there is no such general agreement about a standard of pronunciation. We all have our own opinions as to what is the best pronunciation of English, and many people feel sufficiently concerned to write letters to the newspapers on the subject. It has been said that a man's accent has more significance in this country than anywhere else in the world. However regrettable it may be, there is no denying that some kinds of English speech carry a certain prestige, whereas others may prove a positive disadvantage to the user.

In the first place, if we restrict our study to the accents to be found in Britain and ignore such influential pronunciations of English as are found, for instance, in America, India and Australia, we are faced with a great diversity of *regional accents*, to which we react strongly, even violently. Thus, the Scot or the Northerner may feel that the Londoner's accent is careless, affected or even ugly. The Londoner, on the other hand, is quite likely to enjoy listening to a Scottish accent—so long as it is generally in-

307

telligible to him; he may associate a Northern accent with bluntness of character, plain-speaking. Some regional accents seem to be generally acceptable—Scottish, Irish, West-Country English, for instance. But the local pronunciation of large cities such as London, Birmingham, Liverpool or Glasgow is often held to be ugly. Frequently, too, we may feel that a pronunciation which is different from our own is slightly ridiculous, an object of humour. It is no accident that in all our literature from Chaucer to the present day the comic character is amusing not only for his eccentric behaviour but often also for his local accent.

Yet, in this country, *social distinctions of accent* are of even greater significance than the regional variations. In any region, there is a hierarchy of distinctions of accent corresponding to the structure of our society and depending, for instance, on the social milieu you belong to, your education and your profession. In these days when class distinctions are becoming more and more blurred, the social barriers between accents still exist. Barristers and bus-conductors both tend to have accents appropriate to their situation in society. If we disapprove of an accent, it may mean no more than that we dislike—or fear—another section of society. As a person changes his social status, his accent, too, will often change within the hierarchy of his regional type, frequently without his being aware of the change. Sometimes, indeed, the change of accent may precede the change of status, being simply a first indication of a desire for social advancement. Such a premature change is likely to be resented and ridiculed by the members of the social milieu from which an ambitious person is trying to break away. Alternatively, many speakers match their accent to their actual environment, using one accent at home and another at their work. This is not surprising if we remember that spoken language is a conventional method of communication; it is natural that we should tend to adopt the system of sound values which proves in practice to be the most effective and acceptable means of communication within any particular social situation. Similar adjustments frequently take place when we are faced with someone whose regional accent is very different from our own; we feel considerable pressure to make concessions in our own speech to match that of our companion.

Yet, within this complex pattern of regional and social accents, most of us have a feeling that there is some 'good' or 'correct' pronunciation of English, without markedly regional or social connotations. Many would say that the BBC announcers have such a neutral pronunciation. The BBC encourages this type of pronunciation in its national service announcers mainly because it is widely intelligible —in a way that a regional accent such as that of Scotland or the West Country might not be—and also because it does not generally excite in the minds of listeners the strong prejudices associated with other, more local, accents. But it is not an invention of the BBC, even though it is often referred to as BBC English. It is a style of pronunciation which has had currency and acceptance in this country for a long time; yet it cannot be said to be a 'standard' in the sense that it has been consciously accepted as such or has had its features defined by an official body. Nor can it be called simply 'educated' or 'cultured' English pronunciation, since many highly educated people do not use it—and not all of those who use it give evidence of any degree of culture. It has emerged as a somewhat vaguely accepted form of speech without narrowly prescribed limits, as a result of the interplay throughout our history of many regional and social influences.

There has always been in Britain, as in most other countries, a great regional diversity in speaking the common language—the more remote the period of history, the more striking the diversity. But, especially in the last four centuries, one type of regional pronunciation has acquired a social prestige. This prestige has been attached to the pronunciation of the South-East of England, and more particularly to that of the London region, largely for political and commercial reasons and because of the presence in London of the Court. In 1589, Puttenham in his *Arte of English Poesie* recommends 'the usual speech of the Court, and that of London and the shires lying about London within 60 miles and not much above . . . Northern men,' he says, 'whether they are noblemen or gentlemen, or of their best clerks, use an English which is not so courtly or so current as our Southern English is.' Nevertheless, in Elizabethan England, many of those who frequented the Court continued to use the pronunciation of their own region: we are told, for instance, that Sir Walter Raleigh kept his Devonshire accent. But the speech of the Court, which in its phonetic features was largely that of the London area, acquired an ever-increasing prestige value. By the nineteenth century, with the help of the conformist tradition of the established Public Schools, it may be said to have become relatively fixed as the speech of the influential classes of society. At this point, having lost some of the purely local characteristics of London speech, it was typical of a social stratum rather than of a region. The extension of educational possibilities created a situation in which an educated man might not belong to the upper classes and might have in his speech many regional characteristics; but, if he was eager for social advancement, he probably still felt obliged to modify his accent in the direction of the social standard. Pronunciation was then a marker of position in society.

Today, we call the descendant of this kind of speech *Received Pronunciation*, or RP, suggesting that it is the result of a collective social judgment rather than of a conscious, prescriptive agreement. Still closer to Southern English than to any other regional speech, it is the form of pronunciation upon which our analysis in the preceding pages is based. But it can no longer be said that RP is the exclusive property of any particular social stratum. With the levelling of society itself and as a result of broadcasting, which exposes all of us to this pronunciation, more and more speakers from all regions are influenced by RP, sometimes for conscious social reasons but also quite unconsciously.

It is difficult, however, to give a strict phonetic description of RP which will apply to all users of this style of speech. The speech behaviour of two individuals, even though it falls within the same general category, is never entirely identical. Moreover, the sounds of spoken language are always changing, slowly but constantly. For instance, in addition to a neutral, *general* form of RP, we have at this moment a more archaic or *conservative* type which the older generations use, and an *advanced* variety, used mostly by young people, which gives a possible indication of what the general RP forms are likely to be a century from now. These hints of a future pronunciation are often criticised now—and always have been—by general or conservative RP speakers as affectations or vulgarisms. A contemporary example of such a divergence of RP forms is provided by the diphthong /əʊ/ in the word *home*. The general RP form which we have described consists of glide with a central starting point; but in conservative RP, this glide may begin at a point further back in the mouth and be accompanied by considerable lip-rounding ([oʊ]). On the other hand, advanced RP speech lengthens the central element ([ɜːʊ]) and merely touches very lightly on the [ʊ] element, or, indeed, may start the glide from a relatively front position without lip-rounding ([eʊ]). These variations are less surprising if we remember that this diphthong has developed,

311

over the last thousand years, from the pure vowel stages [ɑː] (a back open unrounded vowel), [ɔː] and [oː] (showing progressively closer and more rounded articulations) before becoming established as diphthongal in Southern English in the nineteenth century. Developments of this kind are likely to continue—more slowly, perhaps, now, because for the first time, through broadcasting, there is a widely disseminated notion of some standard for spoken English, which may act as a brake on change. But speakers differ, not only in the quality of the sounds they use, but also in the phonemes they allocate to groups of words: two RP speakers, both with the same stock of phonemes, may distribute them differently. Thus, two speakers may both have /æ/ and /ɑː/ and agree about their usage in *cat* and *cart*, but differ in the phonemes they use in *lather, transfer*, saying either /ˈlæðə/ or /ˈlɑːðə/ and either /ˈtrænsfɜː/ or /ˈtrɑːnsfɜː/. Or again, they might agree in having /ɒ/ in *cot* and /ɔː/ in *caught*, but one might pronounce *off, cross*, with /ɒ/ and the other with /ɔː/ (a conservative RP form).

Finally, it is not simply a question of using either one of these RP forms or a purely regional type of speech. Many of us have a pronunciation which is largely 'received', but which, at the same time, retains features of our local, regional speech. This is often called *modified* regional speech —modified in varying degrees towards RP. A Northerner might, perhaps, modify his speech simply to the extent of using the RP long open vowel /ɑː/ in *pass*, rather than his own short [a]; or a Cockney might use a /t/ in *water*, rather than his own dialect's [ʔ], and yet keep the Cockney vowel qualities. There is a great deal of 'levelling' of this sort, in the direction of RP, taking place at the moment. It remains to be seen whether it will become even more extensive and whether, as a consequence, dialect speech forms become less and less marked.

No two people use precisely the same sounds in speaking, even though we may identify them as having the 'same' kind of pronunciation. Each one of us has his own configuration of the vocal tract, e.g. the degree of arching of the hard palate, which gives a special quality to the sounds we utter; indeed, we can be identified by the sound of our voices. Nevertheless, we do distinguish between those speakers who have the 'same' pronunciation as ourselves and others whose speech is that of another region or social milieu. Our judgment may be based on any or all of several factors: marked differences in the quality or quantity of sounds, unfamiliar accentual or intonation patterns (see following sections), different phonemic systems, i.e. fewer or more terms in the system, or a different distribution of phonemes in words.

We may need to hear an extensive sample of a person's speech before we know that it is different from our own. In other words, we have to be able to establish the place occupied by the sounds he utters in his total system. Thus, if someone says [paɪnt] by itself, we do not know whether he is a Cockney meaning *paint* or an RP speaker meaning *pint*; or again, the sound pattern [səʊp] has no precise linguistic significance by itself—it may be a form of RP for *soap* or Cockney for *soup*. If we add the word *no*, however, the significance is clear—RP ['nəu 'səʊp] (*soap*) v. ['nəʊ 'suːp] (*soup*) as against Cockney ['nʌʊ 'sʌʊp] (*soap*) v. ['nʌʊ 'səʊp] (*soup*).

We may recognise as different a form of speech which has the same number of phonemes but allophonic realisations of these phonemes which are markedly dissimilar to those typical of, say RP. A speaker of another dialect may have /e/ and /æ/, as in RP, but may realise the /e/ as a very open vowel near to that which the RP speaker would use in *sat*; a consequence of this dissimilarity is that the dialect speaker, in order to keep his phonemes /e/ and /æ/ distinct, also realises /æ/ with a vowel which is much more open than that of RP. Or again, a dialect speaker may oppose the two vowels in *so* and *saw*, but with phonetic values different from those which are characteristic of RP, viz. with a pure long, fairly close back, vowel [oː] in *so* (cf. the glide in RP) and a variety of /ɔː/ which is considerably more open than that which is customary in RP. In all these examples, the RP and dialect systems may be the same, i.e. have the same number of sound oppositions, but there are such marked divergences in the phonetic realisations that the two styles of speech are recognisably dissimilar.

Again, the system may not be disturbed even if the types of allophones relating to a phoneme are different in various dialects. Two allophones of RP /l/ are of markedly different quality—' clear ' before a vowel as in *lit* and ' dark ' following a vowel as in *till*. Some kinds of English have the same type of allophone in both positions, i.e. both relatively clear or both relatively dark. In RP, /r/ occurs only before vowels; in other dialects, *r*- sounds of various kinds occur in pre-consonantal and pre-pausal positions. In these cases, despite the more extensive distribution of /r/, no addition is made to the consonant system (though there are usually repercussions in the vowel system). Or again, similar phonemic oppositions may exist, but are exhibited in words different from those of RP, e.g. /ʊ/ may be opposed to /uː/ as in RP, but /uː/ occurs in *book*, *took*, etc., where RP has /ʊ/.

In the case of other dialects, the systems themselves may not be the same, e.g. the RP opposition /æ/—/ɑː/ may not exist, the distinction between *Sam* and *psalm* being lost, as in some Northern speech, and the pair *cat*—*cart* being kept separate by the pronunciation of /r/ in *cart*; or again, /ʌ/ —/ʊ/ may not be distinguished in such a pair as *cup*, *put*, a vowel near to RP /ʊ/ being used in both cases. /ɜː/ may

314

not exist as a phoneme, being realised, as in some Scottish English, as /ɪ+r/, /e+r/ or /ʌ+r/ in such words as *first, earth, word*; in Cockney the realisation of post-vocalic /l/ as a vowel of the [o] type may lead to confusion of such pairs as *called—cord* and a different assessment of the diphthongal glides in the system. In those Northern dialects where *-ng* is always pronounced [ŋg], [ŋ] does not constitute a distinctive phonemic element as it does in RP (cf. *sin—sing*), since [ŋ] is to be counted as an allophone of /n/ before /k/ or /g/. Sometimes, another dialect shows a complication at some point in the system which is not present in RP, e.g. Scottish English distinguishes *side* /ʌɪ/ and *sighed* /ae/, where RP has /aɪ/ for both.

It will be seen that dialect variants consist particularly of phonemic or non-phonemic differences in the vowels. There is, on the whole, considerable similarity in the number of terms in the consonantal systems of the various types of English (apart from variations such as those concerning /l, r, ŋ/ mentioned above). A confusion of the type /s/—/θ/ in *sin—thin* is typical only of defective speech.

7 ACCENTUAL FEATURES

An utterance, composed of one or more words, is made up normally not only of a changing pattern of sounds of varying length, but also of variations of *stress* (energy or intensity for the speaker, loudness for the listener) and *pitch*. The total effect is that of a continuum, some parts of which stand out, or are *accented*, more than others. Both the word and connected speech may be said to possess variations of *accent* (used here in a more specific sense than that implying a type of pronunciation).

1 *The Word.* The message conveyed by polysyllabic English words is transmitted by the phonemes which compose them and also by the accentual pattern of the word,

315

i.e. by the varying, contrastive prominence of its syllables. The words *over* and *above* are different not only because the phonemes are different, but also because *over* has a strong (accented) syllable followed by a weak (unaccented) syllable, whereas in *above* the accentual balance of the syllables is the reverse. The accentual pattern of English words is *fixed*, in the sense that the main accent normally always falls on the same syllable of a given word; but it is *free*, in that it is not tied to a particular place in all words (cf. the accent which is tied to the penultimate syllable in Polish, or to the first syllable in Czech).

In a word of many syllables, there may be as many degrees of accentuation (prominence) as there are syllables. For most practical purposes, it is sufficient to note three degrees:

> syllables with *primary* accent (here marked with ' before the syllable)—associated with strong stress, full vowel value and a potential change of *pitch direction*;

> syllables with *secondary* accent (here marked with ˌ) associated with rhythmic stress, qualitative or quantitative prominence, and often with a change of *pitch level*;

> *unaccented* syllables (not marked here)—weakly uttered, often with obscuration of a vowel to /ə/, /ɪ/, or /ʊ/, or containing a syllabic consonant as syllable centre.

Thus, the accentual pattern of such words as *over*, *above*, *magazine*, *educate*, *accidental* may be shown as /'əʊvə, ə'bʌv, ˌmægə'ziːn, 'edjʊˌkeɪt, ˌæksɪ'dentl/.

The speaker makes use of quality, quantity, pitch and stress variations in order to convey to a listener an impression of accentual prominence, but, of the four factors, pitch variation appears to be the most effective means of rendering a syllable prominent. Thus, when *over* and *above* are said with the pitch patterns

it is the sharp fall on the first and second syllables respectively, related to greater stress and the full vowels /əʊ/ and /ʌ/, that gives the main cue as to the situation of the accent; in both unaccented syllables, there occurs the typically weak vowel /ə/.

Many two-syllable words of French origin (and some of greater length) distinguish their verb and noun (or adjective) forms by this variation of accentual pattern, usually with associated changes of quality, e.g.

absent	/ˈæbsənt/ (adj.)	/əbˈsent / (vb.)
object	/ˈɒbdʒɪkt/ (n.)	/əbˈdʒekt/ (vb.)
rebel	/ˈrebl/ (n.)	/rɪˈbel/ (vb.)

Sometimes, however, the accentual variation of such pairs is achieved mainly through pitch variation, without quality changes, cf. the noun and verb forms of *import, increase, insult*.

The following list of words illustrates a number of word accentual patterns, in simple words of from two to four syllables :

2 *syllables*—*alone*/əˈləʊn/; *idea*/aɪˈdɪə/; *under*/ˈʌndə/; *placard*/ˈplæˌkɑːd/;

3 *syllables*—*magazine*/ˌmægəˈziːn/; *quantity*/ˈkwɒn-tɪtɪ/; *appetite*/ˈæpɪˌtaɪt/; *important*/ɪm-ˈpɔːtnt/; *tobacco*/təˈbækəʊ/;

4 *syllables*—*remarkable*/rɪˈmɑːkəbl/; *rhinoceros*/ˌraɪ-ˈnɒsərəs/; *enumerate*/ɪˈnjuːməˌreɪt/; *circu-lation*/ˌsɜːkjʊˈleɪʃn/; *caterpillar*/ˈkætəpɪlə/.

Sometimes, the pattern is unstable, e.g. either syllable may receive the main accent in *syringe*; it is said to be 'correct' to place the primary accent on the first syllable in *exquisite*, but many educated speakers put it on the second; similarly, *controversy* 'should' have its first syllable accented, but many educated speakers accent the second; for some *television* is /ˈtelɪvɪʒn/, for others, /ˌtelɪˈvɪʒn/. In a few words, analogy plays part in this instability: *apply* is always /əˈplaɪ/, whence, for reasons of analogy—and rhythm—some would say /əˈplɪkəbl/ (*applicable*) rather than the more 'correct' /ˈæplɪkəbl/. Such instability amongst RP speakers is not to be confused with dialectal variation of accented shape, e.g. Scottish English has *enquiry* with /ˈen/ rather than RP /ˈkwaɪ/, *realise* with /ˈlaɪz/ rather than RP /ˈrɪə/.

The same word patterns may be found in the so-called compound words (i.e. words composed of two or more separable elements). Most frequently it is the first element which receives the main accent and tends to unify the elements of the compound into a single concept, e.g. *air-raid*/ˈeəˌreɪd/; *grandfather*/ˈgrænd͵fɑːðə/; *chamber-maid*/ˈtʃeɪmbəˌmeɪd/; *tape-recorder*/ˈteɪprɪˌkɔːdə/; *musical-box*/ˈmjuːzɪklˌbɒks/. Where the main stress falls on the second element, the first also has potential pitch prominence, so that both elements are strongly meaning-ful, e.g. *downstairs*/ˌdaʊnˈsteəz/; *archbishop*/ˌɑːtʃˈbɪʃəp/; *secondhand*/ˌsekəndˈhænd/; *sergeant-major*/ˌsɑːdʒənt-ˈmeɪdʒə/.

2 *Connected Speech*. Connected speech also has its accentual pattern, i.e. some words or syllables stand out from the others. But the accentuation of connected speech

differs from the relatively fixed form of the polysyllabic word in that the situation of the accent(s) in a sentence is determined by the meaning which the utterance is to convey. (The placing of the accent(s) in connected speech is, nevertheless, determined to some extent by the accentuation of the preceding stretch of speech.) If a polysyllabic word receives an accent in the sentence, the prominence will, however, usually be placed on the syllable normally accented when the word is said in isolation. Thus, in the statement *Everyone likes John*, any of the three words may be selected as the one on which most emphasis is placed, according to the shade of meaning to be conveyed, e.g. primary accent on *everyone* (the first syllable being accented as in isolation) = 'all people without exception', primary accent on *likes* = there is no question of 'disliking', primary accent on *John* = 'although some other person may not be liked'. This primary accent in the sentence is achieved partly by the greater degree of stress placed on the word, but mainly (as in the case of the accentuation of isolate words) by the *change of pitch direction* associated with the word. For instance, if *John* carries the main accent in the above statement, it may be said with a falling tune (compared with the level pitches on the other words);

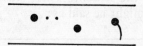

But similar prominence may be gained by rising as well as falling tunes, or combinations of the two (see following section on intonation). This main accent, associated with a pitch glide, is often called the *nucleus* of the group; there may be more than one in a sentence, e.g. both *everyone* and *John* in the present case might have falling (nuclear) tones.

It will be noticed that each word in this sentence which we have taken as an example will always have some prominence, wherever the primary (nuclear) accent falls; they receive secondary accent in the sentence, if they are not nuclear. This secondary prominence is achieved either by a change of *pitch level*, or simply by a rhythmical stress or by the nature of the quality and quantity of the stressed syllable. Thus, our sentence might have the following pitch and accent patterns (retaining the primary accent on *John*):

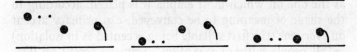

The association of some kind of prominence with each of the words is generally related to the nature of the words. They are semantically important words (e.g. nouns, adjectives, verbs, adverbs, etc.) and are often called *lexical* words.

Other words, such as conjunctions, prepositions, pronouns, articles, etc., are less usually associated with accent; they are *grammatical* words. These, being often totally unaccented, tend to be subject to considerable weakening or obscuration of quality and quantity and have no pitch prominence, e.g. the sentence *There was no chance of his leaving at three* might be said as:

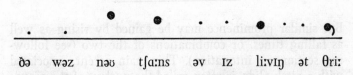

ðə   wəz   nəʊ   tʃɑːns   əv   ɪz   liːvɪŋ   ət   θriː

where *there, was, of, his, at* are all very weakly and rapidly uttered. About sixty of these small grammatical words have a typically weak pronunciation in colloquial, connected speech—a sound value which may be very different from that which they have when said in isolation, e.g.

	Unaccented in connected speech	As said in isolation
an	/ən, n/ (he ate an /ən/ apple)	/æn/
and	/ənd, ən, n, nd/ (two and /ən/ six)	/ænd/
but	/bət/ (but /bət/ John does)	/bʌt/
for	/fər, fə, fr/ (one for /fə/ me)	/fɔː/
has (aux.)	/həz, əz, z, s/ (Jack's /s/ = has gone)	/hæz/
his	/ɪz/ (on his /ɪz/ own)	/hɪz/
is	/s, z,/ (What's /s/ = is this?)	/ɪz/
of	/əv, v, ə/ (one of /əv/ mine)	/ɒv/
than	/ðən, ðn/ (more than /ðən/ enough)	/ðæn/
them	/ðəm, ðm, m/ (he took them /ðəm/)	/ðem/
the	/ðə, ðɪ/ (the /ðə/ dog) (the /ðɪ/ animal)	/ðɪː/
to	/tə, tʊ/ (back to /tə/ school) (nothing to /tʊ/ eat)	/tuː/
was	/wəz/ (Jack was /wəz/ there)	/wɒz/

Notes:

(i) Although grammatical words are typically un-accented and weak, they may be accented, with strong quality, if the meaning requires it, e.g. 'He *is* there', 'his *and* mine', etc.

(ii) Prepositions such as *to*, *from*, *at*, *for*, have strong quality, though unaccented, when final, e.g. *at* in What are you laughing *at?*, and may have weak or strong quality when unaccented and preceding a pronoun, e.g. *at* in He laughed at (/ət/ or /æt/) him. Similarly, auxiliary verbs in a final position have their full form,

321

even when unaccented, e.g. *am* /æm/ and *can* /kæn/ in such sentences as *Look where I am* (with I strongly accented) and *I don't think he can* (with *he* strongly accented), where the reduced forms /əm/ or /m/ and /kən/ or /kn/ would be abnormal.

(iii) Not all monosyllabic grammatical words are weakened in unaccented positions, e.g. *on, or, by, your, my* tend to keep their strong quality except in the most rapid speech.

In connected speech, the syllables carrying a strong accent tend to occur at fairly equal intervals of time; the more numerous the unaccented syllables occurring between the accented syllables, the more rapid the delivery of the weak syllables. (Over an extended stretch of connected speech, the number of unaccented syllables tends to equal or slightly to exceed the number of accented syllables.) The same number of syllables may thus occupy different total periods of time, according to the number of strong accents, cf. the time given to 'Jack and 'Jill 'came 'home 'late (6 syllables—5 accented) and *There are 'two of us 'here* (6 syllables—2 accented), the second sentence occupying less time than the first. Accented syllables may form the hub of a *rhythmic group*, the length of the accented syllable being shorter according to the number of unaccented syllables following in the same group, cf. the decreasing length of the syllable /kʌm/ in *I'll come, no comfort, quite comfortable*. The same phonemic sequence may have different meanings through the variations of length due to rhythmic grouping, cf. the length of /maɪn/ in *minor official*/'maɪnər ə'fɪʃl/ and *mine are official*/'maɪn ərə'fɪʃl/.

8 INTONATION

We are conscious when we speak of varying pitches of the voice—the utterance will normally have a tune, speech on a monotone, such as may sometimes be heard in church, being unusual. The tunes we use are not haphazard, since we make use of speech melody (*intonation*) to convey meaning; and, since we generally interpret correctly the meaning transmitted by others through intonational means, our patterns of intonation may be said to be systematically organised, as are the sound features of the language. There may be similarities between the tunes used in RP and those used in other languages, but the meanings attached to the tunes may be different; or, again, certain melodies are typical of English and rare in other languages. There are disparities of this kind, too, between the intonation of RP and that of other English dialects.

The intonation of RP has, however, more than one linguistic function. It can give prominence to an accented syllable, as we have seen, but at the same time, the type of pitch change used may provide information about the speaker's mood or attitude[1] and is capable of distinguishing sentence types and, sometimes, word meaning. Such divergences in intonation usage as occur between the different English dialects relate especially to the expression of attitude. The following outline is restricted to RP usage.[2]

1   *Accentuation and attitude.* A syllable or word may be highlighted in the utterance by means of pitch prominence, either of a gliding kind or by means of a level pitch which stands out from its environment through being higher or lower. The speaker's attitude to the topic or the listener, e.g. authoritative, bored, surprised, encouraging,

[1] The attitudinal, as well as the accentual, meaning of a tone will, however, be conditioned by the situation in which it is employed.

[2] The signs now to be used for marking tone patterns take the place of those used in earlier pages to indicate accentual patterns: thus, ˈ (previously marking the primary accent) is replaced by a nuclear tone mark, whereas the signs ˈ and ˌ (previously used for primary and secondary accent) are now both used to show syllables carrying secondary accent, according to the relationship of their pitch to the context.

etc., will often be revealed by the type of tune change used (particularly on the accented syllables).

(i) The *primary (nuclear) accent*, on the most important words in the sentence, is shown by means of a change of pitch direction:

(a) Falling tones, with a glide down on one syllable or a marked step down between the accented syllable and a following unaccented syllable, are usually assertive, matter-of-fact, contrastive—the higher the fall, the greater the degree of finality, warmth or contradiction.

Low Fall (ˎ), from a mid to a low pitch,

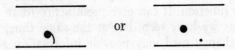

ˎNo (detached); It's riˎdiculous (matter-of-fact); ˎWhen did you? (curt); ˎLook at it (peremptory).

High Fall (ˋ), from a high to a low pitch,

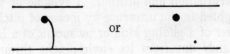

ˋNo! It ˋwasn't! (vigorous contradiction); I ˋdo! (emphatic assertion).

Rise-Fall (ˆ), with a rise preceding the fall, showing added warmth, indignation or sarcasm,

ˆNo! (indignant); ˆReally! (incredulous, sarcastic);

He ˆalways is (impatient).

(b) *Rising* tones, with a rising glide within one syllable, or as an ascent spread over more than one syllable.

Low Rise (ˌ), rising from low to mid pitch, being essentially non-final, polite, appealing, suspicious or grudging,

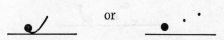

or

ˌNo (tentative, encouraging); ˌWait! (gentle warning);

And ˌthen . . . (introductory); He ˌwouldn't (petulant);

Is there ˌtime? (friendly, polite).

High Rise (ˊ), rising from mid to high pitch, indicating a questioning attitude, or eagerness, concern, indignation, etc.,

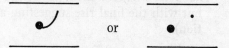

or

ˊNo? ˊWhen? In ˊLondon (questioningly);

You ˊdid? (incredulous question); It was ˊyours! (dismay).

Fall-Rise (ˇ) or (ˆˌ), a fall followed by a rise, combining the contrastive, assertive effect of the fall with the various appealing, continuative or introductory aspects of the rise, within one syllable

325

ˇNo (doubtful, but encouraging) or with a fall on the accented syllable and a rise on the following unaccented syllables,

ˇSlowly! (urgent, but reassuring);

If you ˇwant to (insistence on 'want', but grudging)

or with the rise on a following secondary accent in the same word,

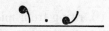

By ˇtelephone (contradictory, but appealing)

or with a rise on a following accented word,

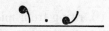

`Do sit ˌdown (compulsive request);

`That's not what I ˌwanted (insistence on 'that', but with the final rise suggesting a qualification).

(ii) *Secondary accent*, with pitch prominence ('), before the nuclear accent, by means of a relatively high level pitch (especially in relation to any preceding unaccented syllables), and, when there are several words carrying secondary accent, by steps down on level pitches, e.g.

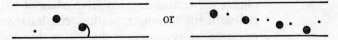

It's 'not ˌfair. 'Can you 'possibly 'come on ˌMonday?

(iii) *Secondary accent*, without pitch prominence (.). Syllables often carry a secondary accent of a mainly rhythmic kind, without pitch prominence.

Before a nuclear accent, they remain relatively low, or, if following a pitch-prominent secondary accent, remain on the level of the latter, e.g.

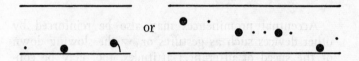

He ˌwasn't ˌthere. 'Can you 'possibly ˌcome on ˌMonday?

Note: The pitch of the syllables preceding, in particular the low falling and low rising nuclear tones has an effect on the impression created. High syllables preceding the nucleus has a lively or cheerful effect; low syllables preceding the nucleus may convey boredom, misery or a note of complaint, e.g.

'Good ˌmorning (cheerful)
ˌGood ˌmorning (routine)

Following a nuclear accent, they remain on a low level (after a fall) or continue the rise (after a rise), e.g.,

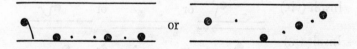

`He ˌdidn't forˌget to ˌcome.   'Will you ˌall be ˌin for ˌtea?

Between a fall and a rise, the syllable(s) carrying a secondary accent remain low, e.g.

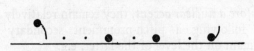

`He was the ˌone who ˌbroke the ˏchair.

Accentual prominences may also be reinforced by other devices such as gestures or by the slowing down of the speed of utterance; attitudes, too, may be conveyed by such non-intonational means as variations of voice quality or rhythm, as well as by the restriction of the intonation pitches employed.

2 *Distinction of sentence types or word meaning.* The same sequence of words may be a statement or a question according to whether a falling or a rising nucleus is used, e.g.

He's ˌlate. (statement)
He's ˊlate? (question)

The meaning of a word may also sometimes rely on the situation of the accent expressed mainly in terms of pitch (where there are no associated qualitative changes), e.g.

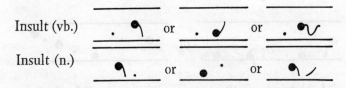

Similarly, words such as *anyone*, *anything*, *anybody* follow-
328

ing a negative may have a different meaning according to their pitch pattern, e.g.

I 'can't 'eat ˌanything   (= I can eat nothing)
I 'can't 'eat ˇanything (= I can eat some things)

9   OTHER FEATURES OF CONNECTED SPEECH

1   *The Word in connected speech.* Just as the realisations of phonemes are different according to their situation in the utterance and the influence exerted on them by contiguous articulations, so words, while retaining a large measure of their identity, may have forms in connected speech which are different from those used when the words are said in isolation. These variations are additional to those already mentioned (p. 320) concerning the weak and strong forms of words in connected speech and isolation.

(i) *Variation of accentual pattern.* The accentuation of the context may influence the accentual (rhythmic) pattern of a word. Such a change takes place particularly in those words which carry two accents in isolation. Thus, *West-minster* may be accented in isolation with a pattern 'West-ˌminster; but when another accent closely precedes, as in *near Westminster*, the syllable /west/ may lose much of its accentual force, the phrase pattern then being 'near West-ˌminster; or again, if a strong accent follows immediately, the syllable /mɪn/ may lose its accent, e.g. in 'Westminster ˌAbbey.

(ii) *Phonemic variations at word boundaries.* The sounds which constitute an utterance are not discrete phonetic entities; contiguous articulations influence each other. This effect is most striking in word final positions, where consonants may be so influenced by the initial consonant in a following word that a word may have one consonant phoneme finally in isolation and another in connected speech.

329

Of all the English consonants, the alveolars /t, d, n, s, z/ are apt to exhibit such phonemic assimilations in rapid speech, e.g.

right/raɪp/ people; red/reg/ currants; one/wʌm/ more, etc., /s, z/ before /j, ʃ/: this/ðɪʃ/ year; those /ðəʊʒ/ shoes, etc., and coalescences of /t, d, s, z/ and /j/ into /tʃ, dʒ, ʃ, ʒ/:

What you/wɒtʃuː/ want; Is this your/ðɪʃɔː/ hat, etc.

(iii) *Elision.* Word final consonantal clusters are frequently simplified by elision, particularly before another word beginning with a consonant, e.g. last/lɑːs/ post, just/dʒʌs/ near, tinned/tɪn→tɪm/ meat, bald/bɔːl/ patch, you mustn't/mʌsn/ lose it; and sometimes before a vowel, especially after syllabic /n/, e.g. he wouldn't /wʊdn/ eat it.

(iv) *Special liaison forms.* Apart from the fact that word final consonants frequently show a marked allophonic change when followed by a word with initial vowel (e.g. the 'clear' [l] of fall-out compared with the 'dark' [l] of fall preceding a pause or a consonant), RP often adds /r/ before an initial vowel in the following word in those words where a spelling r is not pronounced in the isolate form, e.g. here/hɪə/, but here/hɪər/ and there; father /ˌfɑːðə/, but father/ˈfɑːðər/ and mother; more/mɔ/, but more/mɔːr/ or less. The same 'linking r' form occurs on the addition of a morpheme with initial vowel, e.g. hear /hɪə/, but hearing /ˌhɪərɪŋ/. A similar link is often used by many people through analogy after final /ə, ɑː, ɔː/, where it has no justification in the spelling, e.g. Russia and /ˈrʌʃər ənd/ China, the idea of /aɪˈdɪər əv/, Shah of /ˈʃɑːrəv/, awe-inspiring/ˌɔːrɪnˌspaɪərɪŋ/. The 'intrusive' /r/ of these last examples—especially that after /ɔː/—is
330

generally condemned, though it is widely used among educated speakers, particularly after /ə/.

(v) *Juncture.* The previous sections show how a word's phonemic shape may vary in connected speech. A word (or morpheme) may, however, retain features of its isolate (pre-pausal) pronunciation when it occurs within an utterance. A similar sequence of phonemes may be interpreted in one of two ways according to the situation of the word (or morpheme) boundary. This *juncture* between two words or morphemes may be signalled by phonetic cues. Thus, the phonemic sequence /haʊstreɪnd/ may mean either *house-trained* or *how strained*, according to whether the juncture occurs before or after /s/. If the juncture occurs between /s/ and /t/, i.e. with the meaning *house-trained*, the word division may be indicated by the short variety of /aʊ/ before syllable final /s/ and by the strong devoicing of /r/ after syllable initial accented /t/; on the other hand, juncture between /aʊ/ and /s/, i.e. with the meaning *how strained*, is likely to be manifested by the relatively long /aʊ/ (final in a syllable) and by the relatively slightly devoiced /r/ after syllable initial /st/. It should be noted, however, that such junctural cues are potential, and may not always be markedly present in rapid speech.

As a general rule, it may be said that the more rapid the style of speech, the greater the tendency to use elided and assimilated word forms. RP speakers are not normally aware that such modifications take place in their own speech and do not perceive them as sub-standard in the speech of others. At a certain point, however, an excess of elision or assimilation is perceived and characterised as careless speech, e.g. *I'm going to* pronounced as /ˌaɪŋnə/, or *he went away* as /hɪ'wen ə.weɪ/. Very careful (slow) speech, on the other hand, tends consciously to preserve the identity of the word, avoiding elisions, reducing the number of assimilations at word boundaries, frequently using a glottal stop instead of

331

the word final linking /r/ forms, giving marked phonetic cues to indicate junctures, and often avoids the use of the weak pronunciation of grammatical words (which we indicated as typical of their unaccented occurrences in connected speech—p. 320) in favour of the strong isolate form.

2   *Redundancy*. A great deal of the information transmitted in sound by a speaker to a listener is superfluous; in English, the degree of *redundancy* may reach 50 per cent. The situation and context predetermine much of the possible meaning of what we say, in addition to the constraints placed upon an utterance by the sequential probabilities of phonemes and words in our language. It is not, for instance, necessary on a bus to ask for 'One fourpenny ticket'; the word 'four' is sufficient, and may itself be reduced to /ɔː/ and still be understood by the conductor (in opposition to /aɪ/—'five', [ɪʔ]—'six', [eɪʔ]—'eight', etc.). If, at a meal, we are offered /bə`deɪdəʊz/, we readily understand *potatoes*, since there occurs no opposition between /b—d/ and /p—t/ in such a sequence, and, in any case the situation pre-disposes us to understand the vegetable. Or again, if there are apples and pears on a dish and we are asked whether we would prefer *apples* or /beəz/, we understand the fruit rather than the animal even though here there is a meaningful phonemic opposition. Or, *those men have come* might be pronounced /'ðəʊz ˌmæn əv ˌkʌm/, but the pressure of the plural forms /ðəʊz/ and /əv/ is sufficient to make us disregard the singular /æ/ signal said instead of the plural /e/ of *men*. It is possible, in fact, to reduce all the vowel phonemes of English to /ə/—some speakers come near to this by the degree of centralisation which they use—and still retain intelligibility, provided that the vowel lengths and consonantal clusters are retained, e.g. *He wanted to get back at nine* /hə 'wəntəd tə 'gət 'bək ət ˌnəːn/.

It will be seen that, as a result of the constraints imposed by the general context and the characteristics of the language, phonemic oppositions in the word (and, to an even greater extent, the phonetic junctural cues) emerge as of potential significance. This phonemic redundancy is illustrated by the amount of phonemic *neutralisation* which is possible and normal in word forms without loss of intelligibility:

(i) unaccented word forms may often become identical, e.g. /'weəz ðə ˌbʌs ˌstɒp/ = *Where does* (or *is*) *the bus(-) stop?* i.e. /z/ = *does* or *is*; /ðə 'bɔɪz əv 'iːtn ˌfɪʃ/ = *The boys have eaten* (or *of Eton*) *fish*, i.e. /əv/ = *have* or *of*;

(ii) words may become identical through assimilation, e.g. /ə 'ðiːz ðə 'raɪp bəˌnɑːnəz/ = *Are these the ripe* (or *right*) *bananas?*, where the /t/ of *right* may assimilate to /p/ before /b/; ['hæv ə 'gʊd ˌrʌɱ fə jɔː ˌmʌnɪ] = *Have a good rum* (or *run*) *for your money*, where the labio-dental nasal [ɱ] may be an allophone of /m/ or /n/ before /f/;

(iii) simplification of consonantal clusters may lead to apparent confusion of tenses, e.g. /ðeɪ 'rʌʃ ˌpɑːst/ = *They rush* (or *rushed*) *past*, the sequence /ʃtp/ of *rushed past* frequently being reduced in rapid speech to /ʃp/.

In all these cases, the precise meaning of a sequence of phonemic cues is determined by the general context and situation.

10   WRITTEN ENGLISH

Although speech must be considered our primary means of transmitting language, communication through visual signals also plays an important part in our social behaviour. Such visual media include not only the conventional written form of English but also such organised systems of codes and symbols as the Morse code, traffic lights and road signs. It is, however, the written form of English which most nearly approaches in its structure the spoken aspect of the language. In writing, the language is expressed by a linear sequence of visual signs representing words as separate entities and, to an imperfect extent in English, the constituent sounds. Unlike spoken English, our written language now has a standardised form, which we learn as one of the first steps in our education and which permits only a few variations, e.g. *judgment* or *judgement*, *show* or *shew*, *draft* or *draught*, etc. We quickly gain considerable skill in recognising these visual shapes though they may occur in widely differing forms and styles, e.g. the roman print of this page, capital and italicised forms of letters, various sizes and styles of print. Indeed, we acquire such facility in identifying the outlines of words that we need only the smallest visual clues in order to be able to read a text. If you examine the following printed examples, you will find that, though the sense is clear, the letter shapes are imperfect—notice, for instance, in the first example, the arrangement of mere dots and separated lines which we interpret quite easily:

THE ENGLISH

LANGUAGE

She brought him the remains of her lunch and his eyes brightened

Jack and Jill went up the hill

[The foregoing examples are reproduced from Quirk and Smith, *The Teaching of English*, p. 28.]

Or again, if you cover the bottom half of each line on this page, you will still have little difficulty in reading. From this it is clear that, as we gain experience in using the written language, much of the visual information conventionally provided becomes redundant. We also become expert at identifying as the same word quite different visual signals, particularly as a result of the highly idiosyncratic ways in which we draw our letters and join them together when writing by hand. Compare, for instance, the following written forms of the same sentence:

Aunt Dorothy is coming on Monday.

Aunt Dorothy's coming on Monday

Aunt Dorothy's coming on Monday

Aunt Dorothy's coming on Monday

It is evident that the concrete, written representation of a word may vary as much amongst individual writers as does its realisation in sound. An individual may, indeed, in his style of writing, not only eliminate all that is visually redundant but also so obliterate essential cues to recognition that his writing ceases to be generally intelligible to others (and even, after an interval of time, to the writer himself). Writing of this kind, however great the aesthetic appeal of the written pattern, is clearly an ineffective means of transmitting language; as a vehicle for language, it is as inadequate as seriously defective speech.

Though in some cases, e.g. in our numbers and the use of such signs and abbreviations as $=$, $+$, Co., &, £, @, Mr, our writing is purely symbolic, the sign representing a total word form, the spelling of English is basically alphabetic, i.e. the constituent phonemes of a word are represented by letters. But it cannot be said that our present conventional use of the Latin alphabet is consistent or unambiguous. One would expect an efficient alphabetic system of writing to use visual symbols sufficient in number to represent the significant sounds of the spoken language with a one-to-one relationship. Writing would then mirror speech, and the correspondence between the two forms would be so close that reading and writing would be a simple matter. Thus, a phrase such as *good luck* /ˈgʊd ˌlʌk/, now written with eight letters, might more reasonably be expressed with six symbols representing the six phonemes. A child who 'mis-spells' English is often applying such a principle of logical correspondence—writing, for instance, *I must have lost it*, as *I must of lost it*, where the weak form of *have* /əv/ is correctly equated with the weak form of *of*. In the end, he has to think of the written forms of English as complex, established letter patterns, bearing only a rough resemblance to the constituent sounds—a kind of picture-writing. Our present-day spelling of English is, then, highly sophisticated; it is a separate expression of the language, with its own rules and conventions.

However, when the Latin alphabet was first used for English, some thirteen hundred years ago, the speech of the time was represented very much more faithfully than it is today. But the pronunciation of a language changes —more rapidly than ever when a community is not highly organised or literate. For several centuries, especially before the invention of printing, the spelling of English changed too, keeping pace to some extent with the development of speech sounds. Even in Chaucer's time, there was still a fair correspondence between the written and spoken forms of the language.

But during the last five hundred years, though the sounds of the language have changed considerably, there have been no corresponding, radical changes of spelling.

As early as the sixteenth century, there was a movement afoot to reform the spelling of English so that it should conform more closely to the pronunciation. In 1569, John Hart urged the English 'to use as many letters in our writing as we do use voices or breaths, and no more . . . and never to abuse one letter for another, and to write as we speak . . . and, for such sounds as we have no fit letters, we may, without offence to God or reasonable man, choose and use new letters for every one of them'. By the eighteenth century, when English spelling had become finally fixed, largely through the appearance of the great dictionaries of Johnson, Sheridan and Walker, it happened that words which had formerly been pronounced differently now had the same pronunciation, e.g. *meet* had had a vowel similar to the present French *é* and *meat* a vowel similar to French *è*, but in the eighteenth century both words had become, as now, /miːt/. Some letters were retained in the spelling though they no longer had any sound values, e.g. for two hundred years the *gh* of *night* had been silent.

We may say, therefore, that our present-day system of spelling represents roughly the speech of four or five hundred years ago. We now have the choice of at least eight spelling forms for the phoneme /iː/, e.g. *meet, meat, siege, seize, police, key, quay, people*; the letter o has half a dozen different sounds, cf. *donkey, monkey, home, woman, women, who*. Many letters are not pronounced at all, e.g. *r* following a vowel and before a pause or a consonant in RP, *gh* in *thought*, *t* in *castle*; and some combinations of letters can mean various sounds, e.g. *th* is /ð/ in *this*, /θ/ in *thin* and /t/ in *Thomas*. Yet a long-established spelling such as that of English gains such prestige among a literate people that many speakers believe it to be more correct to pronounce words as they are spelt, despite the loss of the original relationship between sound and spelling. Thus, spelling itself may influence pronunciation. Compare, for example, the traditional pronunciation of such words as *forehead* and *nephew* /ˈfɒrɪd, ˈnevjuː/ with the increasingly common /ˈfɔːhed, ˈnefjuː/; earlier /ˈluːɪsəm/ for *Lewisham* has already given way to /ˈluːɪʃəm/.

Nevertheless, however inconsistent the relationship of sound and spelling may be, it can still be maintained that our language has a basically phonemic spelling. On the other hand, certain features of our speech have no reflection in the written language. We have no way of representing the weak vowel /ə/, nor any means of indicating the un-accented forms of grammatical words (except in the apostro-phised spelling *can't* for *cannot*, etc.); the accentual pattern of words and phrases is not indicated, nor is the intonation. (The use of italic print for certain words in phrases gives some hint of accentuation, but punctuation provides only the vaguest information as to intonation, and is, in any case, capable of various interpretations. A parenthesis such as *he complained, she asked, he exclaimed indignantly* may, however, be used to indicate in some measure either the sentence type intended or the speaker's attitude.)

Our written form of English is, therefore, an imperfect representation of the phonemic elements of the spoken language. Yet it can be reasonably argued that there need not necessarily be a strict and complete correspondence between the sound patterns of speech and the visual patterns of writing. We have seen (pp. 332f) that many of the cues to understanding provided in the spoken language are redundant for the purposes of efficient communication; many neutralisations are possible on the phonemic and morphemic levels without loss of intelligibility in a given situation. Written English, too, has very considerable re-dundancy, but it often keeps separate visually those signals which are neutralised in speech, e.g. *of, have* (both often /əv/ in speech, but rarely represented in writing by the same spelling, even by those writers who set out to portray colloquial speech—see Chapter 5, passages 1, 3 5); or it distinguishes visually sequences which in speech may have only the slightest sound contrasts, e.g. *a border-liner, aboard a liner; summer dresses, some addresses* (cf., too, the similar /sʌmə/ sequences written as *some are mine, some of* (often /ə/) *mine*); or again, it retains a distinction of word forms which are homophonous in the spoken language, e.g. *meet, meat; rain, rein, reign; write, rite, right, wright*, etc. Such distinctions on the word and morpheme level, explicit in writing but not in speech, in some measure compensate for the lack of information about such features as intonation and accentuation in the written language.

During the last four centuries, the numerous reformers of our spelling have usually retained the roman alphabet as a basis, though sometimes entirely new letter-shapes have been advocated. It has rarely been made clear that the needs of a writing system which aims to mirror speech and of one which sets out to represent the elements of language may not be identical.

Today, few would seriously maintain that our writing should present an exact record of our speech. If this were the case, we could simply adopt for our reform the principles of the International Phonetic Alphabet, with its roman-based letters for phonemes and its various marks for such distinctive prosodic features as stress and intonation. The resultant form of writing would be a kind of phonetic transcription, providing us with a great deal more information than we need for the visual comprehension of our own language. Either we would quickly learn to ignore in reading and writing a great proportion of the written cues, or our speed in reading and writing would be greatly reduced. (It is worth noting that our present imperfect writing system permits a speed of silent reading at least double that of normal speech.) Moreover, since each of us speaks Eng-

339

lish in a different way and is capable of producing the same utterance with different phonemic and prosodic components according to the style of speech, we would each have our own individual way of spelling the same English language, further complicating the idiosyncracies of cursive writing already mentioned (p. 335). It is clear that a system of writing must have a conventional and institutionalised form which will do service for all users of the language.

If the language system, rather than speech, should provide the basis on which a visual medium of transmission is to be formulated, it is evident that a decision must be made as to the level of linguistic elements which is to be represented. Should, for instance, the sentence, the word, the morpheme or the phoneme provide our basic unit? Whatever level of analysis is chosen, it is important that it should be capable of being represented by an economical number of visual signs.

All the levels mentioned in the last paragraph have been used in the various stages of the development of writing in the history of mankind. The representation by means of pictures (detailed or stylised) of total concepts which may correspond to a sentence or larger unit is found in many kinds of early writing. Our road signs still exemplify this type of visual language. But this is a crude and cumbersome means of visual communication, which is incapable of expressing more than the grosser linguistic messages.

At the other end of the linguistic scale, there is the possibility of establishing a writing system based on the smallest constituent elements of language—the phonemes. Many attempts have been made to bring English spelling back to the more purely phonemic basis that some would claim it had a thousand years ago. The experimental Initial Teaching Alphabet, now being tested, makes modifications and additions of a largely phonemic kind to our existing spelling. It does not, however, depart radically from the traditional forms, since it seeks to provide the child with a more rational vehicle for learning to read before ultimately coming to grips with the conventional orthography. On the other hand, reformed systems, such as that based on the International Phonetic Association's alphabet, are intended to supersede our present form of writing. A system of this last kind does not provide a mirror of any particular form of speech, but adopts conventions (including many features of the traditional orthography) which enhance its linguistic as opposed to its purely phonological validity—e.g. 'Fonetik spelin haz tu difer in meni respekts from transkripʃonz ov pronənsieiʃon'. It is likely that this kind of spelling, with its considerable degree of phoneme-letter correspondence and its thirty letters, would be much more quickly learned by the child. A disadvantage is that, being so closely tied to the phonological structure of the language, such reformed systems would need to be revised at regular intervals in order to match the inevitable changes in pronunciation. Moreover, the spread of English as a world language renders more complex the problems of selecting spelling conventions which will cover the diversity of pronunciation in different parts of the world.

Therefore, both these two extreme linguistic levels may be said to have serious disadvantages as bases for a reform of our spelling. The word or morpheme appear theoretically to be more satisfactory units for the visual representation of language. Languages such as Chinese still use a form of writing where each different morpheme—the 'minimum stretch of meaningful language' (p. 134)—is represented by a single character, as opposed to one or more marks denoting its constituent sounds. But since, in order to achieve even moderate literacy, it is necessary to learn thousands of different characters, this remains an uneconomical form of writing for ordinary purposes—and a most embarrassing one for the printer. There would be the

341

same objection of proliferation of symbols if English were written on the strict basis of one morpheme—one symbol. (We do, of course, already use such morpheme symbolisation, but only to a limited extent, e.g. in such a sentence as ' $5 \times 6 = 30$ ' or '£5 ' as opposed to ' 5 lb '.) A considerable economy can be effected with some languages if phonological syllables rather than morphemes are represented, i.e. the sign is taken to represent a phonemic structure rather than a meaningful unit. Japanese, for instance, has taken over some fifty Chinese characters to represent phonological combinations and has in this way kept its inventory of visual symbols within manageable limits. But Japanese has comparatively simple possibilities of syllable building compared with the very complex syllabic structures of English, which would require many hundreds of syllabic signs.

It may well be that a reform of English spelling should make use of the advantages of both the phonemic and the morphemic levels of analysis. The morphemic structure of English has the advantage of not displaying the great diversity in time and place which vitiate a purely phonemic approach. After all, as we pointed out on p. 339, our writing already expresses the morphemic differences present in such words as *right*, *rite*, *write*, etc. And this differentiation is achieved in a convenient alphabetic form which is unrelated to oppositions of a phonemic kind, since each morpheme is pronounced /raɪt/. Our graphic sign for plurality is most often -*s*, as in *cats*, *dogs*, *horses*, though the phonemic realisations are /-s, -z, -ɪz/. Similarly, we distinguish visually and morphemically between the same phonemic /s/ in *cats*, *cat's*, and *cats'*. Or again, the past tense morpheme spelt conventionally -*ed*, as in *locked*, *tugged*, *waited*, is realised phonemically in these three words as /-t, -d, -ɪd/. Many would claim that these features of our present writing, both the differentiation of certain morphemes of identical phonemic shape and the morphemic identity of others

342

of differing phonemic realisation, constitute visual assets which a purely phonological writing would eliminate. It is conceivable, therefore, that certain alphabetic differences should be retained for the first group, e.g. *rait, rayt, raet*, etc., and that a conventional alphabetic form be devised for the second, e.g. *katz, dogz, horsz*, etc.,—or that new letters or signs should be invented to represent certain morphemic affixes. Such morphemic writing and reading cues could also be extended to those cases where our present spelling is ambiguous, e.g. *read* (in speech /riːd/ or /red/) and *red* (/red/), which might be re-written *rede, read, red*. Rationalisation of this kind is particularly important in the case of monosyllabic morphemes which, within a short alphabetic span, carry a heavy distinctive burden. In the case of many polysyllabic morphemes, e.g. *under, cabbage, mahogany, caterpillar*, etc., the possibility of opposition with a visual shape of similar alphabetic extent lessens. However, those words, referred to on p. 317, which signal their noun/adjective or verb function by a variation of accentual pattern in speech (with or without qualitative variation) e.g. *insult, object*, etc., present a special case. Here, the identity of the written form for the two functions may well be one which the visual representation of the language can tolerate, the constraints of the environment most often determining the function without difficulty. Finally, it is conceivable that those grammatical words which have the greatest relative frequency in a running text, e.g. *the, of, and, to, a/an, that (conj.)*, might be indicated by either abbreviated alphabetic signs or new characters.

The hints at reform mentioned in the last paragraphs would amount to a rationalisation of our present writing system which, by accident and inconsistently, is largely morphemic in nature and alphabetic in expression. It would clearly be unwise to abandon the alphabetic style of writing. It is most economical in terms of the number of characters needed (though a small number of letters could without danger be added to our present inventory); and, at the same time, it is flexible since, if there is no slavish adherence to a one phoneme—one letter principle, considerable complexity of linear patterning is possible. In any case, it becomes evident that, if an efficient system of visual communication is to be achieved, linguistic considerations on a higher level than the phonological should be taken into account.

SUPPLEMENT II

Notions of Correctness

BY

JEREMY WARBURG

*Sometime Professor of English at
Earlham College, Indiana*

Notions of Correctness

W E have seen, especially in Chapters 5, 7 and 8, that many people's notion of correct English is based, not on the actual *usage* of *any* section of the population, but on a sort of 'transcendental' standard which is essentially an amalgam of logic and the grammar of the classical languages. Thus certain forms are held to be 'correct' which are rarely, if ever, used at all; while many other forms, although they are in common use even among educated people, are condemned as 'incorrect'.

These misconceptions are usually acquired, or imposed, at a highly impressionable age, and those who hold them will generally assume their truth to be self-evident. If they assert that in the phrase I *came late due to an accident, due* should be *owing*, or that I *only need two* should be I *need only two*, or that *judgment* spelt without 'the' *e* is wrong, they are likely to do so with unbounded confidence—it just is so. They may even resent it if one asks them to justify their claims; but, still firm in the belief that something more than personal prejudice or preference is involved, they may then refer to some reference or textbook which they assume to be authoritative: 'Well, it says so in the dictionary', they may say.[1] At a more sophisticated level, they may

[1] For example, the *Concise Oxford Dictionary* (1964), as well as numerous textbooks, describes this use of *due* as incorrect. See, however, Sir Ernest Gowers' revision of Fowler's *Modern English Usage* (Oxford 1965), p. 141. Here the usage—condemned as illiterate in the first edition (1926), though even then 'as common as can be'—is described as 'freely employed by BBC announcers' and shown to have 'become literally part of the Queen's English'.

347

appeal to such criteria as reason and analogy ('As it's *about*, it must be *thereabout*, not *thereabouts*'), etymology ('The proper meaning of *horrid*'s really "bristling"—from *horridus*, you know'), or the behaviour of some other language —Latin especially—or of English at an earlier stage ('Of course it's *whom*—accusative'). And still other criteria may be invoked as well: spelling, for example ('There's a *t* in *often*, isn't there? Then why on earth not say it?') or aesthetics ('Ambivalence? It just sounds ugly') . . .[1] At all events, usage—even 'reputable' usage—will be rejected and condemned, except insofar as it confirms their own, or what they feel their own should be[2]—witness this extract from a letter to *The Times* (16 September 1961):

Today you published a photograph of four young people about to spend a year at Soviet universities, together with the information that these were postgraduate students.

The succession: *undergraduate*—one who is reading for a degree, *graduate*—one who has gained a degree, leads one to guess that *postgraduate* means either one who has lost a degree or perhaps, as has been suggested by others, a dead graduate.

Clearly the persons in your photograph are very much alive and, one would suppose, still in possession of their degrees. One is therefore led, albeit reluctantly, to the conclusion that *The Times* is guilty of the furtherance of a pleonasm, and that these persons are graduate students.

This 'transcendental' notion of correctness is very far from new. Broadly speaking, in this country it was popularised, though by no means invented, in the eighteenth and early-nineteenth centuries; at a time, that is to say, when

[1] Cf. Section 7 of Supplement I.
[2] Cf. Leonard Bloomfield, 'Secondary and Tertiary Responses to Language' (1944), in *Readings in Applied English Linguistics*, ed. H. B. Allen (New York 1958), pp. 195-202.

the demand for the formal teaching of English was spreading very rapidly, but—and this is a crucial point to bear in mind—when linguistic science as we know it simply did not exist;[1] when it was widely held, among those who were responsible for meeting the demand, that English had grown, and was growing increasingly, corrupt, that it should be corrected and even permanently fixed, and that logic or reasoning should be invoked to settle questions of disputed use. One of the most influential eighteenth-century writers on English, Robert Lowth, for example, insisted 'that the English Language as it is spoken by *the politest part* of the nation, and as it stands in the writing of *our most approved authors*, often offends against every part of Grammar'.[2] And, almost a hundred years ago, the American, Richard Grant White, maintained: 'There is a misuse of words which can be justified by *no authority*, however great, by *no usage*, however general.'[3] It is, essentially, a doctrine of original linguistic sin,[4] and finds expression, not only in generalised statements such as these, but in countless specific examples:

> Frequent mistakes are made in the formation of the Participle of this Verb [*sit*]. The analogy plainly requires *sitten*; which was formerly in use. . . . But it is now almost wholly disused, the form of the Past Time *sat*, having taken its place. Dr Middleton hath with great propriety restored the true Participle:—'To have *sitten* on the heads of the Apostles' . . .[5]

[1] Cf. C. C. Fries, 'The Rules of Common School Grammars', PMLA, vol. 42 (1927), pp. 221-3.

[2] *A Short Introduction to English Grammar* (London 1762, edn of 1763), p. vii. My italics.

[3] *Words and their Uses* (New York 1870, London edn of 1886), p. 24. My italics.

[4] Fries, in 'The Periphrastic Future with *Shall* and *Will* in Modern English', PMLA, vol. 40 (1925), p. 980, speaks of 'the definite *repudiation of usage*' as 'a doctrine of original grammatical sin'.

[5] Lowth, *op. cit.* pp. 79f.

After the words *than* and *as* this error, of putting the objective for the nominative is very frequently committed: as, 'John was very rich, but Peter was richer than *him.* . . .' It ought to be richer than *he.* . . . It is *reason* which is to be your sole guide.[1]

BALANCE, in the sense of rest, remainder, residue, remnant, is an abomination. Balance is metaphorically the difference between two sides of an account—the amount which is necessary to make one equal to the other. It is not the rest, the remainder. And yet we continually hear of the balance of this or that thing, even the balance of a congregation or of an army![2]

Certainly we suffer from the doctrine nowadays a good deal less. But, in spite of all that linguistic science has done, and tried to do, during the past hundred or so years, such unrealistic attitudes to language, and many such artificial, over-simple or archaic rules for using it, do still persist. They have been handed on from textbook to textbook, and from teacher to teacher, and so they have come down to many of the textbooks, teachers and children of today. No doubt this is partly due to ignorance and inertia. No doubt it is partly due to pedantry and snobbery and an uncritical desire for certainty. No doubt it is partly a matter of profound nostalgia for the things that used to be and for the things that never really were—and very often of distaste for the things that are comparatively new. But, at

[1] William Cobbett, *Grammar of the English Language* (New York 1818, London edn of 1823), pp. 95f.

[2] White, *op. cit.* p. 94. For fuller discussion of, and more detailed reference to, the complex historical aspects of the subject, see, for example, A. C. Baugh, *A History of the English Language* (London 1959); R. F. Jones, *The Triumph of the English Language* (Stanford 1953); S. A. Leonard, *The Doctrine of Correctness in English Usage 1700-1800* (Madison 1929); Susie I. Tucker, *English Examined* (Cambridge 1961); and H. C. Wyld, *A History of Modern Colloquial English* (Oxford 1920).

any rate, the fact remains—whatever the reasons for the fact may be—that such attitudes and rules still have an influential place in the teaching of English, and in our popular linguistic lore.

For example, people still sometimes have it that to use *aggravate* in the sense of 'annoy' is incorrect, because originally it meant 'add weight to'. Originally: in other words, the reason that is given for saying that it is incorrect is 'etymological', and this reason is ridiculous—it would, as was pointed out in Chapter 8, make the correct meaning of *style* 'pointed instrument' and the correct meaning of *like* 'body'; and, one might add, it would make the correct meaning of *nice* 'silly' and the correct meaning of *silly* 'happy' or 'blessed'. What we should bear in mind is this: language changes, and it is perfectly normal that it should. To act as if it does not change, or has not changed, it quite absurd. *Aggravate* in the sense of 'annoy', like *aggravate* in the sense of 'add weight to' or 'make worse', is, in fact, widely established in Standard use today. To claim that using it in such a sense is simply incorrect is simply whimsical.

'Whimsical', of course, may strike one as rather an endearing trait, so I should add at once that correctness of this kind is not necessarily innocuous. Consider this example:

Counsel. Do I understand that you think this condition of my client wholly hysterical?

Witness. Yes, sir; undoubtedly.

Counsel. And therefore won't last long?

Witness. No, sir; not likely to.

Counsel. Well, doctor, let us see; is not the disease called hysteria and its effects hysterics; and isn't it true that hysteria, hysterics, hysterical, all come from the Greek word ὑστέρα?

Witness. It may be.

Counsel. Don't say it may, doctor; isn't it? Isn't an exact translation of the Greek word τέρα the English word 'womb'?

Witness. You are right, sir.

Counsel. Well, doctor, this morning when you examined this young man here, did you find that he had a womb? I was not aware of it before, but I will have him examined over again and see if I can find it. That is all, doctor; you may step down.[1]

True, this etymological browbeating was apparently a court-room trick, and the case is not a recent one. But still, misuses of the etymological approach, certainly no less insidious when unintentional, are not uncommon now, and should be recognised for what they are.

As we have already seen, it is by no means only to vocabulary that this 'transcendental' notion of correctness is applied. Even now there are people who believe that a preposition is something one should not end a sentence with —that it is, quite simply, incorrect. But even Lowth, over two hundred years ago, admitted (if rather grudgingly) that 'This is an Idiom which our language is strongly inclined to'[2]—illustrating the point at the same time as he made it. And of course there is ample precedent for ending sentences (and parts of sentences) with prepositions, in English whose goodness (or should we say, the goodness of which?) is not nowadays considered in dispute— Shakespeare's, Bacon's, Dickens's, Lawrence's, to name a few.

In an interesting and entertaining book, *Grammar Without Tears*, Hugh Sykes Davies has pointed out that it was

[1] Quoted in Francis Wellman, *The Art of Cross-Examination* (New York 1903, edn of 1941), pp. 226f. Cf. L. Glanville Williams, 'Language and the Law', *Law Quarterly Review*, vol. 61 (1945), p. 385; also A. G. Guest, 'A Case of Champagne', *The Listener* (25 May 1961), pp. 927, 930f.

[2] *Op. cit.* p. 141.

Dryden who started all the fuss.[1] He had been using the construction for many years when he declared it was 'a fault', 'not elegant', and he even took the trouble of 'correcting' it (sometimes with rather unfortunate effects) in the course of revising what is probably his finest prose. So, for example, *the end he aimed at* became *the end at which he aimed*, *the age I live in* became *the age in which I live*, *those impertinent people you speak of* became *those impertinent people of whom you speak*, and—more intractable—*would think himself very hardly dealt with* became *would think he had hard measure*.

The fad caught on. Perhaps it was Lindley Murray who had most to do with that. Certainly, throughout the first half or so of the nineteenth century, his Grammar (which was largely a 'compilation' of several later-eighteenth-century ones) was the great authority in schools; and it was in this that he asserted that 'the *fifth* rule for the strength of sentences is, *to avoid concluding them with an adverb, a preposition, or any inconsiderable word*'.[2] At any rate, even though no present-day textbooks I know of insist on the observance of the rule—in fact they tend to scoff at or ignore it—it somehow still hangs on. Popular linguistic lore, it seems, dies hard.

We may be reasonably certain what, at any rate originally, motivated the belief that this stylistic practice made for elegance or strength. As Davies points out, Dryden, for one, had been 'brought up on the grammatical principles of Mulcaster, Greaves, and Hewes, which based English usage on Latin'. In Latin, prepositions very rarely come at the end of sentences. No doubt Dryden made these revisions on the grounds that English is good to the extent that it reflects the behaviour of Latin—the language which he,

<hr />

[1] Cf. 'A Word to End a Sentence with', *Grammar Without Tears* (London 1951), pp. 114-18.

[2] *English Grammar* (York 1795, edn of 1821), p. 306.

and many others both before and since, regarded as a paragon of elegance and strength.[1]

But then, the point is this: Latin is not English, and the habits of an inflected language are not necessarily good habits in a largely uninflected one. It is, in other words, only in Rome that we should think of doing only what the Romans do. That is not to suggest that, in English, ending a sentence with a preposition is always right (or elegant, or strong), any more than it suggests that it is always, or even usually, wrong (or inelegant, or weak). It is, indeed, often a flabby thing to do. But it is often the natural, concise, and vigorous thing to do—the awkward, and pompous, to avoid—in writing, let alone in speech. And then, of course, it often does not really matter which you do, the alternatives are more or less indifferent—some of Dryden's, for example, were. At any rate, the simple, dogmatic prohibition, the simple, generalised preference is quite inadequate. *The circumstances I did it in* seems to me less formal than *The circumstances in which I did it*, and, consequently, my choice of one phrase rather than the other would depend on my estimate of the degree of formality or informality that was needed in a given case. Perhaps it would help if at least one bore in mind some verse which the American, Morris Bishop, wrote about twenty years ago:

> I lately lost a preposition;
> It hid, I thought, beneath my chair

[1] Cf. Noah Webster, *Dissertations on the English Language* (Boston 1789), pp. viiif: '. . . had the English never been acquainted with Greek and Latin, they would never have thought of one half the distinctions and rules which make up our English grammars'. But Latin grammar is not the only possible influence here: etymology (once again) provides another possibility, as G. H. Vallins, in *The Pattern of English* (London 1956), p. 114, points out: 'Perhaps behind all the objections to it is the etymology of the word *preposition* itself (*pre+positum*, "placed in front of") . . .'

354

> And angrily I cried, 'Perdition!
>   Up from out of in under there'.
>
> Correctness is my vade mecum,
>   And straggling phrases I abhor,
> And yet I wondered, 'What should he come
>   Up from out of in under for?'[1]

It is probably also from reverence for Latin that objections to such expressions as *different to*, *to really try* and *who did you see there?* ultimately derive. So far as the last one is concerned, the objection is to the use of the 'nominative case' (*who*) for the object of the verb *see*, which would in Latin (and many other languages, including older forms of English) be—I mentioned this in passing earlier—in the accusative. Consequently, in this situation, only *whom* is recommended by certain textbooks as correct. But this is simply to disregard the facts of usage, the facts of authentic English grammar. Actually, *who* has been in use in such situations for more than three and a half centuries, as the works of Shakespeare and his contemporaries show. In fact, interrogative *whom* has been the object of marked displacement by *who*, through the pressure exerted upon a word by the position it occupies in the sentence—a common enough feature in the more recent history of our language.[2] This tendency to displace it has been particularly marked in direct questions and in speech, but it has certainly been at work in indirect questions and in writing too. It is, in fact, evident that such constructions as *Who did you go to?* and *I don't know who you went to* are widely established in educated use. This is not, of course, to say that they are better than such relatively formal constructions as *Whom did you go to?* and *I don't know*

[1] Quoted in Sir Ernest Gowers, *Plain Words* (London 1948), p. 74.
[2] Cf. Fries, 'On the Development of the Structural Use of Word-Order in Modern English', *Language*, vol. 16 (1940), pp. 199-208.

whom you went to. But there are occasions on which they will be better and there are occasions on which they will be no less good; and it is in terms of their suitability for particular occasions, not in terms of some arbitrary standard of correctness, that the use of linguistic forms should be assessed. It would, no doubt, be wise to remember these lines from a conversation in a play by Shaw:

If it doesnt matter who anybody marries, then it doesnt matter who I marry and it doesnt matter who you marry.

Whom, not who.

Oh, speak English: youre not on the telephone now.[1]

Here is another example, this time one which has to do with the question of agreement (or disagreement) in number, not case. You may recall that Lewis Carroll has the Duchess say, *If everybody minded their own business, the world would go round a good deal faster than it does;* but you may not recall thinking at the time that, so far at any rate as grammar was concerned, this was very wrong. Still, the author of a fairly recent textbook says it was—and he has a lot of other current textbooks on his side—on the grounds that *every* is singular, and the possessive pronoun referring to it should be singular as well. Of course, Carroll 'was quoting, and is not to be accused of ignorance in himself'. So Carroll, one might say, is off the hook, but we (and the Duchess) apparently are not. The correct construction, we are told, is *If everybody minded his or her own business* . . . But if, the author of the textbook adds, we think that that construction sounds a trifle clumsy—as well we might—we should be well advised

---

[1] *The Village Wooing* (London 1934), p. 135. Note that relative *whom* is also liable to displacement. But for fuller discussion of the ramifications of *who/whom* usage, see Gowers-Fowler, *Modern English Usage*, pp. 707-11, and R. Quirk and J. Svartvik, *Investigating Linguistic Acceptability* (The Hague 1966), esp. pp. 76f.

to say, *Everybody should mind his own business.*[1] Yet there is ample precedent for the construction which the Duchess used, and it is certainly established in educated use today. In fact, it is perfectly intelligible, and surely often more natural than its counterpart. Of course, expressions of this kind may not be logical, at least from certain points of view, but then there is more convention than logic in language, as Professor Quirk has pointed out in Chapter 7, and there is much that is logical, from any point of view, which purists themselves do not accept.[2]

As for which of the expressions one should use, again this may not even matter, but, if it does, it matters because functions vary, *not* because one has to conform, regardless of function, to merely absolutist and irrelevant rules. Either *everybody . . . his* or *everybody . . . their* may do, in both the spoken and the written forms; and one should try to choose whichever seems likely to do best.

I have tried to show that a certain, rather common notion of correctness is misguided and misleading. Noah Webster, another (but unusually enlightened) eighteenth-century grammarian, said of Lowth that he 'criticised away more phrases of *good* English, than he . . . corrected of *bad*', and even substituted for them, by arbitrary rules, 'phrases that have been rarely, or never used at all'.[3] And many people since have done the same, constructed, or at least given credence to, models of verbal behaviour which do not adequately match experience, which falsify the linguistic facts of life. It is certainly not too much to say— and it is curiously ironical—that in doing so they, too, not only add to the ammunition of intolerance and untruth,

[1] J. E. Metcalfe, *The Right Way to Improve your English* (London 1958), pp. 68f.
[2] Cf. my *Verbal Values* (London 1966), pp. 84f., and R. Quirk, 'On English Usage', *Journal of the Royal Society of Arts*, vol. 114 (1966), pp. 845f.
[3] *Dissertations*, p. 287.

waste time and energy, but actually provoke the very thing, bad English, which they themselves deplore: affected phrases, stilted speech, a gutless, neutered, or incongruous prose—the products of confusion, pedantry, or fear. 'Young gentlemen,' wrote Webster about one hundred and eighty years ago,

> YOUNG gentlemen who have gone through a course of academical studies, and received the usual honors of a University, are apt to contract a singular stiffness in their conversation. They read Lowth's Introduction, or some other grammatical treatise, believe what they read, without examining the grounds of the writer's opinion, and attempt to shape their language by his rules. Thus they enter the world with such phrases as, *a mean, averse from, if he have, he has gotten,* and other which they deem *correct*; they pride themselves, for some time, in their superior learning and peculiarities; till further information, or the ridicule of the public, brings them to use the language of other people.[1]

That is still, essentially (and in many inessentials), profoundly true today; and far more true of writing than Webster says it is of speech.

This is not, of course, to say that we should have no standards, anything goes, whatever is is right; only that we should have realistic, helpful ones. To think of correctness in terms of educated usage is helpful, because this kind of usage is so much more widely acceptable, so much more widely communicable and more generally cohesive than usage of an uneducated kind—the I *never had none*'s and the *aint*'s.[2] But to condemn the expression *vacuum-cleaner*, as one man did, on the grounds that nobody would want to clean a vacuum—that is *not* realistic and helpful. To maintain, as one textbook writer has maintained, that

[1] *Op. cit.* p. vii.
[2] Cf. *Verbal Values*, pp. 85-7.

bathing pool (without a hyphen) means a pool which is bathing—*that* is not realistic and helpful. To claim, as people do, that such forms as *I'm averse to, they were intrigued, quite a number, it's me,* or *idea-r-of* (spoken with intrusive *r*), are incorrect or wrong—*that* is not realistic and helpful. We should rid our minds of such figments, and bear in mind: first, that within the whole realm of English the area of usage *in dispute* is unquestionably small; second, that such disputed usages undoubtedly exist, providing forms which it is quite unprofitable to regret, and distinctions which it is positively foolish to ignore.

And, of course, textbooks can be useful here, insofar as *they* reflect a sense of proportion in matters of this kind, insofar as they deal with English in a realistic and not an arbitrary way.

Even so, it should be recognised, textbooks cannot do everything; they are, at best, static, cumbersome, and indirect. We should try to think of them as guides to language, not as language itself; otherwise we may find that our talent for language is merely inhibited by textbook rules. We learn above all by taking part in the actual situations in which English is used, by living the language as fully as we can, by attending, and attending to, what Webster called 'that excellent school, the world'.[1] It is a part which textbooks certainly can help us with, but only we can play.

[1] *Ibid.*

Some Recommended Reading

I A First Reading List

BARBER, C., *Linguistic Change in Present-Day English*, Edinburgh 1964.

ENKVIST, N., SPENCER, J. and GREGORY, M., *Linguistics and Style*, London 1964.

FRANCIS, W. N., *The English Language*, New York 1963.

GIMSON, A. C., *An Introduction to the Pronunciation of English*, London 1962.

O'CONNOR, J. D. and ARNOLD, G. F., *The Intonation of Colloquial English*, London 1961.

ROBERTS, P., *English Syntax*, New York 1964.

STRANG, B. M. H., *Modern English Structure*, London 1962.

THOMAS, O., *Transformational Grammar and the Teacher of English*, New York 1965.

ULLMANN, S., *Words and Their Use*, London 1951.

WARBURG, J., *Verbal Values*, London 1966.

II Suggestions for Further Study

ARNOLD, G. F., *Stress in English Words*, Amsterdam 1957.

BOLINGER, D. L., *Forms of English: Accent, Morpheme, Order*, Cambridge, Mass. 1965.

CARROLL, J. B., *Language, Thought and Reality: Selected Writings of Benjamin Lee Whorf*, New York 1956.

361

CHERRY, C., *On Human Communication*, London 1957.

CHOMSKY, N., *Syntactic Structures*, The Hague 1957.

——*Aspects of the Theory of Syntax*, Cambridge, Mass. 1965.

DENES, P. and PINSON, E. M., *The Speech Chain*, Murray Hill, N.J. 1963.

GLEASON, H. A., *Linguistics and English Grammar*, New York 1965.

GORDON, I. A., *The Movement of English Prose*, London 1966.

HALLIDAY, M. A. K., MCINTOSH, A. and STREVENS, P., *The Linguistic Sciences and Language Teaching*, London 1964.

HOCKETT, C. F., *A Course in Modern Linguistics*, New York 1958.

JESPERSEN, O., *A Modern English Grammar*, 7 vols., London 1909-49.

LEECH, G. N., *English in Advertising*, London 1966.

——*A Linguistic Guide to English Poetry*, London 1968.

LEES, R. B., *The Grammar of English Nominalizations*, Bloomington 1960.

LYONS, J., *Introduction to Theoretical Linguistics*, Cambridge 1968.

MARCHAND, H., *The Categories and Types of Present-Day English Word-Formation*, Wiesbaden 1960.

MENCKEN, H. L., *The American Language*, ed. R. I. McDavid, New York 1963.

PALMER, F. R., *A Linguistic Study of the English Verb*, London 1965.

QUIRK, R. and SMITH, A. H., *The Teaching of English*, London 1959.

QUIRK, R. and SVARTVIK, J., *Investigating Linguistic Acceptability*, The Hague 1966.

ROBINS, R. H., *General Linguistics*, London 1964.

SEBEOK, T. A., *Style in Language*, New York 1960.

362

SVARTVIK, J., *On Voice in the English Verb*, The Hague 1966.

TURNER, G. W., *The English Language in Australia and New Zealand*, London 1966.

ULLMANN, S., *Semantics: An Introduction to the Science of Meaning*, Oxford 1962.

——*Language and Style*, Oxford 1964.

WELDON, T. D., *The Vocabulary of Politics*, Harmondsworth 1953.

WRENN, C. L., *Word and Symbol*, London 1967.

Index

365

366

Acknowledgements

We are grateful to the following for permission to include copyright material:

George Allen & Unwin Ltd. and Holt, Rinehart and Winstone Inc. for an extract from *Language* by Leonard Bloomfield; Sri Aurobindo Ashram for an extract from his poem in *Trance of Waiting*; William Blackwood & Sons Ltd. for the poem *Empty Vessel* by Hugh McDiarmid; Geoffrey Bles Ltd. for an extract from *No Moaning at the Bar* by Geoffrey Lincoln; the British Council for extracts from their *Annual Report for 1960-61*; the Estate of the late Roy Campbell for an extract from *Flowering Reeds: The Olive Tree 1*; the author and Jonathan Cape Ltd. for an extract from *Flight to Italy* by C. Day Lewis; Cassell & Co. Ltd. for an extract from *Cassell's New English Dictionary*; W. & R. Chambers Ltd. for an extract from *Chambers' Twentieth Century Dictionary*; The Clarendon Press, Oxford for extracts from the *New English Dictionary* (N.E.D.), *Concise Oxford Dictionary*, *Shorter Oxford English Dictionary*, *Pocket Oxford English Dictionary* and the *Little Oxford Dictionary*; the *Daily Telegraph* for a verse by Peter Simple and letters; J. M. Dent & Sons Ltd. for an extract from *Nine Sharp* by the late Herbert Farjeon; Faber & Faber Ltd. and Farrar, Straus & Cudahy, New York for an extract from The Music of Poetry from *On Poetry and Poets* by T. S. Eliot; Faber & Faber Ltd. and Harcourt, Brace and World Inc. for extracts from *Four Quartets—East Coker* and *Sweeney Agonistes* from Collected Poems by T. S. Eliot; Faber & Faber Ltd. and Random House Inc. for an extract from *1929*, from *Poems—1930* by W. H. Auden; Editions Gallimard for an extract from *Parlez-vous Franglais?* by Titti Etiemble; Alfred A. Knopf Inc. for a verse by David McCord from *Logic and Language* by B. F. Huppé and J. Kaminsky; author and Methuen & Co. Ltd. for an extract from 'Idanre' by Wole Soyinka from *Collected Poems*; *The New Yorker* for a verse by Morris Bishop, reprinted by permission, Copr. © 1947 The New Yorker Magazine Inc.; the executors of the late C. K. Ogden for a translation of an Ode by Horace, Book I, xxxvi, in Volume 18 of *Psyche*; Criterion Books Inc. and the literary agents of John Osborne and Anthony Creighton for an extract from *Epitaph for George Dillon*; Random House Inc. for an extract from *American College Dictionary*; Routledge & Kegan Paul Ltd. for an extract from Malinowski's supplement to I. A. Richards & C. K. Ogden: *The Meaning of Meaning*; Martin Secker & Warburg Ltd. for an extract from *Studies in Communication* by J. Z. Young; S. J. Sharpless for an extract from his article in

The Observer of 27 December 1953; The Times Newspapers Limited for an extract from 'Cheers & Tears In Kentucky' which appeared in *The Times* of 5 March 1963; the *Sunday Times* for extracts from letters; the executors of the estate of the late Dylan Thomas and J. M. Dent & Sons Ltd. for extracts from *Love's First Fever* and *Out of the Sighs*; Eduard Wancura Verlag for an extract from *Des Deutschen Bürgers Plunderhorn* by F. U. Gass; Frederick Warne & Co. Ltd. for an extract from *Nuttall's Standard Dictionary*; The World Publishing Company, Cleveland, Ohio for an extract from *Webster's New World Dictionary*; and the Yorkshire Dialect Society for an extract from the author's article on *Dialects in Standard English* in Transactions of the Yorkshire Dialect Society, vol. 10 (1958). The block on page 334 is from the *Teaching of English*, edited by Quirk and Smith, by permission of Martin Secker & Warburg.

for the construction of sentences are still rudimentary and of uncertain status. Clearly, they do not refer to the manipulation of 'real', finished sentences like 'The man was wise' but rather to the manipulation of much more abstract entities. But what kind of abstractions and in what sense they are manipulated are matters of continuing controversy. (A recent beginner's guide to the application of *transformational* and *generative* theory to English, by Owen Thomas, is included in the First Reading List, p. 361.)

Nevertheless, it seems worthwhile to try to bypass these difficulties in seeking to establish a small set of simple sentences whose patterns could be used to account for a very large number of more complicated ones. We shall here explore the proposition that there are three such basic types of pattern:

A. The man is wise.
B. The women danced beautifully.
C. The boy admired fighters.

Each of these must, however, be expanded by adding subtypes. Thus in addition to

A.1 The man is wise

we might include

A.2 The planes are fighters

to account for the formation (and our understanding) of *The fighter planes* analogously to *The wise man*. And yet another

A.3 The man is in the corner

is necessary to account for the very common type of post-

213

modified nominal group, *The man in the corner*. Type A is thus a basically tripartite predication consisting of a nominal group as subject, the verb *to be*, and a third element which may be an adjective, a nominal group (of which normally only the head is abstracted for use in premodification), or a prepositional phrase. We cannot hope to exhaust with these few sub-patterns all the relations expressible with *be*[1] (contrast, for example, the sub-classificatory *The plane is a fighter*—which allows the production of the nominal group *The fighter plane*—with the classificatory A/*The plane is a machine*, for which we cannot derive **The machine plane*), but A.3 may remind us of one related pattern involving *be* that we must not ignore. If instead of the definite article we had used the indefinite article to illustrate A.3 (*A man is in the corner*), it would have seemed an improbable sentence or at any rate a highly restricted one—appearing in a stage-direction, perhaps. It would at once have occurred to us that we would normally have formed the sentence quite differently: *There is a man in the corner*. This 'existential' formula, we recognise, is one that is especially common in initiating a discourse; we also see that in some sense it 'says' just what A.3 says, but that the existential formula focuses *a man* into the post-verb part of the sentence where new information is normally expected—and of course everything is new at the outset of a new discourse (a story, for example).

Nor is this the only such focusing device to be associated with the type A sentence pattern. By pronominalisation of a whole sentence, we can of course produce sequences like

She is beautiful. It (*i.e. what has preceded*) is true.

But English grammar also allows us, in effect, to reverse this

[1] Cf. Y. Olsson, *On the Syntax of the English Verb* (Gothenburg 1961), pp. 119f, 152f, and elsewhere.

pronominalisation so that *it* can 'stand for' what follows instead of what precedes:

It is true that she is beautiful.

And as an extension of this process, we have the so-called 'cleft-sentence' which enables us to focus the subject, complement or adjunct of a sentence. For example, beside

John bought the car in London.

we have

It was *John* that bought the car in London.
It was *the car* that John bought in London.
It was *in London* that John bought the car.

But to return to existential *there*. This item, unstressed and hence normally pronounced /ðə/, must not be confused with locative *there*, pronounced /ðɛə/. It is not, after all, tautologous to say

There is a man there now.

nor contradictory to say

There is a man here now.

These last examples remind us of the need to provide in all types of sentence pattern for the possibility of introducing an adverbial adjunct of place or time: not adjuncts of all kinds, since—for example—type A will not admit adjuncts of manner.

When we turn to type B, however, we not merely find that manner adjuncts must be possible but that this sentence pattern is the *locus classicus* for them:

B.1 The women danced beautifully.

With a very restricted sub-type, in fact, an adjunct is obligatory:

> B.2 Students live frugally.

Even with B.1, however, it is appropriate to illustrate the pattern with the adjunct present, since the simplest form of the intransitive sentence (for example, *Birds sing*) is of extremely rare occurrence. This the reader can easily test by trying to find one in his daily paper or by trying to supply a plausible context for one he invents.

Just as processes can be suggested to derive nominal groups like *The wise man* from the type A pattern, so there are nominal groups for which type B constitutes the underlying sentence: for example, *The dancing of the women*, where a nominalisation of the verb becomes the head and where the subject enters a structure of postmodification. There is also the agentive type, *The beautiful dancers*, where the noun head denotes the performer of an action. The ambiguity that can arise through abbreviative and assumptive processes is notably exemplified in the latter instance, since it may relate to a type A sentence, *The (women) who dance are beautiful*, or to a type B sentence, *The (women) dance beautifully*.

The processes for introducing adjuncts constitute in many ways the obscurest part of English grammar and much work still needs to be done. The difficulty can be illustrated by the following examples which show *naturally* operating in three quite distinct relationships:

> He walked with a naturally proud air.
> He walked naturally.
> Naturally, he walked.

It is clearly significant, however, that the 'open' class of adverbs are directly and uniformly related to adjectives (*beautiful ~ beautifully*), and that most seem to be related to adjectival modification (in an abbreviative and assumptive way, we might add) through a small number of abstract nouns having very general meaning:

> . . . highly praised ~ praised to a high *degree*
> . . . danced beautifully ~ danced in a beautiful *manner*

The third of our main patterns is illustrated with the sentence:

C.1 The boy admired fighters.

The pattern thus admits complements identical with those found in A.2, but the selections are sharply different. In A.2 the selection of subject and complement is interdependent: thus (with exceptions more apparent than real) if one is singular, the other must be singular; if one is animate, so must the other be. In C, the selection of subject and complement is mediated by the verb, with which they both have interdependence in selection. Thus while one can have

> The boy (*or* The boys) admired fighters (*or* the girl *or* the picture).
> The rabbit frightened the grasshopper.

one cannot have

> *The picture admired the fighter.
> *The rabbit frightened the picture.

As with type B, so with type C there is a related nominal group structure, *The (rabbit's) frightening of the grasshopper*, again with the verb nominalised as head, but this time with the subject (if retained) as a genitive premodifier while the complement appears in the postmodification structure. An important property of C.1 is to admit operation

217

of that focus-shifting phenomenon known as the passive, which enables us—when we wish—to delete the active subject:

> The picture was admired (by the boys).

We thus see that

> Everyone looked at the picture.
> Everyone stopped at the roadside.

have only a superficial resemblance since the former shares the type C pattern in allowing the passive (*The picture was looked at by everyone*), while the type B character of the latter is matched by the fact that the passive is not possible (**The roadside was stopped at by everyone*).

Not all sentences sharing type C's selectional characteristics admit the passive (for example, *The dress—or That behaviour—becomes her*), and while such sentences are very miscellaneous, we should single out those formed with the verb *to have* as an important sub-type:

> C.2 The man has two cars.

Part of the importance of C.2 is that it appears to underlie the possessive (though Lyons and others disagree); compare the rejoinder in the following short conversation:

> 'John's two cars are very —'
> 'Oh, so John has two cars now!'

We thus have here another of the abbreviative processes in the formation of nominal groups, such that we can see

> John's pretty, gracefully swimming goldfish in that bowl (came from . . .)

in terms of the explicit sentences

218

John has a goldfish (C.2)
The goldfish is pretty (A.1)
The goldfish is in that bowl (A.3)
The goldfish swims gracefully (B.1)

Another important feature shown by *have* is its adaptiveness to existential statement. We may compare the effective similarity between the pair

A clock has two hands.
There are two hands on a clock.

So, too, when we invoke metaphor to proceed from I *have a car* (which might be alternatively expressed as I *own*—or *possess*—*a car*) to I *have an idea*, the latter becomes little more than a device for announcing the existence of an idea, together with some indication of its relation to the speaker (though this relationship can no longer be paraphrased with the verbs *own* or *possess*). We should also note that when we say We *have a man* (*here*) *who can do it* or You *have a visitor waiting to see you*, there is close similarity to *There is a man* (*here*) *who can do it* and *There is a visitor waiting to see you* respectively. But there is an additional and more fundamental resemblance to the more elementary forms A *man can do it* and A *visitor is waiting*, and we thus see again the focus-shifting potentiality of existential statement that we noticed earlier in comparing A *man is in the corner* with *There is a man in the corner*. In this respect, however, we are regarding the sentence You *have a visitor waiting* as having as its third element or complement an entire embedded sentence, as though we were able to say

*You have (that) a visitor is waiting.

And, with this relationship in mind, we can conveniently
219

introduce the next sub-class of type C where such a relationship is obvious:

C.3 The man thought that the girl was pretty.

Some verbs taking a finite verb clause as complement will permit the passive with the clause initially placed in the normal subject position; for example, *That the man had a scar was remembered by the witness*. But such usages tend to be rare and in many instances are not regarded as acceptable. It is nevertheless a fact that English grammar permits clauses as passive subjects, as is clear from the ready acceptability of the passive when the anticipatory *it* process is used to keep the 'real' subject in post-verb position: *It was thought (by the man) that the girl was pretty*.

When sentences are embedded in sentences, a number of important non-finitisation and deletion processes are available, as we have already seen, thus allowing us to abbreviate them and take some of their features for granted. Beside the explicitness of

He expected that the girl would swim gracefully.

we therefore have

He expected the girl to swim gracefully.

Indeed, there are constructions with certain embedded sentences of type A (especially A.1), in which even the non-finite verbal group is usually deleted and its retention thought clumsy:

The man thought the girl $\begin{cases} \text{(to be) pretty.} \\ \text{(to be) a genius.} \end{cases}$

With the embedded sentence in its non-finite or in its verb-

220